Italian Cuisine
The Gourmet's Companion

Jeffrey A. Sadowski

JOHN WILEY & SONS, INC.

New York   Chichester   Weinheim   Brisbane   Singapore   Toronto

Copyright © 1997 by Jeffrey A. Sadowski
Published by John Wiley & Sons, Inc.

Library of Congress Cataloging-in-Publication Data

Sadowski, Jeffrey A.
    Italian cuisine : the gourmet's companion / Jeffrey A. Sadowski.
        p.   cm.
    Includes bibliographical references.
    ISBN 0-471-14909-8 (paper : alk. paper)
    1. Food—Dictionaries.   2. Cookery, Italian—Dictionaries.
    3. Italian language—Dictionaries—English   4. English language—
    Dictionaries—Italian   5. Food—Dictionaries—Italian
    6. Cookery, Italian—Dictionaries—Italian   I. Title.
    TX349.S235   1997
    641.5945′03—dc20   96-18807

Printed in the United States of America

10 9 8 7 6 5 4 3 2 1

Come home with me and eat.

— *I Kings 13:15*

Preface

Italian Cuisine: A Gourmet's Companion takes a unique approach to genuine Italian cookery. It is made up of two sections. Part I offers hundreds of authentic recipe summaries, alphabetized and arranged by course. For most diners, the recipe summaries will serve as a quick picture of the dish—its ingredients, cooking preparation, and service. Although no ingredient amounts, oven temperatures, cooking times, etc., are given, knowledgeable chefs will be able to reproduce a particular dish simply by knowing the ingredients and methods used.

Part II is really an Italian culinary dictionary. Thousands of entries are alphabetically listed, and concise, accurate definitions are presented. Cooking terms, ingredients, pastas, regions and regional specialties, wines and liqueurs, and cooking methods are all covered. Italian cooking terms often appear to be synonymous with each other; this, of course, is usually not the case. This section will end confusion and broaden the knowledge of anyone who consults it.

This book is intended as a convenient reference tool for those possessing an advanced knowledge of food and cooking—chefs, culinary students and instructors, and serious amateur cooks. Cooking terms are commonly used throughout the book, particularly in Part I. To the professional and dedicated amateur, these are part of the everyday language used in the kitchen.

Italian Cuisine: A Gourmet's Companion will also, however, be a handy companion for restaurant goers negotiating their way through Italian menus at home and abroad. Referring to the alphabetical list of dishes in Part I will allow them to ascertain how a dish is prepared and what ingredients it contains.

Jeffrey A. Sadowski

Acknowledgments

I would like to thank the following people for making this book possible: Laurie Sadowski, Claire Thompson, Maria Colletti, Theresa Moffa, Kira deLong, Tyler Shippen, Robin Riessman, and the staff at Wiley, particularly Ira Brodsky. A very special thanks to Rob Ansaldo and Mary Ansaldo for their expertise, patience, and willingness to help.

Contents

PART I — Italian Dishes, by Course   **1**

Antipasti—Appetizers   3

Minestra, Brodetto, e Zuppa—Soups   9

Pasta—Pastas   15

Riso e Risotto—Rice   27

Polenta e Gnocchi—Polenta and Dumplings   34

Pizze e Focacce—Pizzas and Foccacias   37

Pesce—Fish   39

Pollame—Poultry   49

Agnello e Montone—Lamb and Mutton   54

Manzo—Beef   57

Maiale—Pork   61

Vitello—Veal   64

Salsiccia—Sausage   69

Verdure—Vegetables   70

Legumi—Legumes   80

Insalate—Salads   81

I Dolci—Sweets   84

PART II — Italian Food and Beverage Vocabulary   **89**

Italian Pronunciation Key   90

Part I

Italian Dishes, by Course

ANTIPASTI — APPETIZERS

Acciughe Anchovies.
— *all'ammiraglia* Fresh anchovy fillets marinated in olive oil and lemon juice; seasoned with salt, pepper, fresh basil, and oregano.
—, *pasticcetti con* Preserved anchovy fillets wrapped in pastry dough and deep-fried.
— *con peperoni gialli* Marinated anchovies garnished with sautéed yellow peppers, capers, chopped hard-cooked eggs, and fresh chopped herbs; drizzled with olive oil and lemon juice.
— *alla piemontese* Fresh anchovies marinated in olive oil, balsamic vinegar, and seasonings; garnished with white truffles.
Anguilla Eel.
— *marinata* Eel pieces dredged in flour and fried in oil; covered with olive oil, vinegar, garlic, onions, lemon juice, and seasonings and allowed to marinate; served cold.
Antipasto alla contadina Thinly sliced cooked ham and cooked ox tongue marinated in olive oil with quartered artichokes and fresh herbs; arranged on a platter and garnished with chopped hard-cooked eggs, olives, small pickles, and lettuce leaves.
Antipasto di funghi Whole medium-sized mushrooms sautéed in olive oil with chopped garlic and onions, fresh tarragon, and seasonings; cooled; vinegar and lemon juice added; chilled completely before serving.
Antipasto di lesso marinato Cubed boiled meat marinated in olive oil and vinegar with fresh herbs, capers, chopped garlic, anchovies, and onions; garnished with gherkins, olives, and chopped hard-cooked eggs.

Antipasto di riso pallino Cooked rice combined with ground pork, Parmesan cheese, chopped sautéed onion, and seasonings; bound with egg; formed into small balls and baked; served with tomato sauce.
Aragosta all'arancia Uncooked boneless lobster chunks sautéed in butter with onions, and seasonings; deglazed with brandy; freshly squeezed orange juice and heavy cream added and simmered until lobster is cooked and sauce has thickened; served over pasta, rice, and so on.
Aringhe salate all'italiana Salted herring well rinsed and drizzled with a dressing composed of oil, vinegar, mustard, fresh basil, chopped gherkins, and capers.
Arrosticini all'abruzzese Lamb shoulder cut into bite-sized chunks and marinated in olive oil with salt, pepper, and garlic; skewered and grilled.
Asparagi alla parmigiana Blanched asparagus tips tossed with melted butter, salt, and pepper; sprinkled with grated Parmesan cheese and baked until golden brown.
Avocado in coppa Fresh ripe avocado, cheese, and smoked salmon all diced and bound with olive oil or mayonnaise; arranged in a cup over shredded lettuce.
Avocado con gorgonzola Ripe avocados mashed with Gorgonzola

Avocado con gorgonzola (cont.) cheese; spread on toasted bread slices.

Avocado ripieni Roughly chopped cooked shrimp combined with fresh herbs, capers, and hard-cooked eggs; bound with mayonnaise and stuffed in avocado half.

Bagna cauda See Part II.

Bastoncini di carota marinati Blanched carrot sticks marinated in olive oil, wine vinegar, garlic, fresh herbs, and salt and pepper.

Bocconcini fritti An assorted platter composed of mozzarella cubes, chunks of mortadella, sliced pancetta, and so on, all breaded and fried.

Bresaola See Part II.

Bruschetta See Part II.

Canestrelli trifolati Sea scallops sautéed in olive oil with garlic, roasted peppers, capers, and parsley; dusted with bread crumbs and browned in the oven.

Caponata See Part II.

Cappelle di funghi ripiene Mushroom caps stuffed with diced pancetta, anchovy paste, eggs, bread crumbs, cream, and seasonings; baked until tender.

Carpaccio See Part II.

Cipolle farcite con purea di tonno Blanched white onions hollowed out and stuffed with tuna (*canned*) puree, chopped onion pulp, capers, salt, and pepper; served cold.

Conchiglie al cartoccio Raw half-shell clams sprinkled with lemon juice and brandy and topped with raw egg yolks; dusted with Parmesan cheese; wrapped lightly in foil and baked.

Coppe di gamberetti alla marinara Poached, chilled shrimp arranged in a small bowl over sliced tomatoes; drizzled with mayonnaise that has been seasoned with Worcestershire sauce, lemon juice, and tomato puree; garnished with chopped hard-cooked eggs and fresh herbs.

Coppe di gamberoni Cooked, chilled crayfish sprinkled with vinegar and brandy and served in a small bowl over shredded lettuce; drizzled with thinned mayonnaise.

Cozze in antipasto Mussels poached in water and white wine; marinated in mayonnaise thinned with the poaching liquid.

Cozze e vongole passate ai ferri Poached clams and mussels on the half-shell topped with bread crumbs seasoned with olive oil, garlic, and parsley; drizzled with olive oil and baked in hot oven; served with lemon wedge.

Crespelle Crepes.

— **alla fiorentina** Crepes stuffed with fresh chopped spinach sautéed in olive oil with onions, garlic, and diced pancetta; seasoned with Parmesan cheese; topped with *besciamella* and baked.

— **con il ragù** Crepes stuffed with a mixture of *bolognese* sauce (tomato sauce with meat) and *besciamella*; topped with the same sauce and baked.

Crocchette di pollo Diced, cooked chicken seasoned and bound with a thick *besciamella*; formed into balls and dipped in beaten eggs and bread crumbs; deep-fried.

Crostini Small pieces of bread, toast, and sometimes polenta serving as the base for various appetizers.

— *con burro di acciughe* Toasted bread slices spread with anchovy butter.

— *coi fegatini di pollo e prosciutto* Diced prosciutto and chicken livers sautéed in butter with salt, pepper, sage, and parsley; mounded on small toast pieces and served hot.

— *al gorgonzola* Thin slices of fried polenta topped with Gorgonzola cheese; placed briefly in a hot oven until cheese has melted.

— *del marchese* Small toast squares spread with a pureed mixture composed of chicken, chicken livers, sautéed onions, garlic, capers, anchovies, and cognac; served hot.

Erbazzone reggiano A savory pastry stuffed with chopped cooked spinach, diced ham, Parmesan cheese, ricotta, and seasonings; served hot or cold.

Fagottini See Part II.

Fantasia alla recchelina Sliced squid, whole shrimp, clams, and mussels (all cooked, shelled, and chilled) tossed with olive oil, balsamic vinegar, garlic, fresh herbs, and seasonings; arranged in bowl and garnished with colored sweet peppers.

Farfalline al salmone Cubed salmon sautéed in butter and simmered in cream until fish is cooked and sauce has thickened; tossed with cooked *farfalline* pasta; served hot.

Fettunta See Part II.

Formaggio tonnato Chopped *(canned)* tuna combined with ricotta and Parmesan cheese; unsweetened whipped cream folded in; served cold with toasted bread slices.

Frittata An egg dish similar to a flat omelet; the egg is combined with various ingredients and cooked like a pancake on both sides in a frying pan.

— *al basilico* Beaten eggs combined with chopped basil, Parmesan cheese, and black pepper; cooked in olive oil.

— *al formaggio* Beaten eggs combined with Gruyère and Parmesan cheese; cooked in butter and served immediately.

— *fredda alla rustica* Beaten eggs combined with sautéed onions, green peppers, eggplant chunks, and sliced artichokes; seasoned with salt and pepper and cooked in olive oil; served cold.

— *di porri* Sautéed leeks combined with beaten eggs, salt, and pepper; cooked in olive oil and served hot.

Fritteda alla palermitana (*Marinated vegetables*) Chopped garlic; sliced onion, artichokes, celery, cooked fava beans, and cooked peas all sautéed in olive oil; seasoned with sugar, vinegar, salt, and pepper; served at room temperature.

Funghi imbottiti Mushroom caps coated with olive oil, salt, and pepper; stuffed with cooked ground sausage, anchovy paste, bread crumbs, eggs, salt, and pepper; baked until caps are tender; served hot.

Funghi alla trasteverina Whole mushrooms sautéed in olive oil and marinated in vinegar, tomato paste, onions, garlic, and seasonings; served cold.

Gamberetti all'olio e limone Cooked, shelled baby shrimp marinated in olive oil, lemon juice, salt, and pepper; served at room temperature.

Gonfietti See Part II.

Insalata di riso Chilled cooked rice combined with chopped anchovies, diced onions and celery, black olives, and vinegar bound with mayonnaise; garnished with hard-cooked eggs and sliced tomatoes.

Involtini di mortadella Sliced mortadella layered with roasted red peppers, capers, and black olives; rolled and pierced with a toothpick.

Melanzane alla marinara Cubed, poached eggplants marinated in olive oil, vinegar, garlic, salt, pepper, oregano, and basil; raisins, pine nuts, and red pepper strips added prior to serving; served chilled.

Melanzane, sandwich di ricotta, Parmesan cheese, and chopped cooked ham stuffed between slices of eggplant; coated with seasoned flour and dipped in beaten eggs and bread crumbs; fried in olive oil on both sides until crispy.

Melone col prosciutto Fresh, ripe melon wedges wrapped with thinly sliced prosciutto; seasoned with freshly ground black pepper and served chilled or at room temperature.

Mozzarella in carrozza See Part II.

Mozzarella ai ferri Mozzarella slices (½-inch thick) grilled on both sides in a very hot skillet until nicely browned and crusted.

Mozzarella fresca con pomodori e acciughe Fresh mozzarella slices topped with sliced ripe tomato and anchovy fillets; drizzled with olive oil and seasoned with fresh ground black pepper and chopped basil.

Mozzarella fritta Mozzarella cheese cut into rectangles; dredged in seasoned flour and dipped in beaten eggs and bread crumbs; deep-fried and served with various cold sauces.

Olive all'aglio Canned black olives marinated in olive oil and fresh chopped garlic.

Olive farcite Olives stuffed with anchovy paste, capers, and seasonings.

Olive nere all'umbra Large black olives marinated in olive oil seasoned with garlic and bay leaf.

Ostriche Oysters.

— *alla tarantina* Raw shucked oysters arranged on the half-shell and sprinkled with seasoned bread crumbs; drizzled with olive oil and baked; served with lemon wedges.

— *alla Napoleone* Raw shucked oysters arranged on the half-shell and drizzled with brandy, lemon juice, salt and pepper; served cold over crushed ice with parsley and lemon wedges.

— *alla parmigiana* Raw shucked oysters arranged on the half-shell; sprinkled with bread crumbs mixed with Parmesan cheese and fresh ground pepper; moistened with melted butter and olive oil and baked.

— *vellutate* Oysters poached in fish stock and white wine; shelled; poaching liquid thickened with roux and cream; oysters covered with sauce and served hot or cold.

Pane ripieni Mozzarella cheese and sliced ham layered between slices of dry bread; dipped in beaten eggs and cooked on a griddle.

Panini alla frutta Toasted bread slices topped with Mozzarella cheese, smoked ham, sliced apples, and oranges; baked briefly in hot oven.

Panini ripiene al formaggio Hollowed-out bread rolls filled with diced ham and mozzarella cheese and bound with softened butter; baked in hot oven until cheese has melted.

Panzanella, la See Part II.

Peperonata See Part II.

Peperoni e acciughe Flat, canned anchovy fillets (rinsed well in cold water) and strips of roasted sweet peppers marinated in olive oil; seasoned with garlic, capers, fresh chopped oregano, and seasonings.

Peperoni imbottiti piccanti Halved parcooked sweet peppers stuffed with a mixture of bread crumbs, olive oil, anchovy paste, capers, pine nuts, raisins, salt, and pepper; baked.

Peperoni e pere Multicolored sweet bell peppers and ripe pears cut into strips; drizzled with olive oil, lemon juice, salt and pepper, and chopped parsley; served at room temperature.

Piadine al pomodoro Flat bread (*piadine*) spread with a mixture of ricotta, diced pancetta, and chopped parsley; topped with sliced tomato; served at room temperature.

Pisci d'ovu Fritters composed of eggs, Parmesan cheese, bread crumbs, and seasonings; deepfried in oil.

Pizzette al basilico Sliced bread topped with shredded mozzarella, diced tomatoes, and chopped fresh basil; baked in hot oven until cheese has melted.

Polenta fritta Chilled polenta cut into various shapes and panfried in olive oil until browned; seasoned with salt and pepper.

Polenta e funghi Small polenta squares fried in olive oil until browned; topped with sautéed mushrooms seasoned with garlic, chopped parsley, and salt and pepper; served hot.

Polenta, sandwich di Sliced Gruyère cheese and prosciutto (or ham) sandwiched between chilled polenta squares; dredged in flour and dipped in eggs and bread crumbs; pan fried in olive oil until golden brown.

Pomodori al forno Large ripe tomatoes stuffed with rice; seasoned with sautéed onions, garlic, salt, and pepper; baked until tender.

Pomodori coi gamberetti Prepared as for *Pomodori ripieni di tonno*, substituting chopped cooked shrimp for the tuna.

Pomodori ripieni di tonno Tomatoes hollowed out and stuffed with

DISHES BY COURSE

Pomodori ripieni di tonno (cont.) flaked tuna (*canned*) mixed with mayonnaise, prepared mustard, capers, and lemon juice.

Porcini in gratella Whole porcini mushrooms tossed with olive oil, chopped garlic, salt, and pepper; grilled or broiled slowly; served hot.

Porrata See Part II.

Ricotta alle erbe Fresh ricotta seasoned with fresh chopped parsley, basil, and oregano; salt and pepper. Served with toasted bread pieces.

Sarde in carpione Fresh sardines dredged in flour and deep-fried; marinated in vinegar, herbs, and spices.

Sfogliatine See Part II.

Sformato freddo di tonno e patate Mashed potatoes combined with flaked tuna (*canned*), melted butter, cream, and seasonings; placed in a mold and chilled; unmolded and served with mayonnaise thinned with lemon juice.

Spuma fredda di salmone Cold cooked salmon blended smooth with olive oil, lemon juice, salt, and pepper; folded into whipped cream; served with toast squares.

Strisce colorate Multicolored sweet peppers, eggplant, zucchini, and red onion cut into strips; arranged alternately in a casserole with cherry tomatoes; sprinkled with salt and pepper, chopped garlic, and olive oil; baked in slow oven until tender.

Supplì di riso See Part II.

Tartine al salmone Small buttered bread squares topped with thinly sliced smoked salmon; seasoned with lemon-flavored mayonnaise.

Tartine di pollo Cooked diced chicken bound with mayonnaise and seasoned with salt, pepper, and chopped parsley; spread on small toasted bread squares and garnished with poached asparagus tips.

Tartine fantasia Small bread squares spread with a mixture of Parmesan cheese, diced ham, chopped hard-cooked egg, and capers, diced seeded cucumbers, and chopped herbs bound with softened butter; served cold.

Tartine rustiche Herbed ricotta (see *Ricotta alle erbe*) spread on buttered toast squares; served immediately.

Teste di funghi farcite Mushroom caps stuffed with chopped sautéed onions, mushroom stalks, and garlic; bread crumbs, oregano, and salt and pepper; baked until mushrooms are tender.

Tortini di riso e tonno Cooked rice, flaked tuna (*canned*), chopped olives and capers combined with beaten eggs and cream; baked in a pastry-lined mold; cut into small pieces and served hot or cold.

Tramezzini al gorgonzola con noci Small bread squares topped with sliced ham, Gorgonzola cheese, and walnuts; baked briefly in hot oven.

Triangolini pasticciati Puff pastry squares stuffed with various fillings and folded into triangles; baked in hot oven until golden brown.

Uova Eggs.

— *farcite al limone* Halved hard-cooked egg whites stuffed with the mashed yolks, mayonnaise, lemon juice, salt, peppers, and capers; served chilled.

— *farcite al prosciutto* Halved hard-cooked egg whites stuffed with the mashed yolks, diced prosciutto, mayonnaise, chopped dill pickles, and seasonings; served chilled.

— *alla fiorentina* Halved hard-cooked egg whites stuffed with the crushed yolks, ricotta, Parmesan cheese, and softened butter; coated with *besciamella* and grated cheese and baked until lightly browned.

— *ripiene* Hard-cooked eggs stuffed with the yolks, anchovy paste, chopped capers, chopped garlic, and chopped green olives; bound with mayonnaise.

— *sode in salsa verde* Halved hard-cooked egg whites stuffed with the mashed yolks combined with olive oil, capers, anchovy paste, chopped parsley, prepared mustard, garlic, salt, and pepper.

Verdure e funghi saltati in padella Blanched baby carrots and potato cubes, pearl onions, small whole mushrooms, and sliced zucchini sautéed in olive oil; seasoned with salt and pepper and served hot.

Verdure marinate Olive oil, vinegar, sugar, salt, pepper, and garlic heated to boiling and chilled; marinade tossed with uniformly cut vegetables, e.g., cauliflower, onions, eggplant, zucchini, sweet peppers, broccoli, and black and green olives. Marinated up to two days.

MINESTRA, BRODETTO, E ZUPPA — SOUPS

Acqua cotta See Part II.

Brodetto di sogliole all'anconetana Garlic, celery, tomatoes, and fresh herbs sautéed in olive oil and added to fish stock (in which sole was poached); poured over toasted bread slices and poached sole; served immediately.

Brodetto alla triestina Assorted fish simmered in white wine and water with tomatoes, garlic, onions, wine vinegar, and parsley.

Brodo Broth.

—, *cappelletti in* Tortellini served in clear chicken or beef broth with freshly grated Parmesan cheese.

—, *gnocchetti di riso in* Small rice dumplings in beef or chicken broth; sprinkled with grated Parmesan cheese.

—, *gnocchetti di semolina in* Small semolina dumplings in beef or chicken broth; sprinkled with grated Parmesan cheese.

—, *lattughe ripiene in* Small lettuce leaves stuffed with bread crumbs, ground meat, and eggs; served in beef broth seasoned with pesto.

— *di manzo* Beef marrow bones, beef, aromatic vegetables, and herbs simmered in water; reduced until desired flavor and consistency is attained; strained.

—, *alla paesana, riso in* Sautéed onions, garlic, and tomatoes simmered in stock with rice; seasoned with salt and pepper.

—, *passatelli di carne in* Ground beef combined with fresh bread

DISHES BY COURSE

Brodo, passatelli di carne in (cont.) crumbs, eggs, and grated Parmesan cheese; formed into small dumplings and cooked in broth; served with grated pecorino cheese.

— **di pesce con taglierini** Sautéed onions, celery, carrots, and tomatoes simmered in white wine and water; *taglierini* noodles and white fish added and simmered until tender.

— **pieno alla calabrese** Beaten eggs, bread crumbs, and Parmesan cheese whisked into boiling chicken broth; brought to a boil and served immediately.

— **di pollo** Chicken bones, aromatic vegetables, and herbs simmered in water; reduced until desired consistency and flavor is attained; strained.

—, **semolino in** Semolina sprinkled into simmering broth and cooked until soft; served with freshly grated Parmesan cheese.

— **spinaci e riso** Chopped spinach, onions, garlic, and celery sautéed in butter and added to boiling stock; raw rice added and simmered until tender; served with grated Parmesan cheese.

—, **taglierini in** Fresh *taglierini* served in piping hot broth with grated Parmesan cheese.

Busecca See Part II.

Caciucco di ceci See Part II.

Cipollata See Part II.

Crema di sedani Sautéed celery, carrots, and onions simmered until tender; pureed and strained; enriched with cream and egg yolks.

Crema di verdure Lettuce, spinach, watercress, potatoes, celery, onions, leeks, and carrots simmered in water until tender; pureed, strained, and enriched with cream and butter.

Incavolata See Part II.

Jota, la See Part II.

Minestra Soup.

— **con battuta alla ligure** Garlic, onions, pancetta, and fresh basil sautéed in lard and added to boiling broth; dried linguine added and simmered until tender.

— **di broccoli alla romana** Broccoli, garlic, and tomatoes sautéed in bacon fat; simmered in stock with pasta and served with grated Parmesan cheese.

— **di bue** Sautéed onions, garlic, spinach, celery, and carrots simmered in beef stock; rice added and simmered until al dente; tender-cooked beef cubes added and seasoned with grated cheese.

— **alla campagnola** Chopped tomatoes, garlic, and onions sautéed in olive oil; simmered in stock with pasta; enriched with eggs and Parmesan cheese.

— **di cavolfiore** Sauteed onions, cauliflower florets, raw rice, and parsley added to boiling stock; enriched with butter and grated cheese.

— **di ceci alla contadina** Sautéed onions, garlic, pancetta, tomatoes, and herbs added to boiling stock; chickpeas added and simmered until tender; served hot over toasted bread and sprinkled with grated cheese.

— **di crostacei alla trapanese** Garlic, onions, tomatoes, crayfish meat and fresh herbs simmered in fish (or lobster) stock; served over boiled rice.

— *di fagioli* Onions, garlic, and tomatoes sautéed in lard; simmered in stock with cooked cannellini beans, raw noodles, and fresh herbs until pasta is tender; served with grated Romano cheese.

— *di fagioli alla bolognese* Garlic sautéed in olive oil and added to hot tomato puree; seasoned with salt, pepper, and fresh herbs; cooked beans and pasta added and served with grated cheese.

— *e fegatini* Onions and diced chicken livers sautéed in butter and added to boiling stock; served over cooked rice.

— *di lenticchie e bietola* Onions, garlic, green peppers, and celery sautéed in olive oil; simmered in stock with lentils and chopped chard; served with grated Parmesan cheese.

— *della nonna* Sautéed leeks and spinach simmered in stock with potatoes, rice, and chopped tomatoes; topped with grated cheese.

— *di pasta e fagioli* Red kidney beans, onions, celery, carrots, tomatoes, garlic, and ham rind simmered in broth; small soup pasta added and served with grated cheese.

— *di riso e fagioli alla genovese* Red kidney beans, spinach, potatoes, onions, leeks, rice, and garlic simmered in broth; seasoned with pesto.

— *di riso e luganega* Sausage, cubed potatoes, onions, garlic, and rice simmered in beef broth; enriched with butter and grated Parmesan.

— *di riso e piselli* Sautéed onions, peas, diced pancetta, and rice simmered in stock; enriched with egg yolks and grated cheese; served immediately with toasted bread.

— *di riso e scarola* Onions and chopped escarole sautéed in olive oil; simmered in chicken stock with raw rice until tender; served with grated Parmesan cheese.

— *di riso e verze* Cabbage, garlic, and onions sautéed in olive oil; simmered in stock with rice and parsley; sprinkled with grated Parmesan cheese.

— *siciliana di riso e asparagi* Diced pancetta, onions, garlic, and parsley sautéed in olive oil and added to hot broth; cooked rice and poached asparagus tips added; sprinkled with grated cheese and served immediately.

— *di verdure alla primaverile* Fresh peas and dried beans simmered in stock until half done; diced potatoes, green beans, mushrooms, zucchini, tomatoes, and small soup pasta added; seasoned with pesto.

— *di zucchine* Sautéed potatoes, garlic, and onions simmered in stock; diced zucchini and *pastina* added and cooked until tender.

Minestrone A hearty vegetable soup.

— *alla brianzola* Green beans, onions, celery, potatoes, tomatoes, carrots, and cabbage sautéed in lard and added to boiling broth; raw soup pasta added and sea-

Minestrone alla brianzola (cont.) soned with fresh herbs and grated cheese.

— *di broccoli e manfrigul* Onions, garlic, and leeks sautéed in olive oil and added to boiling stock; *manfrigul* (see Part II) and broccoli florets added and simmered until tender; served with grated Parmesan cheese.

— *alla contadina* Pancetta, onions, celery, carrots, and garlic sautéed in olive oil and added to boiling broth; simmered with potatoes, cabbage, cooked cannellini beans, spinach, and tomatoes; served with toasted bread and grated Parmesan cheese.

— *con il lardo* Chopped bacon, garlic, onions, tomatoes, carrots, and celery sautéed in bacon fat and added to hot stock; dried beans, diced potatoes, and pasta added (taking into account the various cooking times) and simmered until tender; seasoned with fresh basil and grated cheese.

— *estivo* Chopped tomatoes, garlic, onions, lettuce, cabbage, carrots, zucchini, and fresh basil cooked slowly in olive oil in a covered pot until tender; cooked beans added; served with grated cheese.

— *freddo alla milanese* *Minestrone alla milanese* fortified with rice and seasoned with freshly chopped basil and grated Parmesan cheese; served at room temperature.

— *alla milanese* Onions, garlic, celery, potatoes, zucchini, tomatoes, and carrots sautéed in lard and added to boiling broth; red

kidney beans and rice added and simmered until tender; served with grated cheese.

— *alla romagnola* Onions, carrots, celery, and garlic sautéed in olive oil and added to boiling stock; simmered with parcooked cannellini beans, potatoes, cabbage, green beans, squash, and tomatoes; seasoned with salt, pepper, and grated Parmesan cheese.

— *semplice* Sautéed onions and garlic added to stock; simmered with green beans, celery, potatoes, peas, and small pasta noodles; sprinkled with grated Parmesan cheese.

— *siciliano di pasta e carciofi* Chopped onions, garlic, and celery sautéed in lard and added to boiling broth; diced tomatoes, chopped artichokes, and raw pasta added; simmered until tender and served with grated cheese.

— *toscano* Dried cannellini beans simmered in stock with sautéed pancetta, onions, celery, cabbage, garlic, tomatoes, and carrots; raw pasta added and cooked until tender; seasoned with fresh herbs.

Pancotto See Part II.

Paparot See Part II.

Passatelli See Part II.

Passato A smooth soup.

— *di castagne* Sautéed onions, celery, and fresh sage combined with chestnut puree; thinned with milk or cream and heated to simmering; strained and served with toasted bread.

— *di fagioli* Onions, garlic, ham, and cannellini beans simmered in stock until tender; pureed, strained, and seasoned; served with toasted bread.

— *di spinaci* Onions, carrots, celery, and spinach sautéed in butter and added to boiling broth; simmered until vegetables are soft; pureed, seasoned with salt and pepper, and served with toasted bread and grated cheese.

— *di verdure* Onions, garlic, carrots, leeks, spinach, cabbage, and tomatoes sautéed in olive oil and simmered in stock until tender; pureed, strained and seasoned; served with grated Parmesan cheese and toasted bread.

Preboggion col pesto See Part II.

Risi e bisi See Part II.

Stracciatella See Part II.

Zuppa A hearty soup served with bread.

— *all'aglio* Sautéed onions simmered in stock; thickened with bread crumbs and pureed; seasoned with grated cheese and served with toasted bread slices.

— *di asparagi* Sautéed onions and celery simmered in stock; asparagus tips added and cooked until tender; poured over toasted bread and sprinkled with grated cheese.

— *di calamari e carciofi* Squid simmered in stock with olive oil, white wine, garlic, onions, and fresh herbs until tender; sliced artichokes and freshly grated black pepper added; served with toasted bread.

— *di cannellini con aglio e prezzemolo* Onions sautéed in olive oil; simmered in stock with cooked cannellini beans; sea-

soned with salt, pepper, and parsley; served with toasted bread.

— *di cavolo nero* Pancetta, garlic, onions, carrots, and celery sautéed in olive oil and added to boiling broth; simmered with red cabbage, tomatoes, sliced sausage links, and cooked cannellini beans; served with toasted bread.

— *di ceci* Onions sautéed in olive oil; simmered in stock with cooked chickpeas, tomatoes, and parsley; seasoned with salt, pepper, and rosemary.

— *di ceci e pasta* Small cooked soup pasta added to *zuppa di ceci*.

— *di cipolle* Sautéed onions simmered in stock and thickened with flour and butter; sprinkled with grated cheese and served with toasted bread.

— *di cozze* Sautéed leeks, onions, and potatoes simmered in fish stock; poached mussels added and thickened with bread crumbs; enriched with cream.

— *ai frutti di mare* Clams, mussels, and shrimp poached in white wine and water; seafood removed and stock added to sautéed onions, tomatoes, and garlic; poured in a bowl over toasted bread and the poached seafood.

— *di lenticchie* Sautéed ham, celery, onions, and tomatoes simmered in stock; cooked lentils added and seasoned with salt, pepper, and fresh sage; served over toasted bread and sprinkled with grated Parmesan cheese.

— *di merluzzo* Sautéed leeks, onions, garlic, tomatoes, and cod chunks simmered in fish stock;

DISHES BY COURSE

Zuppa di merluzzo (cont.)
seasoned with saffron, fennel, and red pepper; served with toasted bread.

— **di patate e cipolle** Onions sautéed in butter and added to boiling stock; simmered with potatoes, salt, pepper, and fresh parsley; served with grated Parmesan cheese.

— **pavese** Poached egg and toasted bread served in chicken or beef broth.

— **di pesce al finocchio** Onions, garlic, tomatoes, fennel, and parsley sautéed in olive oil and added to hot fish stock; assorted seafood added and simmered until fish is cooked; served immediately.

— **di pesce con i gamberi** Shrimp, white fish, onions, garlic, celery, and fresh thyme and parsley sautéed slowly in butter; simmered in stock until tender, pureed, and strained; thickened with cream and seasoned with saffron. Served with toasted bread.

— **di piselli e patate** Onions and carrots sautéed in olive oil; simmered in broth with fresh peas, potatoes, and chopped parsley; seasoned with salt, pepper, and grated Parmesan cheese.

— **di piselli e vongole** Onions, garlic, and tomatoes sautéed in olive oil and added to boiling clam stock; fresh peas added and simmered until tender; cooked clams added and served with toasted bread.

— **di porri** Leeks, onions, and parsley slowly cooked in butter; sprinkled with flour and sim-mered in stock until thick; served with grated Parmesan cheese and toasted bread.

— **povera** Onions, cabbage, potatoes, garlic, and lima beans sautéed in olive oil and added to boiling stock; seasoned with tomato puree, salt and pepper, and fresh herbs.

— **primavera** Garlic, onions, leeks, potatoes, artichokes, and carrots sautéed in olive oil; simmered in stock with fresh peas and herbs until tender; served with grated Parmesan cheese and toasted bread.

— **di riso e cavolo** Onions and cabbage sautéed in butter and added to boiling stock; simmered with raw rice and fresh herbs until rice is tender; served with grated Parmesan cheese.

— **spagnola** Garlic, onions, tomatoes, and parsley sautéed in olive oil and added to boiling stock; rice and codfish added and cooked until tender.

— **di trippa alla trentina** Fresh herbs, aromatic vegetables, potatoes, diced tomatoes, and beef tripe simmered in stock; served over toasted bread.

— **della valsesia** Onions, leeks, potatoes, celery, garlic, and herbs simmered in stock; sprinkled with grated *Toma* cheese and served with rye bread.

— **vegetale con polpettini** Diced onions, carrots, celery, garlic, peas, and tomatoes simmered in beef stock; small soup noodles and meatballs added; sprinkled with grated Parmesan cheese.

— *di vongole* Sautéed garlic and tomatoes simmered in white wine and fish stock; poached clams added and seasoned with chopped parsley; poured over toasted bread.

— *di zucca* Pumpkin chunks slowly cooked in butter; pureed and enriched with cream; seasoned with salt and pepper and served with toasted bread.

PASTA—PASTAS

Acciughe e pomodoro alla pugliese, con Garlic, minced anchovies, and tomatoes sautéed in olive oil, mashed until a paste is formed; seasoned with salt, pepper, and parsley and tossed with cooked pasta.

Aglio e olio alla napoletana, con Garlic and diced chili peppers or red pepper flakes sautéed in olive oil; tossed with cooked spaghetti or vermicelli and sprinkled with fresh chopped parsley.

Ajo e ojo See Part II.

Alfredo, all' Butter and heavy cream simmered until thick; tossed with cooked fettuccine or *tagliatelle* and grated Parmesan cheese; seasoned with freshly ground black pepper and a pinch of nutmeg; served immediately.

Amatriciana, all' Onions, garlic, pancetta, and red pepper flakes sautéed in olive oil; diced tomatoes with juice added; seasoned with salt and freshly ground black pepper and tossed with *bucatini*; sprinkled with grated pecorino cheese.

Aragosta, all' Cooked lobster chunks marinated in olive oil with garlic and herbs; hot pasta tossed with chilled marinade and served at once.

Arrabiata, all' Pancetta, onions, garlic, anchovies, and red pepper flakes sautéed in olive oil; fresh chopped tomatoes added; seasoned with salt and tossed with cooked pasta; sprinkled with freshly grated Parmesan cheese; served immediately.

Asparagi, con Blanched asparagus tips, onions, and garlic sautéed in olive oil; fresh chopped tomatoes and juice added and slightly reduced; tossed with cooked pasta and sprinkled with grated Parmesan cheese.

Asparagi, al sugo di With asparagus sauce. (See Part II, *Asparagi, sugo di.*)

Bagaria Cubed eggplant, onions, garlic, and capers sautéed in olive oil; canned diced tomatoes, fresh herbs, and green olives added and simmered until slightly thickened; seasoned with salt and pepper and tossed with cooked drained pasta; served immediately with grated cheese.

Barese, alla Turnip sprouts, onions, and garlic sautéed in olive oil; tomato puree, fresh basil, and salt and pepper added; tossed with cooked spaghetti or linguine and served immediately.

Basilico, con Garlic, parsley, chopped fresh tomatoes, and a generous amount of fresh basil sautéed in olive oil; seasoned with salt and pepper and tossed with cooked pasta; served with freshly grated cheese.

Bavette alla livornese Garlic, onions, tomatoes, and fish chunks sautéed in olive oil; seasoned with salt, pepper, and basil and tossed with cooked pasta noodles.

Bavette e pesce Garlic, onions, tomatoes, sweet peppers, and fresh herbs sautéed in olive oil; tomato juice added and simmered with shrimp, octopus, and various other seafood; tossed with cooked pasta.

Beccacce, e Boned woodcock pieces sautéed in butter with garlic and fresh herbs; red wine, brandy, and tomato juice added and simmered until meat is tender; tossed with cooked pasta and topped with grated cheese.

Bisi, e Chopped chicken livers, fresh sage, and fresh cooked peas sautéed in butter; tossed with cooked pasta and sprinkled with grated cheese.

Bolognese, alla Onions, garlic, celery, carrots, fresh basil, and ground beef sautéed in olive oil; chopped tomatoes with juice and white wine added; seasoned with salt and pepper and tossed with cooked pasta; served with freshly grated Parmesan cheese.

Boscaiola, alla Garlic, fresh mushrooms, fresh or reconstituted dry wild mushrooms, and sausage sautéed in olive oil; canned diced tomatoes with juice added and seasoned with salt, pepper, and chopped parsley; tossed with cooked pasta and sprinkled with grated cheese.

Briciolata See Part II.

Broccoli, con i Garlic sautéed in olive oil; canned diced tomatoes, pine nuts, currants, and broccoli florets added and simmered until florets are tender; seasoned with salt and pepper and tossed with cooked pasta; sprinkled with freshly grated Parmesan cheese and served immediately.

Broccoli e acciughe, di Onions, garlic, parsley, and anchovies sautéed in olive oil and mashed to a paste; seasoned with salt and pepper and tossed with blanched broccoli and cooked pasta; served with grated cheese.

Bucaniera, alla Garlic, onions, and red pepper flakes sautéed in olive oil; white wine, chopped fresh tomatoes, and poached seafood added; seasoned with salt and freshly ground black pepper and tossed with cooked pasta.

Burro e formaggio, al Cooked pasta tossed with hot butter and sprinkled generously with freshly grated Parmesan cheese; served immediately.

Cacciatore, del Mushrooms, garlic, and onions sautéed in olive oil; tomato puree and seasonings added; enriched with cream and tossed with hot pasta; sprinkled with grated Parmesan cheese.

Cacio e pepe, col Hot cooked pasta tossed with olive oil and generous amounts of freshly ground black pepper and grated pecorino cheese.

Canestrelli, coi Garlic, red pepper flakes, parsley, and scallops sautéed in olive oil; tossed with spaghetti or vermicelli and toasted bread crumbs.

Cannelloni Garlic, pancetta, and ground beef sautéed in olive oil; cooled and bound with ricotta and *besciamella*; stuffed into cooked cannelloni pasta and covered with ragù sauce; sprinkled with grated cheese and baked.

— *della nonna* Cannelloni stuffed with ground beef, chopped cooked spinach, grated Parmesan cheese, and eggs; topped with *besciamella* and Parmesan cheese and baked.

— *con ricotta* Cannelloni stuffed with ricotta, Parmesan cheese, eggs, and seasonings; topped with *besciamella* and baked.

— *della vigilia* Cannelloni stuffed with fresh chopped sautéed spinach, ricotta, Parmesan cheese, eggs, and seasonings; topped with *besciamella* and baked.

Cappelletti in brodo Cappelletti served in broth and accompanied with freshly grated Parmesan cheese.

Capriolo, al Venison pieces, onions, and fresh herbs browned in butter; stock added and simmered until venison is tender; enriched with cream and cognac and tossed with cooked pasta; served immediately.

Carbonara alla See Part II.

Carciofi, con Garlic, tomatoes, pancetta, and artichokes sautéed in olive oil; white wine added and reduced until flavors intensify; seasoned with salt, pepper, and fresh herbs; tossed with ziti, rigatoni, penne, and so on; sprinkled with grated pecorino cheese.

Carrettiera, alla Garlic, chopped tomatoes, and fresh basil sautéed in olive oil; seasoned with salt and freshly ground black pepper and tossed with cooked pasta; sprinkled with grated pecorino cheese.

Caviale di tonno, con Tuna roe sautéed in olive oil and mashed to a paste; seasoned with salt, pepper, and parsley; tossed with hot pasta.

Cavolfiore, con Garlic, blanched cauliflower, and chopped parsley sautéed in olive oil; canned diced tomatoes, pine nuts, anchovy fillets, and golden raisins added; seasoned with salt and pepper and tossed with cooked and drained pasta; served piping hot with freshly grated pecorino cheese.

Cavolfiore, col sugo di Blanched cauliflower, garlic, and parsley sautéed in olive oil; seasoned with anchovy puree, salt, and freshly ground black pepper; tossed with cooked pasta.

Chitarra See Part II.

Cibreo See Part II.

Cipolla, alla Onions and leeks sautéed in butter; tossed with hot pasta and sprinkled with grated Parmesan cheese.

Cipolle e porri, alle Onions, leeks, and scallions sautéed in olive oil and tossed with hot cooked pasta; sprinkled with grated Parmesan cheese.

Cipolle, col sugo di Onions and diced pancetta sautéed in olive oil and bacon fat; white wine added and reduced; seasoned with salt and pepper and tossed with chopped parsley and spaghetti; sprinkled with freshly grated Parmesan cheese.

Coniglio, al Garlic and cubed rabbit meat sautéed in butter; deglazed with red wine; tomato puree and rabbit stock added and reduced until desired consistency is attained; strained and tossed with cooked pasta and pureed rabbit livers; sprinkled with freshly grated Parmesan cheese and served piping hot.

Coniglio alla sarda, con Ground rabbit meat browned in olive oil with sage and parsley; simmered in white wine and stock and enriched with heavy cream; tossed with hot pasta.

Contadina, alla Onions, garlic, and tomatoes sautéed in olive oil; seasoned with salt, pepper, and fresh oregano; tossed with pasta and served immediately with grated Parmesan cheese.

Corzetti alla rivierasca Corzetti pasta tossed with cooked salmon pieces in a tomato and basil sauce; garnished with chopped walnuts.

Dolce, al Cooked chilled pasta tossed with mayonnaise, vinegar, diced beetroot, shredded carrots, and diced celery; served chilled.

Dorate, alle Fresh bread crumbs, garlic, and fresh herbs browned in butter and tossed with cooked pasta; seasoned with freshly ground black pepper and sprinkled with grated Parmesan cheese; served at once.

Fegatini, con Diced chicken livers, tomato strips, fresh blanched peas, and garlic sautéed in butter; seasoned with salt and freshly ground black pepper and tossed with hot drained pasta; served with grated cheese.

Fegatini, con il ragù di Cooked pasta tossed with chopped sautéed chicken livers and *bolognese* sauce; served with freshly grated Parmesan cheese.

Fegatini, al sugo di Onions, garlic, and chopped chicken livers sautéed in olive oil; flour added to make a roux; chicken stock and white wine added and simmered until thickened; tossed with hot cooked pasta.

Fiaccheraia, alla Onions, garlic, red pepper flakes and tomato pulp sautéed in olive oil; tossed with cooked pasta and served with grated cheese.

Finocchio alla siciliana, con Onions and fresh blanched fennel sautéed in olive oil; broth, raisins, pine nuts, and boneless fresh sardine chunks added and simmered until fish is cooked; seasoned with salt and pepper and tossed with cooked pasta and toasted bread crumbs; sprinkled with more bread crumbs and served piping hot.

Forno col ragù, al Cooked ziti or similar pasta tossed with *bolognese* sauce and *besciamella*; sprinkled with freshly grated Parmesan cheese and baked.

Frutti di mare, ai Onions, garlic, and tomatoes sautéed in olive oil; tomato juice and fresh raw seafood added; simmered slowly until seafood is cooked; seasoned with salt, pepper, and fresh basil; tossed with spaghetti or linguine and served immediately.

Funghetto, pasta verde al Mushrooms and garlic sautéed in olive oil; white wine and chopped tomatoes added and simmered until thickened; seasoned with salt and freshly ground black pepper and tossed with green spinach noodles; served with grated cheese.

Funghi, con i Fresh white mushrooms, fresh or reconstituted dried wild mushrooms, and garlic sautéed in butter; seasoned with salt and pepper, and tossed with hot cooked pasta; sprinkled with grated cheese.

Gaetana, alla Ground pork, onions, and garlic sautéed in olive oil; white wine and stock added and simmered with fresh herbs, chopped calf's liver, and black olives; tossed with cooked pasta and served with grated pecorino cheese.

Gamberetti, col sugo di Garlic and chopped drained tomatoes sautéed in butter; deglazed with white wine; heavy cream and fresh raw shrimp added and simmered gently until sauce thickens and shrimp is cooked; seasoned with chopped parsley and freshly ground black pepper; tossed with cooked pasta.

Garganello, al Wild duck boned and browned in butter; simmered in *salsa bianca* fortified with red wine and flavored with capers and anchovies; tossed with cooked pasta and served immediately.

Golosa, alla Diced prosciutto, sliced mushrooms, tomatoes, and fresh sage sautéed in butter; heavy cream added and reduced until thickened; seasoned with salt and freshly ground black pepper and tossed with cooked pasta; sprinkled with chopped parsley and grated cheese.

Gorgonzola, al Cooked pasta tossed with hot butter and crumbled Gorgonzola; sprinkled with freshly grated Parmesan cheese.

Gratinata See Part II.

Lasagne A wide, flat noodle sometimes having a curly edge.

— **alla Cacciatore** Strips of rabbit meat, pancetta, onions, and mushrooms sautéed in olive oil; white wine and fresh chopped tomatoes added and simmered until thickened; seasoned with salt, pepper, and chopped parsley; tossed with pasta squares (about two- to three-inch squares); served immediately.

— **coi carciofi** Lasagne noodles layered with artichoke hearts cooked in butter and *besciamella* mixed with grated Parmesan cheese; topped with more *besciamella* and grated cheese and baked.

— **alla ferrarese** Shelled walnuts ground in a mortar with olive oil, salt, and freshly ground black pepper; thinned with cream and layered between cooked lasagne noodles; sprinkled with grated cheese and baked.

— **coi funghi e prosciutto** Lasagne noodles layered with white and wild mushrooms cooked in butter, tomato sauce, and freshly grated Parmesan cheese; layers repeated and topped with *besciamella* and grated cheese; baked.

— **alla genovese** Large pasta

Lasagne alla genovese (cont.)
squares tossed with meat sauce; served with grated Parmesan cheese.

— **con melanzane** Lasagne noodles layered with tomato sauce, fried breaded eggplant, and *besciamella*; baked.

— **pasticciate** Lasagne noodles layered alternately with *bolognese* sauce, *besciamella*, and freshly grated Parmesan cheese; baked.

— **al pesto** Layers of lasagne noodles alternating pesto sauce and *besciamella*; baked.

— **col pesto di ricotta** Small lasagne squares spread with pesto and ricotta and topped with more pasta squares; sprinkled with grated Parmesan cheese and served immediately, unbaked.

— **piccanti** Lasagne noodles layered with hot sausage, Parmesan cheese, and tomato sauce seasoned with red pepper; layers repeated and topped with *besciamella*; baked.

— **primavera** Lasagne noodles alternately layered with *besciamella* and fresh cooked spring vegetables; topped with *besciamella* and baked.

— **verdi casalinghe** Onions, garlic, ground beef, and ground sausage meat browned in olive oil; fresh herbs, beef stock, and fresh chopped tomatoes added; sauce layered alternately with *besciamella* and cooked spinach lasagne noodles; sprinkled with freshly grated Parmesan cheese and baked.

— **verdi al forno** Spinach lasagne noodles layered with tomato sauce and *besciamella*; topped with *besciamella* and grated cheese; baked

— **verdi alla ligure** Spinach lasagne noodles layered alternately with tomato sauce and ground beef; topped with *besciamella* and baked.

Laziale, alla Garlic, onions, mushrooms, pancetta, tomato strips, and ground beef sautéed in butter; white wine, diced cooked lamb's brains, and fresh herbs added; stuffed into cannelloni shells and covered with meat sauce (see *Manzo, al sugo di*; this section) and grated Parmesan; baked.

Lepre, con la Boneless hare pieces sautéed with onions, garlic, fresh herbs, and the animal's liver; simmered in a covered pot in red wine and stock until tender; sauce pureed and tossed with hot pasta.

Livornese, alla Diced pancetta, ham, onions, garlic, and basil sautéed in olive oil; deglazed with brandy and tossed with hot pasta.

Lucana con fagioli, alla Garlic, red pepper flakes, and lima beans sautéed in lard; seasoned with salt, freshly ground black pepper, and chopped parsley; tossed with cooked pasta and served immediately.

Lumache, e Cooked snails sautéed with garlic in olive oil; deglazed with white wine and seasoned with salt, pepper, and garlic; tossed with thick noodles and served immediately.

Lusso, di Cooked pasta sautéed

quickly in butter with diced ham; beaten egg yolks, grated Parmesan cheese, and cream combined and tossed with hot pasta; sprinkled with minced truffles and grated cheese.

Maccheroni trinacria al forno Cooked macaroni tossed with tomato sauce flavored with anchovies; topped with fried eggplant slices and grated cheese; baked.

Maniche di frate alla caprese Large macaroni stuffed with ground sausage, tomatoes, and seasonings; arranged in a baking dish lined with *besciamella*; topped with fried breaded eggplant slices and coated with more *besciamella*; sprinkled with grated Parmesan and baked.

Manicotti imbottiti Mozzarella cheese, grated Parmesan cheese, fresh ricotta, eggs, and chopped parsley combined and stuffed into cooked manicotti shells; coated with tomato sauce and grated Parmesan and baked.

Manzo, al sugo di Onions, garlic, celery, carrots, and boneless beef chunks sautéed in olive oil; beef stock added and sauce reduced until beef is tender; seasoned with salt and pepper and tossed with cooked pasta; served with freshly grated Parmesan cheese.

Marinara Onions and garlic sautéed in olive oil; canned diced tomatoes added and simmered with fresh basil, oregano, and freshly ground black pepper; anchovy paste stirred in and tossed with cooked drained pasta; served immediately with grated pecorino cheese.

Mascarpone, al Mascarpone cheese, heavy cream, grated Parmesan cheese, and egg yolks mixed well and heated gently; tossed with cooked pasta and served immediately.

Mascarpone, col Hot cooked pasta tossed with hot butter and softened mascarpone cheese; served immediately.

Melanzane, con le Diced eggplant sautéed in olive oil until tender; onions, chopped tomatoes, and garlic added; seasoned with salt, freshly ground black pepper, and chopped parsley; tossed with cooked spaghetti or vermicelli.

Napoletana, alla Tomato sauce cooked with ground sausage, diced salami, and white wine; seasoned with salt, red and black pepper, and ricotta; tossed with cooked pasta.

'Ncasciata alla siciliana Onions, garlic, carrots, diced ham, and boneless pork chunks sautéed in olive oil; tomato strips and beef stock added and simmered, covered, until pork is tender; layered in a baking dish with sauce, cooked pasta, hard-cooked egg slices, and grated Parmesan; layers repeated, ending with sauce and Parmesan cheese; baked.

Nero, al See Part II.

Nursina, alla Minced black truffles, chopped garlic, and anchovies gently sautéed in olive oil; seasoned with salt and freshly ground black pepper and tossed with cooked spaghetti or vermicelli; served immediately.

Ortolano, dell' Onions, garlic, car-

Ortolano, dell' (cont.)
rots, celery, and fresh herbs sautéed in butter and tossed with
pasta; sprinkled with grated Parmesan cheese.

Paglia e fieno alla ghiotta Onions,
garlic, and pancetta sautéed in
butter; heavy cream and fresh
cooked peas added and simmered
until thickened; seasoned with
salt and pepper and tossed with
egg fettuccine and spinach
fettuccine; sprinkled liberally with
freshly grated Parmesan cheese
and served immediately.

Panna, con la Butter and heavy
cream simmered until thickened;
seasoned with salt and white pepper and tossed with cooked pasta;
freshly grated Parmesan cheese
served on the side.

Panna e funghi, alla Onions, mushrooms, truffles, and garlic sautéed
in butter; heavy cream added and
reduced until thick; seasoned and
tossed with pasta.

Passato di pesce alla genovese, con
Onions and garlic sautéed in olive oil with cubed sea fish (various); simmered in white wine and
water until tender; pureed and
seasoned with freshly ground
black pepper and fresh herbs;
tossed with pasta.

Pasticcio di fegatini e maccheroni
Cooked macaroni arranged in a
baking dish and covered with tomato sauce mixed with chopped
chicken livers; covered with more
macaroni and topped with *besciamella*; sprinkled with grated Parmesan cheese and baked.

Pasticcio di maccheroncelli alla

toscana Onions, garlic, ground
beef, chicken livers, and tomatoes
sautéed in butter; moistened with
broth and seasoned with salt, pepper, and fresh herbs; tossed with
cooked short pasta (ziti, rigatoni,
macaroni, and so on) and grated
Parmesan cheese; placed in a
pastry-lined tin and baked.

Pasticcio di pasta Cooked spaghetti
tossed with *ragù* sauce, eggs, and
Parmesan cheese; placed in an
buttered mold lined with bread
crumbs and baked; unmolded
before serving.

Patate, e Peeled potato cubes sautéed in olive oil with diced onions
and garlic; canned diced tomatoes
added and simmered until potatoes are tender; seasoned with
salt, freshly ground black pepper,
and chopped parsley; tossed with
cooked pasta and sprinkled with
grated pecorino cheese.

Peperoni, ai (1) Sweet peppers, onions, carrots, parsley, and pancetta
sautéed in olive oil; seasoned with
salt and freshly ground black pepper and tossed with cooked pasta;
served immediately with grated
Parmesan on the side. (2) Garlic,
sweet peppers, and chopped fresh
tomatoes sautéed in olive oil; seasoned with salt, freshly ground
black pepper, and fresh basil and
tossed with cooked pasta; served
with grated Parmesan cheese.

Pescatore, del Garlic and chopped
tomatoes sautéed in olive oil; tomato puree, seasonings, and raw
shrimp added; simmered slowly
until shrimp is cooked; tossed with
ziti, rigatoni, penne, and so on.

Pesce, al sugo di Onions, parsley, tomatoes, and garlic sautéed in olive oil; white wine, fish stock, and fish puree added and reduced until thick; tossed with spaghetti or vermicelli and served immediately.

Pesto, con Fresh basil crushed in a mortar with fresh garlic cloves, grated Parmesan, and olive oil; seasoned with freshly ground black pepper and tossed with piping hot cooked and drained pasta.

Pesto di formaggio Piping hot cooked and drained pasta tossed with pesto (see *Pesto, con*; this section) and sprinkled generously with freshly grated Parmesan and pecorino cheeses and served immediately.

Piccanti alla calabrese Garlic, red pepper flakes, and anchovy paste sautéed in olive oil; seasoned with fresh parsley and freshly ground black pepper and tossed with hot cooked pasta.

Piovra, con la Chopped cooked octopus sautéed in olive oil with onions and garlic; fish stock added and simmered; tossed with hot pasta.

Piselli e peperoni, coi Roasted red pepper slices, diced prosciutto, and garlic sautéed in butter; cooked peas and heavy cream added and reduced until thickened; tossed with cooked pasta and sprinkled with freshly grated Parmesan cheese.

Piselli e ricotta, con Diced pancetta, onions, and parsley sautéed in butter; cooked peas added and seasoned with freshly ground black pepper; tossed with fresh ricotta and cooked pasta and sprinkled with grated cheese.

Pizzicotti dei romani See Part II.

Pizzoccheri/pizzòcher See Part II.

Polpettine di carne, con Pasta served with meatballs in tomato sauce; sprinkled with grated Parmesan.

Pommarola See Part II.

Pomodoro al forno, al Tomatoes, pancetta, anchovies, and fresh parsley and basil baked together in olive oil; tossed with hot pasta and seasoned with salt and pepper.

Pomodoro e funghi secchi, al sugo di Reconstituted dried wild mushrooms, onions, garlic, and sausage sautéed in olive oil; diced tomatoes with juice added and seasoned with salt and black pepper; tossed with cooked pasta and sprinkled with grated cheese.

Pomodoro fresco, al Fresh diced tomatoes, garlic, olive oil, and fresh basil simmered together until desired flavor is attained; seasoned with salt and freshly ground black pepper and tossed with cooked pasta; served immediately with grated Parmesan cheese.

Pomodoro e acciughe, al sugo di Garlic, onions, and anchovies sautéed in olive oil; chopped tomatoes with juice added; seasoned with salt, pepper, and parsley; tossed with cooked pasta.

Pomodoro e panna, con sugo di Onions, garlic, carrots, and celery sautéed in butter; canned diced tomatoes with juice added and reduced until flavors intensify; heavy cream added and sim-

DISHES BY COURSE

Pomodoro e panna, con sugo di
(cont.)
mered until thickened; seasoned
with salt and pepper and tossed
with cooked pasta; served with
grated pecorino cheese.

Pomodoro e peperoni, con Onions,
garlic, sweet peppers, and fresh
chopped tomatoes sautéed in olive oil; seasoned with salt and pepper and tossed with cooked pasta.

Pomodoro, con salsa semplice di
Garlic sautéed in olive oil; tomato
puree and a dash of sugar added
and seasoned with salt, freshly
ground black pepper and bay
leaves; simmered until slightly
thickened and tossed with cooked
pasta; sprinkled with grated
cheese.

Poverella, alla Cooked pasta sautéed
in bacon fat with pieces of cooked
bacon; beaten eggs slowly added
and tossed in hot pan; seasoned
with freshly grated black pepper
and grated pecorino cheese.

Puttanesca, salsa alla See Part II.

Quattro formaggi, ai Mozzarella
cheese, fontina cheese, and Gorgonzola cheese slowly melted in
butter; heavy cream and grated
Parmesan added and cooked gently until creamy; seasoned with salt
and freshly ground black pepper
and tossed with hot cooked pasta.

Ragù d'agnello, col Boneless lamb
pieces, onions, garlic, and green
peppers sautéed in olive oil; white
wine and canned diced tomatoes
added and simmered, covered,
until meat is tender; seasoned
with salt and pepper and tossed
with cooked pasta.

Ragù al tonno, con With tuna sauce;
see Part II, *Tonno, salsa di.*

Raviolini al gratin Small cooked
ravioli stuffed with ricotta, Parmesan cheese, bread crumbs, and
eggs; arranged in a baking dish
and coated with tomato sauce;
sprinkled with grated cheese and
baked.

Ravioli Square, round, or half-
moon shaped stuffed pasta.

— ***alla mantovana*** Ravioli stuffed
with ricotta, Parmesan cheese,
fresh herbs, and eggs; cooked in
salted boiling water and tossed
with *ragù* sauce.

— ***alle noci*** Garlic, walnuts and
fresh bread crumbs sautéed in olive oil; pureed, enriched with
cream and tossed with cooked
ravioli; sprinkled with grated Parmesan cheese and served immediately.

— ***alla panna gratinati*** Cooked
ravioli stuffed with ground sausage, eggs, grated Parmesan,
bread crumbs, and seasonings;
placed in a baking dish and coated
with *besciamella* and Parmesan
cheese; baked.

— ***alla romagna*** Cooked ravioli
stuffed with ricotta, grated
pecorino cheese, grated Parmesan
cheese, and beaten eggs; placed
in a baking dish and coated with
meat sauce (see *Manzo, al sugo di*;
this section) and grated cheese;
baked.

— ***verdi alla ricotta*** Green ravioli
stuffed with fresh chopped basil,
Parmesan cheese, and ricotta;
cooked in salted boiling water and
tossed in butter.

Ricotta, con la Ricotta thinned with heavy cream and seasoned with salt, pepper, cinnamon, and sugar; gently heated and tossed with hot cooked pasta.

Romagnola, alla Ravioli, tortellini, *agnolotti,* or other stuffed pasta filled with ricotta, grated Parmesan, bread crumbs, eggs, and seasonings; cooked; tossed with hot butter and sprinkled with grated cheese and freshly ground black pepper.

Rosmarino, col Garlic and fresh rosemary gently cooked in butter; seasoned with salt and freshly ground black pepper and tossed with cooked pasta; sprinkled with grated Parmesan cheese.

Rotolo di pasta See Part II.

Salsa di noci, con With walnut sauce; See Part II, *Noci, salsa di.*

Salsiccia, con la Ground sausage browned in olive oil with garlic and onions; white wine and canned diced tomatoes added and simmered until flavors blend; tossed with cooked pasta and served with grated cheese.

Sarde, con le Fresh sardines sautéed in olive oil, mashed until incorporated into oil; seasoned with raisins, pine nuts, cooked wild fennel, and wine vinegar; tossed with *bucatini* and sprinkled with toasted bread crumbs.

Sarde, con Sardines sautéed in olive oil with garlic and onions and mashed to a paste; tossed with cooked pasta and served piping hot.

Sbirraglia, alla Layers of plain cooked lasagne noodles coated with cream sauce flavored with brandy, chopped truffles, and seasonings; sprinkled with grated Parmesan cheese and baked.

Scheggino, pasta di See Part II.

Seppie e pisellini, con Thinly sliced squid, garlic, and tomatoes sautéed in olive oil; white wine and fresh cooked peas added and reduced; tossed with cooked pasta and chopped parsley; served immediately.

Siciliana, alla (1) Onions, garlic, tomatoes, and sweet peppers sautéed in oil; anchovies added and simmered with fresh herbs; tossed with hot pasta and sprinkled with grated pecorino cheese. (2) Diced eggplant sautéed in olive oil until tender; onions, garlic, and tomatoes added; tossed with cooked pasta and fresh ricotta and seasoned with salt, pepper, and fresh basil; sprinkled with freshly grated pecorino cheese.

Siracusana, alla Onions, garlic, sweet peppers, and eggplant chunks sautéed in olive oil; chopped fresh tomatoes, anchovy paste, black olives, capers, and fresh herbs added; seasoned with salt and pepper and tossed with cooked pasta; served with freshly grated pecorino cheese.

Spinaci e ricotta, con Fresh chopped spinach and minced onions slowly stewed in butter and seasoned with salt and freshly ground black pepper; tossed with rigatoni or penne and fresh ricotta; sprinkled generously with freshly grated Parmesan cheese.

Telline, con le Garlic sautéed in ol-

Telline, con le (cont.)
ive oil; fresh chopped tomatoes, canned diced tomatoes (with juice), clam juice (or mussel broth), and cooked mussels added; tossed with cooked pasta and seasoned with salt and pepper.

Torta di pasta Cooked pasta tossed with tomato sauce, browned sausage meat, grated Parmesan cheese, eggs, and seasonings; stuffed in a pastry-lined pie pan and covered with pastry; baked and served hot.

Tortellini alla bolognese Cooked tortellini stuffed with minced mortadella, Parmesan cheese, diced prosciutto, eggs, and seasonings; topped with meat sauce and sprinkled with grated Parmesan cheese.

Tortellini al gorgonzola Tortellini stuffed with crumbled Gorgonzola, freshly grated Parmesan, ricotta, and bread crumbs; cooked in boiling salted water and tossed with tomato sauce; sprinkled with grated Parmesan cheese and served immediately.

Tortelli di piccione Cooked *Tortelli* stuffed with ground squab meat, Parmesan cheese, diced prosciutto, eggs, and seasonings; tossed in hot butter and Parmesan cheese.

Tortelloni alla casentina *Tortelloni* stuffed with sausage, Parmesan cheese, bread crumbs, tomato puree, and seasonings; tossed in sage butter and sprinkled with grated Parmesan cheese.

Toscana, alla Onions, sweet peppers, garlic, and carrots sautéed in pork fat; white wine, tomato puree, and seasonings added; tossed with hot pasta.

Toscana con la lepre, alla Marinated hare cut into sections and browned in olive oil with onions, celery, carrots, and pancetta; red wine and fresh herbs added and simmered, covered, until hare is tender; sauce strained and finished with whole butter; tossed with cooked pasta and served with grated Parmesan cheese.

Trenette col pesto Cooked *trenette* tossed with pesto; served immediately with freshly grated Parmesan cheese.

Trenette con salsa di carciofi Garlic, mushrooms, and artichokes sautéed in olive oil; deglazed with white wine; chicken stock and tomato puree added and thickened with roux; tossed with *trenette*.

Trippate, pasta alle See Part II.

Veneta, alla Onions, garlic, ground veal, and ground sausage sautéed in olive oil; deglazed with red wine and stock and thickened with heavy cream; tossed with hot pasta and served with grated Parmesan cheese.

Veneziana, alla Cooked pasta tossed with cooked fish chunks, tomato sauce, and pine nuts; arranged in a baking pan and topped with *besciamella*; layers repeated and topped with grated Parmesan cheese; baked.

Verde, pasta Cooked and drained pasta tossed with hot garlic-butter, grated Parmesan cheese, and a generous amount of fresh chopped parsley; seasoned with salt and pepper and served immediately.

Verdure piccanti, alle Onions, garlic, celery, spinach, and carrots sautéed in olive oil; deglazed with white wine and seasoned with red and black pepper; tossed with hot pasta and served with grated Parmesan cheese.

Verdure, con sugo di Onions, garlic, celery, carrots, and fresh basil sautéed in olive oil; canned diced tomatoes added and simmered until thickened; tossed with cooked pasta and sprinkled with grated cheese.

Vongole, alle Chopped clams sautéed in olive oil with garlic, parsley, tomatoes, black pepper, and red pepper flakes; tossed with spaghetti or linguine and served piping hot.

Vongole bianche, al sugo di Chopped clams, onions, garlic, parsley, black pepper, and red pepper flakes sautéed in butter; heavy cream added and reduced until thick; tossed with spaghetti, vermicelli, and so on.

Zucchine, con le Sliced zucchini, garlic, and seasonings sautéed in olive oil; tossed with cooked pasta and sprinkled with grated cheese.

RISO E RISOTTO—RICE

Arancini di ricotta Cooked rice mixed with ricotta; formed into balls and dipped in seasoned flour, beaten eggs, and bread crumbs; fried in oil and seasoned with salt

and pepper; may also be sprinkled with powdered sugar and served as a dessert.

Arancini alla siciliana Cooked rice mixed with grated pecorino cheese, tomato puree and beaten eggs; formed into small balls stuffed with seasoned ground beef; rolled in flour, eggs, and bread crumbs; deep-fried and served with grated pecorino cheese and tomato sauce.

Asparagi, con punte di Onions sautéed in olive oil; raw rice added and tossed with hot oil; stock added and simmered, covered, until rice is cooked al dente; freshly grated Parmesan cheese, cooked asparagus tips, and butter mixed in and served immediately.

Bisati, e Fresh eel chunks, garlic, and onions sautéed in olive oil until browned; raw rice added and tossed in hot oil; stock, white wine and fresh herbs added and simmered, covered, until rice is al dente; freshly grated Parmesan cheese stirred in and served piping hot.

Bisi alla veneta, e Onions, garlic, fresh chopped parsley, and pancetta sautéed in lard; raw rice and blanched fresh peas added and tossed with hot fat; covered with stock and simmered, covered, until rice is cooked al dente; grated cheese stirred in and served immediately.

Boscaiola, alla Mushrooms, garlic, onions, and tomato strips sautéed in olive oil; seasoned with salt and freshly ground black pepper and

Boscaiola, alla (cont.)
served over hot cooked rice; sprinkled with grated Parmesan cheese.

Cagnun, in Garlic, minced onions, and bacon sautéed in butter; canned diced tomatoes added and seasoned with salt and freshly ground black pepper; reduced until slightly thickened and tossed with cooked rice; sprinkled with grated cheese and served at once.

Carciofi, con Blanched artichokes, diced pancetta, garlic, and chopped parsley sautéed in olive oil; raw rice added and tossed in oil to brown slightly; white wine and stock added and simmered, covered, until rice is cooked al dente; butter and grated Parmesan cheese stirred in and served immediately.

Castrato, con Onions, tomato strips, and boneless lamb chunks sautéed in butter; stock added, seasoned with cinnamon, and simmered, covered, until lamb is nearly tender; raw rice added to stock and cooked until al dente.

Caviale, al Raw rice and onions sautéed in butter; white wine and stock added and simmered, covered, until rice is cooked al dente; tossed with butter and caviar and served immediately.

Chnolle, e Cooked rice tossed with small polenta balls, grated cheese, and melted butter; placed in a baking dish and cooked in the oven until hot and slightly browned; served with Parmesan cheese on the side.

Crocchette di riso Cooked rice mixed with eggs, grated cheese, and seasonings; rolled in seasoned flour, eggs, and bread crumbs; deep-fried in oil.

Crocchette di spinaci Cooked rice, chopped cooked spinach, and grated cheese combined and formed into balls; rolled in seasoned flour, beaten eggs, and bread crumbs; deep-fried in oil.

Filante con la mozzarella Onions, chopped parsley, and raw rice sautéed in olive oil; broth and fresh basil added and simmered, covered, until rice is cooked al dente; freshly grated Parmesan cheese and shredded mozzarella cheese mixed in; served piping hot.

Fiocchetti di riso Cooked chilled rice mixed with diced ham, grated cheese, walnuts, and seasonings; formed into balls and rolled in flour, eggs, and bread crumbs; deep-fried in oil and served with tomato sauce.

Gamberi all'imperiale, e Garlic sautéed in butter and deglazed with white wine; curry powder, heavy cream, and crayfish or shrimp added and simmered until sauce is thickened and shrimp are nearly cooked; seasoned with salt and pepper and served over cooked rice.

Indiana, all' Onions and garlic sautéed in butter; raw rice added and browned in butter; seasoned with curry powder and covered with stock; simmered, covered, until rice is cooked al dente; salt, pepper, and heavy cream mixed in and served immediately.

Indivia belga con riso Sliced endive, minced onions, sliced mushrooms, raw rice, stock, and butter combined in a baking dish and sealed tightly; baked until rice is cooked al dente; heavy cream, fresh parsley, salt, and pepper stirred in and served at once with freshly grated Parmesan cheese on the side.

Lattughe, con le Onions, garlic, pine nuts, and raw rice sautéed in olive oil; white wine, stock, and chopped lettuce added and simmered, covered, until cooked al dente; seasoned with salt and pepper and freshly grated Parmesan cheese stirred in; served piping hot.

Limone, al Very hot cooked rice tossed with a mixture of beaten eggs, grated Parmesan cheese, fresh lemon juice, salt, and pepper; whole butter stirred in and served immediately.

Luganega, e Onions, garlic, fresh sage, and ground Italian sausage browned in butter; raw rice and broth added and simmered, covered, until rice is cooked al dente; heavy cream, butter, and grated Parmesan cheese stirred in; seasoned with salt and freshly ground black pepper and served immediately.

Lumache, con le Onions, garlic, and canned snails sautéed in olive oil; deglazed with white wine; stock and raw rice added and simmered, covered, until rice is cooked al dente; sprinkled with fresh chopped parsley and served with grated cheese on the side.

Mantovana, alla Onions, garlic, and fresh parsley sautéed in butter; raw rice added and lightly browned; stock added and simmered, covered, until rice is cooked al dente; cooked ground sausage and grated Parmesan cheese mixed in and served immediately.

Mignestris di ris vert See Part II.

Nido di riso giallo Onions and raw rice sautéed in olive oil; stock and fresh herbs added and simmered, covered, until rice is cooked al dente; half of the rice layered in a baking dish; covered with chopped sautéed chicken livers, fresh cooked peas, and shredded cheese; covered with remaining rice and drizzled with melted butter; baked.

Noci, con Onions and fresh chopped parsley sautéed in olive oil; raw rice and walnut pieces added and tossed in hot oil; covered with stock and simmered, covered, until rice is cooked al dente; seasoned with freshly ground black pepper and grated Parmesan cheese.

Patate al pesto, e Cubed peeled potatoes, onions, and raw rice lightly browned in olive oil; stock and white wine added and simmered, covered, until rice is cooked al dente; tossed with butter, salt and pepper, and cooked shrimp; served immediately.

Risi e bisi Onions, prosciutto, and raw rice lightly browned in butter; broth added gradually; when rice is nearly done, cooked fresh peas added; seasoned with freshly

Risi e bisi (cont.)
ground black pepper and grated Parmesan cheese.

Risotto Like boiled rice and pasta, risotto can be prepared in numerous ways. The basic method of cooking risotto involves cooking *arborio* rice in butter or olive oil until slightly toasted; while stirring, hot broth is added, a little at a time and only when the rice has absorbed the previously added broth. The finished rice should be creamy and tender but a bit firm to the bite.

— *in bianco* Onions and raw rice lightly browned in butter; chicken broth added gradually until rice is cooked al dente; seasoned with salt, freshly ground black pepper, and grated Parmesan cheese; served piping hot.

— *in bianco con agliata* See Part II, *Agliata, risotto in bianco con.*

— *con carciofi* Poached artichoke hearts, garlic, onions, and pancetta sautéed in olive oil; raw rice tossed in and lightly browned; broth added gradually, until rice is cooked al dente; salt, freshly ground black pepper, and grated Parmesan cheese stirred in; served immediately.

— *ai frutti di mare* Onions, garlic, celery and raw rice browned in olive oil; white wine and a light fish stock added gradually until rice is cooked al dente; cooked mussels, clams, and shrimp tossed in; seasoned with salt and freshly ground black pepper.

— *con funghi* Onions, reconstituted dried Porcini mushrooms, and raw rice browned in butter; white wine, chicken broth, and the strained water from soaking the mushrooms added gradually until rice is cooked al dente; seasoned with salt and pepper and sprinkled with grated Parmesan cheese.

— *con gamberetti in bianco* Garlic, fresh chopped parsley, and minced onions sautéed in olive oil; raw rice tossed in and browned; broth and white wine added gradually until rice is cooked al dente; enriched with whole butter and garnished with sautéed shrimp; seasoned with freshly ground black pepper.

— *alla maggiorana* Rice sautéed in butter until lightly browned; broth added gradually until rice is cooked; tomato strips, fresh marjoram, and salt and pepper stirred in; sprinkled with freshly grated Parmesan cheese and served piping hot.

— *di mare* Raw rice browned in butter with onions and garlic; white wine and a light fish broth added gradually until rice is cooked al dente; cooked shellfish (crab, shrimp, scallops, and so on.) tossed in and seasoned with salt and freshly ground black pepper.

— *alla marinara* Garlic, onions, fresh chopped parsley, and raw rice sautéed in olive oil; white wine and fish stock mixed with tomato paste gradually added until the rice is cooked al dente; seasoned with ground black pepper and served immediately.

— *alla milanese* Diced beef marrow and onions sautéed in butter; raw rice tossed in and lightly browned; white wine and broth gradually added until rice is cooked; seasoned with salt, pepper, and saffron; served piping hot with grated cheese on the side.

— *alla monzese* Onions and raw rice sautéed in butter; broth seasoned with saffron and white wine added gradually until rice is cooked al dente; cooked sausage slices tossed in and sprinkled with freshly grated Parmesan cheese.

— *alla paesana* Onions, garlic, blanched fresh peas, asparagus tips, and sliced carrots sautéed in olive oil; raw rice tossed in and lightly browned; broth added gradually, stirring constantly; when rice is nearly cooked, tomato strips and sliced zucchini added; butter and grated Parmesan cheese stirred in and seasoned with salt and pepper.

— *alla parmigiana* Onions, garlic, celery, chopped parsley, wild mushrooms, ground sausage, and carrots sautéed in olive oil; canned diced tomatoes, chicken livers, and broth added and simmered until thickened; poured over risotto (see *Risotto in bianco*) and served immediately with Parmesan cheese.

— *primavera* Onions, garlic, celery, carrots, and leeks sautéed in butter; raw rice tossed in and lightly browned; broth added gradually; when rice is nearly cooked, sliced zucchini and small broccoli florets added; seasoned with ground black pepper, salt,

and chopped parsley; sprinkled with grated cheese.

— *con punte di asparagi* Raw rice sautéed lightly in butter; broth added gradually until rice is nearly cooked; asparagus tips added and simmered until rice and asparagus are done; seasoned with freshly ground black pepper and grated Parmesan cheese.

— *alle quaglie* Onions, pancetta, quail pieces, and fresh herbs sautéed in olive oil; white wine and chicken stock added and simmered, covered, until quail is tender; poured over risotto (see *Risotto in bianco*); sprinkled with grated cheese and served immediately.

— *col ragù* Onions, garlic, carrots, celery, and ground beef browned in olive oil; canned diced tomatoes and seasonings added and simmered until thickened; poured over risotto (see *Risotto in bianco*); sprinkled with freshly grated Parmesan cheese and served immediately.

— *al ramerino* (*From Tuscany*) Garlic, chopped parsley, fresh rosemary, and raw rice sautéed in olive oil; red wine and broth added gradually until rice is cooked al dente; seasoned with freshly ground black pepper and served immediately.

— *con salsicce* Onions, garlic, and ground Italian sausages browned in butter; raw rice tossed in and lightly browned; broth added gradually until rice is cooked al dente; seasoned with salt and pepper and sprinkled with grated cheese.

DISHES BY COURSE

— *alla sbirraglia* Boneless chicken and beef cubes sautéed in olive oil with onions, carrots, and garlic; white wine and canned diced tomatoes added and reduced until thickened; served over *risotto in bianco*; sprinkled with freshly ground black pepper and grated Parmesan cheese; served immediately.

— *con scampi* Onions, garlic, celery, and fresh herbs sautéed in butter; raw rice tossed in and lightly browned; deglazed with brandy; white wine and broth added gradually until rice is cooked al dente; cooked shrimp mixed in and seasoned with salt and pepper.

— *col sedano* Onions and celery sautéed in butter; raw rice tossed in and lightly browned; broth added gradually until rice is cooked al dente; ground black pepper and freshly grated Parmesan cheese stirred in; served immediately.

— *agli spinaci* Fresh chopped spinach, onions, garlic, and green onions sautéed in butter; raw rice tossed in and lightly browned; broth added gradually until rice is cooked al dente; whole butter and heavy cream stirred in and sprinkled with freshly grated Parmesan cheese; served immediately.

— *alla toscana* Onions, celery, garlic, carrots, and ground beef browned in olive oil; canned diced tomatoes and red wine added and simmered until slightly thickened; seasoned with salt and ground

black pepper and poured over piping hot risotto (see *Risotto in bianco*); sprinkled with grated cheese and served immediately.

— *verde* Onions and garlic sautéed in butter; raw rice tossed in and lightly browned; broth added gradually; when rice is nearly cooked, fresh chopped spinach and heavy cream added and cooked until rice is al dente; sprinkled with freshly grated cheese.

— *con le vongole* Onions, garlic, chopped parsley, and raw rice sautéed in olive oil; white wine and clam juice added gradually until rice is cooked al dente; cooked clams, salt, and freshly ground black pepper stirred in; served immediately.

— *con le zucchine* Onions, garlic, and raw rice browned in butter; broth added gradually, stirring constantly; when rice is nearly al dente, sliced zucchini added; salt, pepper, whole butter, and grated Parmesan cheese stirred in; served immediately.

Rognone al porto, con Onions, garlic, parsley, lamb kidneys, and mushrooms sautéed in butter; dusted with flour and port wine added; simmered until thickened and seasoned with salt and pepper; served over cooked rice and sprinkled with grated cheese.

Salsiccia, alla Onions, garlic, and ground sausage browned in butter; fresh chopped tomatoes and juice added and seasoned with salt, pepper, and fresh herbs.

Scampi, con Onions, garlic, fresh

blanched peas, and fresh herbs sautéed in butter; raw rice added and browned slightly; covered with stock and simmered, covered, until rice is cooked al dente; freshly ground black pepper, cooked shrimp, and grated Parmesan cheese stirred in and served immediately.

Seppie in umido con riso Onions, garlic, cleaned and sliced cuttlefish, and chopped parsley sautéed in olive oil; canned diced tomatoes, white wine, and seasonings added and simmered, covered, until fish is tender; served over cooked rice.

Siciliana, al forno alla Onions, garlic, capers, and sweet peppers sautéed in olive oil; canned diced tomatoes, canned tuna, black olives, and anchovies added and simmered until thickened; layered alternately in a baking dish with cooked rice; sprinkled with freshly grated pecorino cheese and baked; served piping hot.

Supplì al telefono See Part II.

Timballo di riso giallo Onions, garlic, and raw rice sautéed in butter; white wine, stock, and fresh herbs added and simmered, covered, until rice is cooked al dente; half of the rice placed in a baking dish, layered with sautéed chicken livers, blanched fresh peas, and shredded cheese; covered with remaining rice and drizzled with melted butter; baked.

Tricolore Cooked rice tossed with hot butter and placed in serving bowl; one half topped with tomato sauce, the other with pesto;

sprinkled with freshly grated Parmesan cheese and served immediately.

Vagone, del Onions, and tomato strips sautéed in butter; raw rice tossed in and lightly browned; stock and white wine added and simmered, covered, until rice is cooked al dente; rice arranged in a serving bowl and topped with sautéed sausage slices and brussels sprouts; sprinkled with grated Parmesan cheese and served immediately.

Veneta, alla Onions, garlic, thinly sliced fresh fennel, and chicken chunks sautéed in butter; stock, white wine, and raw rice added and simmered, covered, until rice is cooked al dente; grated Parmesan cheese and butter stirred in and served immediately.

Veneziana, e uva alla Garlic, chopped fresh parsley, and raw rice sautéed in olive oil until browned; stock added and simmered, covered, until rice is cooked al dente; fresh grapes and freshly grated Parmesan cheese stirred in and served immediately.

Verde freddo Chilled rice tossed with pesto sauce, canned tuna, capers, and green olives; sprinkled with freshly ground black pepper and grated Parmesan cheese.

Verza, con la Onions, garlic, and cabbage sautéed in olive oil; raw rice and broth added and simmered, covered, until rice is cooked al dente; grated Parmesan and mozzarella cheese, ground black pepper, and chopped fresh parsley stirred in; served immediately.

Vitello con riso Ground sausage browned in butter and olive oil with minced onions and garlic; raw rice tossed in and coated with hot oil; canned diced tomatoes and stock added and simmered, covered, until rice is tender; grated pecorino stirred in; mounded on a serving platter and topped with panfried veal cutlets (see *Cotolette di vitello*, Part I).

POLENTA E GNOCCHI—POLENTA AND DUMPLINGS

Gnocchetti gialli al burro e salvia Cornmeal dumplings (made from cooked polenta) arranged in an oiled baking dish and drizzled with sage-flavored butter; sprinkled with grated Parmesan cheese and baked until lightly browned.

Gnocchetti alla Maddalena Blanched artichoke hearts, onions, garlic, chicken chunks, and fresh sage and rosemary sautéed in olive oil; served over semolina gnocchi (see *Gnocchi di semola*) and sprinkled generously with freshly grated Parmesan cheese.

Gnocchetti di semola alle zucchine Heavy cream, butter, salt, pepper, and zucchini puree simmered until thickened; when sauce has reached desired consistency, toss with thinly sliced zucchini, gnocchi (see *Gnocchi di semola*), and grated Parmesan cheese; seasoned with nutmeg and served piping hot.

Gnocchi Dumplings made from semolina flour, wheat flour, or potatoes.

— *alla bava* Cooked potato gnocchi alternately layered (two to three times) with shredded Fontina cheese in an oiled baking dish; topped with melted butter and baked until golden brown.

— *di farina gialla* Freshly made hot polenta poured into an oiled baking dish; topped with sliced Italian sausage, tomato sauce, and grated Parmesan cheese; covered with more polenta; refrigerated; when completely chilled and firm, topped with tomato sauce and baked; served piping hot with grated cheese.

— *filanti* Heavy cream and butter brought to a simmer; Fontina and mozzarella cheeses added and stirred until melted; tossed with cooked potato gnocchi and sprinkled generously with freshly grated Parmesan cheese; served piping hot.

— *alla fiorentina* Finely ground semolina sprinkled into boiling milk and cooked, stirred constantly, until thickened; chopped cooked spinach, eggs, and grated Parmesan cheese mixed in; formed into small ovals and arranged in an oiled baking dish; coated with *besciamella* and baked until lightly browned; served piping hot with grated cheese on the side.

— *fritti* Semolina, eggs, grated Parmesan cheese, salt, olive oil, and water kneaded until smooth; cut into bite-sized pieces and fried in oil; served hot or cold.

— *gialli* Pumpkin puree, eggs, flour, salt and pepper, and grated cheese kneaded together; cut into bite-sized pieces and cooked in boiling salted water.

— *alla parmigiana* Flour whisked all at once into boiling water combined with milk and butter; stirred vigorously until a ball has formed and is pulling away from the sides of the pan; eggs, salt, and pepper beaten in; formed into bite-sized nuggets and cooked in boiling water; drained, placed in a baking dish, and covered with *besciamella* and a generous amount of Parmesan cheese; baked.

— *di patate* Milled boiled potatoes kneaded with flour, eggs, salt, and pepper; formed into bite-sized nuggets and cooked briefly in boiling salted water.

— *di patate con formaggio* Cooked potato gnocchi tossed with hot butter, freshly ground black pepper, and grated Parmesan cheese; topped with shredded mozzarella and baked until nicely browned.

— *di patate con pesto* Hot potato gnocchi tossed with pesto; served immediately with freshly grated Parmesan cheese on the side.

— *di patate alla romana* Onions, garlic, and fresh chopped tomatoes sautéed in olive oil; seasoned with salt and freshly ground black pepper and tossed with hot potato gnocchi; sprinkled with grated pecorino cheese.

— *alla romagnola* Onions, garlic, carrots, celery, and ground beef sautéed in lard; canned diced tomatoes, red wine, beef stock, and seasonings added and reduced until thickened; served over hot potato gnocchi and sprinkled with

freshly grated Parmesan cheese; served immediately.

— *alla romana* See *Gnocchi di semola alla romana.*

— *di semolina* Finely ground semolina, salt, and olive oil kneaded together into a smooth dough; cut into bite-sized nuggets and cooked in boiling salted water.

- *alla romana* Fine semolina sprinkled into boiling milk and butter and whisked constantly until a thick gruel has formed; egg yolks and grated Parmesan cheese stirred in; spread on an oiled marble surface about one-half-inch thick and left to cool; cut into rounds or squares and layered in a baking dish, with butter and Parmesan cheese between layers; baked until golden brown.

— *verdi* Cooked chopped spinach, butter, ricotta, and seasonings slowly heated together; eggs, flour, and grated Parmesan cheese beaten in; cooled; formed into bite-sized nuggets and poached in boiling salted water.

- *in brodo* Gnocchi verdi cooked and served in seasoned broth; served hot with grated Parmesan cheese.

- *al burro e formaggio* Hot *gnocchi verdi* tossed with melted butter and sprinkled generously with grated Parmesan cheese; baked until cheese has lightly browned.

— *alla veronese* Mushrooms, onions and diced brains sautéed in butter; deglazed with brandy;

Gnocchi alla veronese (cont.)
cooked potato gnocchi tossed with *besciamella* and topped with brain mixture and freshly grated Parmesan cheese; baked and served immediately.

Polenta Coarsely ground cornmeal sprinkled into boiling salted water, constantly stirred until a thick gruel has formed (up to one hour); may be served as a mush or chilled and sliced.

—, aringhe e Grilled sliced polenta topped with seared herring fillets and olive oil; seasoned with freshly ground black pepper.

— con besciamella Chilled sliced polenta alternately layered (two to three times) in an oiled baking dish with *besciamella* and grated cheeses; topped with *besciamella* and baked until piping hot and lightly browned; allowed to settle a few minutes after removing from the oven and before cutting.

— in bianco al forno Chilled sliced polenta layered alternately (three times) with shredded cheese in a greased baking dish; covered with *salsa bianca* and mozzarella and Parmesan cheeses; baked and served piping hot.

— al burro e formaggio Hot freshly cooked polenta tossed with butter and grated Parmesan cheese; seasoned with freshly ground black pepper; served immediately.

— falcadina Shredded cheese melted in cream and butter; tossed with chilled polenta that has been cut into bite-sized nuggets and dropped in boiling water to warm; sprinkled with freshly grated Parmesan cheese and served piping hot.

— fritta con erbe e funghi Onions, wild mushrooms, and garlic sautéed in olive oil; seasoned with salt, freshly ground black pepper, and fresh tarragon; served over fried polenta slices.

— col Gorgonzola Chilled sliced polenta drizzled with butter and toasted in a hot oven until browned and crispy; sprinkled with crumbled Gorgonzola cheese and served immediately.

— con intingolo di coniglio Onions, garlic, tomatoes, and boneless rabbit meat browned in butter and olive oil; white wine, stock, and fresh sage added and simmered, covered, until rabbit meat is tender; served over grilled polenta slices.

— mantecata Polenta prepared with mozzarella and Gorgonzola cheeses; poured into an oiled baking dish and sprinkled with grated Parmesan cheese; baked until lightly browned and hot.

— d'oropa (*From Piedmont*) Shredded Fontina and mozzarella cheeses stirred into hot freshly made polenta; sprinkled with freshly grated Parmesan cheese and drizzled with melted butter; served piping hot.

— Pasticciata Chilled sliced polenta alternately layered (two to three times) in a oiled baking dish with *besciamella, salsa alla bolognese* sauce (see *Bolognese, salsa*; Part II), and grated Parmesan cheese; topped with the two sauces and baked until heated through.

- *con funghi* Onions, garlic, mushrooms, and fresh herbs sautéed in olive oil; a small amount of diced canned tomatoes added and seasoned with salt and pepper; sauce spread between two layers of chilled sliced polenta in a baking dish and drizzled with melted butter; baked and sprinkled with grated Parmesan cheese.

— *alla pistoiese* Onions, garlic, mushrooms, leeks, and sweet Italian sausage sautéed in olive oil; canned diced tomatoes and red wine added and reduced until thickened; cooked quail meat added; served piping hot over hot freshly made polenta.

— *e salsiccie* Freshly made hot polenta topped with cooked Italian sausage and tomato sauce; sprinkled with grated Parmesan cheese.

— *polpettine di* Chilled diced polenta mixed with thick *besciamella* and shredded cheese; spread on a flat oiled surface and chilled; cut into rounds and dipped in flour, eggs, and bread crumbs; deep-fried.

Topini di patate See Part II.

PIZZE E FOCACCE — PIZZAS AND FOCACCIAS

Bruschetta Sliced Italian bread toasted and rubbed with a fresh garlic clove; drizzled generously with olive oil and seasoned with salt and freshly ground black pepper; served warm.

Calzone di magro Pizza dough filled with fresh tomatoes, anchovy fillets, onions, capers, and seasonings; prepared as for *Calzone alla napoletana*.

Calzone alla napoletana Pizza dough rolled into a small thin round; one half of the dough topped with diced salami, shredded mozzarella, grated Parmesan, ricotta, and seasonings; folded over as for a turnover and pinched around the edges to secure enclosure; baked in a hot oven until lightly browned and crisp.

Consum See Part II.

Crescia See Part II.

Focaccia A flat bread typically seasoned with herbs and olive oil.

— *coi ciccioli* Bread dough kneaded with crisp chopped pancetta and rolled thin; dusted with coarse sea salt, freshly ground black pepper, and olive oil; baked in a hot oven until lightly browned.

— *farcita* Bread dough rolled into a thin circle and topped with ground beef or sausage cooked with minced onions in olive oil, shredded cheese (provolone, mozzarella, *cacciocavallo*, and so on), and grated Parmesan; covered with another layer of dough and sealed securely; brushed with beaten egg and baked until crisp.

— *al ramerino e aglio* (*From Tuscany*) Bread dough flavored with rosemary rolled flat, but not terribly thin; drizzled with olive oil, salt, freshly ground black pepper, rosemary, and minced garlic; baked in a well-oiled pan until crisp.

— *col sale* Bread dough rolled fairly thin and sprinkled with coarse sea salt and freshly ground black pepper; drizzled with olive oil and baked in a hot oven until crisp.

— *con la salvia* Bread dough kneaded with fresh chopped sage and rolled fairly thin; sprinkled with sage, coarse sea salt, freshly ground black pepper, and olive oil; baked in a hot oven until crisp.

Piadina/piadone See Part II.

Pizza An open pie made typically of flat bread dough spread with toppings and baked.

— *bianca* Prepared as for *Pizza bianca alla romana*, omitting the anchovy fillets.

— *bianca alla romana* Thinly rolled dough topped with olive oil, anchovy fillets, shredded mozzarella, grated Parmesan, fresh chopped basil, and salt; baked in a hot oven until lightly browned and crispy.

— *con cipolle* Pizza dough rolled thin and topped with caramelized onions; seasoned with salt, pepper, dried oregano, and grated cheese; drizzled with olive oil and baked until crisp.

— *con funghi* Pizza dough rolled into a thin round; topped with olive oil, sliced mushrooms, tomato slices, salt, and freshly ground black pepper; baked in a hot oven until edges become lightly browned and crispy.

— *Margherita* Pizza dough rolled thin and topped with pureed tomatoes, shredded mozzarella, ol-

ive oil, and dried oregano, baked in a hot oven until edges become golden brown and crispy.

— *alla marinara* Thinly rolled dough topped with tomato puree, olive oil, and coarse sea salt; baked in a hot oven.

— *alla napoletana* Pizza dough rolled thin and topped with tomato sauce, shredded mozzarella, anchovy fillets, salt, pepper, and dried oregano; drizzled with olive oil and baked until crisp.

— *rustica Pasta briciolata* (see Part II) rolled thin and topped with shredded smoked mozzarella, diced ham, diced salami, minced onions, garlic, salt, and pepper; topped and sealed with another sheet of pastry and brushed with beaten egg, baked in a hot oven until lightly browned.

— *con salsicce* Pizza dough rolled thin and topped with tomato sauce, cooked ground Italian sausage, salt, and freshly ground black pepper; drizzled with olive oil and baked until crisp; served immediately.

— *alla siciliana* Pizza dough rolled thin and topped with tomato sauce, anchovy fillets, and grated pecorino cheese; drizzled with olive oil, salt, and pepper and baked in a hot oven until crisp; served immediately.

Schiacciata con remerion *(From Tuscany)* Yeast dough rolled thin and seasoned with salt, freshly ground black pepper, and rosemary; drizzled with olive oil and baked until crisp.

Sfinciuni di San Vito Yeast dough

rolled into a thin round and topped with cooked ground beef, minced onions, garlic, *caciocavallo* cheese, grated pecorino cheese, salt and pepper; covered with another sheet of dough and pinched around the edges to securely enclose filling; baked in a hot oven until lightly browned and crisp.

PESCE—FISH

Alborelle arrosto Fresh gutted sprats seasoned with salt and pepper and fried in olive oil; drizzled with white wine and fresh lemon juice.

Alici Anchovies.

— ***agreganate alla napoletana*** *(From Campania)* Fresh boned and gutted anchovies arranged in a baking dish; brushed with olive oil combined with garlic, wine vinegar, salt, pepper, and fresh oregano; baked in a hot oven until fish is cooked.

— ***casalinghe con pomodoro*** Fresh cleaned anchovies arranged in a shallow baking dish; coated with a sauce composed of sautéed garlic, fresh parsley, and tomato puree; sprinkled with bread crumbs and baked.

— ***in tortiera*** Fresh boned and gutted anchovies layered in an oiled baking dish and drizzled with olive oil, garlic, salt, and pepper; covered with tomato sauce and baked.

Anguilla Eel.

— ***arrostita al lauro*** Skinned and gutted eel pieces dredged in seasoned flour and fried in oil; arranged in a baking dish with lemon slices and bay leaves; seasoned with salt and pepper and baked.

— ***allo spiedo*** Eel pieces, bread slices, and bay leaves threaded alternately on a skewer; brushed with seasoned olive oil and grilled.

— ***alla veneta*** Eel pieces dredged in seasoned flour and fried in olive oil; removed from pan and placed in a dish; onions, garlic, carrots, and fresh herbs sautéed in the remaining oil; wine vinegar and seasonings added; poured over eel and covered tightly for up to two days.

Aragosta Lobster.

— ***alla diavola*** Parboiled lobster tails split in half lengthwise; spread with a mixture of brown mustard, softened butter, cognac, salt, and pepper; sprinkled with bread crumbs and baked until golden brown and lobster is cooked.

— ***ai ferri*** Live lobster boiled in court bouillon; cooled in liquid; split in half lengthwise and brushed with olive oil seasoned with salt, pepper, and garlic; cooked on a grill and served with the remaining basting oil.

— ***alla partenope*** Diced cooked lobster meat well chilled and mixed with brown mustard, olive oil, fresh herbs, and seasonings; served on a bed of lettuce and sprinkled with fresh lemon juice.

Arselle alla maniera di Vasto *(From Abruzzi)* Onions, garlic, and chili pepper sautéed in olive oil; white

Arselle alla maniera di Vasto (cont.) wine, tomato puree, clam juice, fresh herbs, and seasonings added; poached shelled clams tossed in; served in a bowl over toasted garlic bread slices.

Arselle al pomodoro e basilico Onions, garlic, and fresh basil sautéed in olive oil; fresh chopped tomatoes and clam juice added and simmered until thickened; poached shelled clams tossed in the sauce to heat; served immediately.

Baccalà Dried, salted codfish.

— **in agrodolce** Soaked and rinsed salted cod dredged in flour and panfried; water, vinegar, currants, fresh mint and sugar added and simmered until fish is cooked.

— **alla fiorentina** Reconstituted dried salted cod dredged in seasoned flour and browned in olive oil with garlic; tomato puree added and seasoned with fresh herbs and ground black pepper; simmered until fish is cooked; served in sauce.

— **e peperoni** Soaked and rinsed salt cod dredged in flour and fried in oil; in a separate pan, onions, garlic, and sweet red peppers sautéed in olive oil; fresh chopped tomatoes, salt, and pepper added and bought to a simmer; sauce served over fish.

— **alla portoghese** Onions, garlic, potatoes, and tomato fillets sautéed in olive oil; soaked and rinsed salted codfish chunks, pitted olives, and fresh herbs added and cooked until potatoes are tender.

— **alla trasteverina** Onions, garlic,

potato cubes, and pine nuts sautéed in olive oil; raisins, capers, fresh herbs and anchovy paste added; poured over salt cod that has been rinsed, floured, and panfried; baked in a hot oven and drizzled with lemon juice and chopped parsley.

— **in umido** Minced onions sautéed in olive oil; tomato puree, raisins, pine nuts, and seasonings added and bought to a boil; reconstituted and rinsed salt cod added to pan and simmered until tender.

Bianchetti, frittata di Beaten eggs, salt, pepper, and whitebait mixed together and cooked on both sides in a frying pan; may be eaten hot or cold.

Branzino con salsa di olive Onions, pimentoes, capers, black and green olives, and fresh herbs sautéed in olive oil; white wine and tomato puree added and seasoned with salt and pepper; poured over panfried bass.

Branzino con salsa gustosa Poached bass served with a cold spicy sauce composed of mayonnaise, capers, diced artichokes, onions, chopped gherkins, and red chili peppers.

Brodetto, in (*A method of preparing fish*) Onions, garlic, and chopped parsley sautéed in olive oil; canned diced tomatoes, white wine, stock, and seasonings added; whole small fish or fillets added and simmered until fish is tender; served piping hot in broth.

Cacciucco alla livornese Squid, eel, octopus, dog fish, and red mullet sautéed briefly with onions, garlic, and red pepper; white wine, stock, canned diced tomatoes, and fresh herbs added and stewed until fish is cooked; served piping hot over crusty bread.

Calamaretti alla barese Skinned and gutted baby squid arranged in a baking dish and topped with a sauce composed of tomato puree seasoned with sautéed garlic, fresh herbs, salt, and pepper; baked, covered, until squid is cooked.

Calamaretti fritti Skinned and gutted baby squid slices dipped in seasoned flour and fried; drizzled with lemon juice and seasoned with salt.

Calamari Squid.

— ***neri*** Squid cut into rings, dredged in seasoned flour, and sautéed in olive oil; onions, sweet pepper, garlic, white wine, stock, and the ink sac from the squid added; simmered until squid is cooked; served piping hot with fresh parsley and lemon wedges.

— ***ripieni*** Skinned and gutted squid stuffed with sautéed garlic and squid tentacles, bread crumbs, olive oil, and fresh herbs; arranged in a baking dish and drizzled with olive oil and white wine; seasoned with salt and pepper and baked until tender.

— ***ripieni stufati al vino bianco*** Stuffed squid (see *Calamari ripieni* above) seared in olive oil; arranged in a baking dish and covered with olive oil, white wine, canned diced tomatoes, and seasonings; tightly sealed and cooked

in the oven until squid is tender.

— ***in salsa rossa*** Onions, garlic, and sliced squid sautéed in olive oil; canned diced tomatoes, salt, pepper, and fresh herbs added; reduced until sauce has thickened; served with pasta and crusty bread.

— ***in zimino*** Onions, garlic, carrots, and squid pieces sautéed in olive oil; deglazed with white wine; tomato puree and chopped cooked spinach added and stewed until squid is tender; seasoned with salt and pepper and served piping hot.

Capitone Female eel.

— ***fritto*** Skinned and cleaned female eel chunks dredged in seasoned flour and fried in oil; served very hot with lemon slices.

— ***alla livornese*** Skinned and gutted female eel chunks, onions, carrots, garlic, and celery sautéed in olive oil; canned diced tomatoes added and stewed until eel is cooked; ladled over toasted bread slices and served piping hot.

— ***marinato*** Skinned and gutted female eel placed in a pot and covered with olive oil, vinegar, and seasonings; poached until eel is cooked; cooled in liquid and marinated for two to three days.

Cartoccio, al (*A method of preparing fish*) Fresh fish placed on waxed paper or aluminum foil and drizzled with olive oil, white wine, minced onions and garlic, and salt and pepper; wrapped loosely but securely and baked in a moderate oven; served immediately.

Coda di rospo con pomodoro e olive
Monkfish fillets placed in an oiled baking dish and sprinkled with salt, ground white pepper, and olive oil; topped with chopped tomatoes and sliced green olives; baked.

Cozze Mussels.

— *crude al limone* Raw cleaned mussels served chilled on the half-shell with freshly ground black pepper and lemon wedges.

— *gratinate all'aglio* Steamed or boiled mussels detached but not removed from the half-shell; hot garlic butter poured over mussels and sprinkled lightly with seasoned bread crumbs; baked until very hot and bread crumbs have browned.

— *alla pugliese* White sauce (*salsa bianca*) mixed with grated Parmesan and tinted with tomato sauce; poured over poached and shelled mussels and sprinkled with bread crumbs; baked in a hot oven until nicely browned.

— *in tecia alla veneta* Steamed mussels removed from the shell and arranged in a baking dish; sprinkled with olive oil, white wine, minced garlic, chopped parsley, and bread crumbs; seasoned with salt and pepper and baked until nicely browned.

Dentice con funghi Red snapper dredged in seasoned flour and browned on both sides in olive oil; baked. Mushrooms, garlic, and onions sautéed in olive oil until dry; seasoned with salt and pepper and spooned over the baked fish.

Fette di pesce alla casalinga Firm-fleshed fish steaks (swordfish, halibut, tuna, and so on) seared in olive oil; stewed in white wine, canned diced tomatoes, and seasonings; placed on a serving dish and topped with the braising liquid; served immediately.

Finocchi freschi, coi (*A method of preparing fish*) Fresh sliced fennel simmered in water, olive oil, and seasonings until tender; small fish or fillets added and covered; simmering continued until fish is cooked; fish served with fennel and drizzled with the braising liquid.

Frittatine della festa A thin round omelette stuffed with sautéed baby shrimp and rolled; drizzled with melted butter and sprinkled with fresh chopped parsley.

Frittelle di pesce Bite-sized stuffed pastries filled with raw ground fish mixed with eggs, bread crumbs, and seasonings; deep-fried and served immediately with lemon wedges and various cold sauces.

Frittelle di pesciolini Washed and cleaned minnows roughly chopped and placed in a bowl with eggs, garlic, olive oil, grated cheese, flour, fresh herbs, and seasonings; poured on a hot griddle and cooked as for pancakes; served immediately.

Frittura di pesce Assorted fish and seafood dredged in seasoned flour and deep-fried; served with assorted cold sauces, lemon wedges, and parsley sprigs.

Funghi, con (*A method of preparing fish*) Fresh and rehydrated dried mushrooms sautéed in olive oil with garlic, onions, and fresh herbs; deglazed with white wine and the strained liquid used to reconstitute the mushrooms; poured over hot poached fish.

Gamberi Shrimp.

— *dell'Adriatico, spiedini di* Fresh peeled and deveined shrimp tossed with olive oil, bread crumbs, minced garlic, chopped parsley, salt, and pepper; threaded on a skewer and grilled over a live flame; sprinkled with lemon juice and served at once.

— *dorati* Fresh peeled and deveined shrimp dipped in batter composed of water, eggs, yeast, flour, and salt and pepper; fried in oil until golden brown; served immediately.

— *alla panna* Heavy cream combined with butter, salt, and freshly ground black pepper; heated to a simmer and reduced until sauce has thickened; tossed with poached shrimp and sprinkled with chopped parsley.

Gamberoni in agrodolce Minced anchovy fillets, garlic, and capers gently sautéed in olive oil; vinegar and sugar added; marinade poured over boiled prawns; allowed to cool before serving.

Gransevola gratinata (From Veneto) Cooled boiled crab cut open and insides removed; meat chopped and combined with *besciamella*, brandy, egg yolks, and grated cheese; mixture stuffed into crab shell and baked in a hot oven until nicely browned.

Granchio alla gran diavola Minced onions, mushrooms, garlic, and red pepper sautéed in butter; shelled and picked crab meat added and deglazed with cognac; heavy cream added and reduced until sauce has thickened; seasoned with salt and pepper and served immediately.

Gratella, in (*A method of preparing fish; from Tuscany*) Whole boned and gutted fish brushed with olive oil seasoned with salt, ground black pepper, and lemon juice; grilled over live coals, basting often.

Limone e maggiorana, al (*A method of preparing fish*) Small whole fish or firm-fleshed fillets dredged in seasoned flour and cooked in butter with garlic and marjoram; transferred to a serving plate and sprinkled with freshly squeezed lemon juice and the remaining pan juices; served at once.

Livornese, alla (*A method of preparing fish*) Onions, garlic, celery, carrots, and fresh herbs sautéed in olive oil; tomato puree added and seasoned with salt and ground black pepper; fish fillets added and stewed until tender.

Lumache Snails.

— *con l'aglio all'italiana* Canned snails placed in snail shells or small pastry cases; filled with softened butter mixed with garlic, minced onions, salt, and pepper; baked and served piping hot.

— *col pomodoro alla romana* Garlic, onions, and red pepper flakes sautéed in olive oil; fresh chopped tomatoes, white wine, broth, and canned snails added; simmered until sauce has slightly thickened.

— *alla siciliana* Canned snails, garlic, and onions sautéed in olive oil and butter; tomato puree, fresh herbs, salt, and pepper added and simmered until sauce has slightly thickened; served piping hot in sauce.

Mitili ripieni Steamed or boiled mussels detached but not removed from the half shell; stuffed with bread crumbs mixed with butter, eggs, and seasonings; baked in a hot oven until nicely browned; served immediately.

Moscardini alla camoglina (From Liguria) Octopus chunks seared in olive oil and stewed in tomato sauce with hot and sweet peppers until octopus is cooked.

Muggine all'italiana con tartufi e asparagi Mullet fillets dredged in seasoned flour and fried in oil; arranged in a greased baking dish and surrounded with poached asparagus tips; drizzled with grated Parmesan cheese and lemon juice and baked; topped with sliced truffles.

Nasello alla brace alla sarda Boned and cleaned hake cut into chunks and alternately threaded on a skewer with bay leaves; seasoned with salt and pepper and brushed with olive oil; grilled over live coals.

Nasello alla toscana, trancio di Poached hake drizzled with hot sage butter; lightly seasoned with salt and freshly ground white pepper.

Ostriche gratinate Fresh raw oysters removed from shell and arranged in a baking dish; sprinkled with grated Parmesan cheese, melted butter, salt, pepper, and bread crumbs; baked until golden brown and oysters are cooked.

Pagelli arrosto Sea bream brushed with olive oil seasoned with garlic, chopped parsley, white wine, and freshly ground black pepper; baked in a hot oven and served immediately with the hot oil.

Pagelli profumati Cleaned and gutted sea bream stuffed with garlic and fresh herbs; brushed with olive oil and baked; drizzled with hot oil and served immediately.

Palombo alla francese Onions, garlic, chopped parsley, and mashed anchovy fillets sautéed in olive oil; deglazed with white wine; poured over panfried dogfish slices; drizzled with fresh lemon juice.

Palombo fritto Boneless dogfish fillets dipped in milk and then seasoned flour; panfried in oil and served with fresh parsley sprigs and lemon wedges.

Palombo ai piselli Onions, garlic, and thinly sliced dogfish fillets sautéed in olive oil; fresh tomatoes, herbs, and fresh blanched peas added; simmered, covered, until fish is tender.

Peoci alla bulgara (From Veneto) Poached mussels removed from the shells and dredged in seasoned flour, beaten eggs, and bread crumbs; deep-fried in oil and served with fried onion rings, lemon wedges, and assorted cold sauces.

Persico Perch.

—*, cotolette di pesce* Perch fillets dredged in flour, dipped in beaten eggs, and coated with bread crumbs; fried in oil and served with lemon wedges and parsley.

—, *involtini di pesce* Fresh perch fillets spread with a mixture of bread crumbs, anchovy paste, eggs, and seasonings; rolled, placed in an oiled oven-proof dish, and baked.

— *alla milanese, filetti di pesce* Perch fillets marinated in olive oil, lemon juice, and seasonings; dredged in flour, dipped in beaten eggs, and coated with bread crumbs; panfried in butter; drizzled with the remaining pan juices.

Pesce arrosto Fresh whole fish boned and gutted and arranged in a baking dish; brushed with olive oil seasoned with minced garlic, fresh herbs, salt, and pepper; sprinkled with fresh lemon juice and baked just until fish is cooked.

Pesce bollito Onions, carrots, celery, garlic, black peppercorns, parsley, bay leaf, salt, white wine, and water combined to make a light aromatic stock; heated to a bare simmer and fish added; poached until just cooked; whole fish may be cooled in the stock.

Pesce al pangrattato Whole small fresh fish boned and gutted arranged in an oiled baking dish; sprinkled with toasted bread crumbs mixed with olive oil, minced garlic, chopped parsley, salt, and pepper; baked until fish is cooked and topping is golden brown.

Pesce spada Swordfish.

— *alla griglia* Swordfish steaks brushed with olive oil seasoned with minced garlic, fresh lemon juice, chopped herbs, and salt and pepper; cooked under flame or heat, basting occasionally; do not turn.

— *al limone* Swordfish steaks dredged in seasoned flour and fried in olive oil and butter; cooked swordfish transferred to a serving plate and excess fat poured from frying pan; dab of butter added to pan and swirled to melt; fresh lemon juice and capers added and drizzled over fish; served piping hot.

— *piccante al forno* Swordfish steaks marinated in olive oil, fresh lemon juice, fennel, salt, pepper, and garlic; covered and baked until half-cooked; uncovered and cooked until tender.

— *alla stimirata* *(From Lazio)* Swordfish steaks dredged in seasoned flour and browned in olive oil; garlic, onions, celery, and capers added and briefly sautéed; wine vinegar, salt, and pepper added and cooked down to a syrupy consistency; fish transferred to a serving plate and drizzled with the pan juices.

Pesce da taglio con salsa di prezzemolo Garlic, onions, chopped parsley, and capers sautéed in olive oil; contents sprinkled with flour; broth added and simmered until sauce has thickened; seasoned with anchovy paste, wine vinegar, salt, and pepper; served over hot poached fish.

Pescetti in carpione Small whole fish

Pescetti in carpione (cont.)
dredged in seasoned flour and fried in olive oil; stacked in a glass jar and covered with onions, wine vinegar, and seasonings; allowed to marinate, covered, about twenty-four hours.

Rane all'italiana Fresh cleaned frogs' legs dipped in beaten eggs and coated with seasoned bread crumbs; fried in olive oil; sprinkled with salt and served with tomato sauce.

Salmone in salsa verde Poached salmon coated with *salsa verde* (see *Verde, salsa*; Part II) and allowed to marinate for one to two days; served with sliced tomato.

Saraghine alla brace *(From Emilia-Romagna)* Small fresh sardines gutted and cleaned and brushed with olive oil seasoned with salt and pepper; grilled over live coals and served at once with fresh lemon wedges.

Sarde fritte alla ligure Fresh boned and gutted sardines stuffed with bread crumbs, diced mushrooms, eggs, grated Parmesan cheese, and seasonings; dipped in flour, then in beaten eggs, and coated with bread crumbs; deep-fried and served with lemon wedges and parsley sprigs.

Sarde in saor *(From Veneto)* Fresh cleaned sardines dredged in flour and fried in oil; stacked in a dish and covered with a mixture of olive oil, wine vinegar, sugar, pine nuts, and seasonings; marinated for twenty-four hours.

Sardine fritte con verdure Fresh boned sardines dredged in sea-soned flour and panfried; served over fresh greens and garnished with cucumber slices, tomatoes, and red onions slices; served immediately.

Sardine ripiene Fresh boned sardines stuffed with bread crumbs, eggs, butter, and seasonings; coated with *besciamella* and baked.

Scampi Prawns.

—, grigliata di Large shrimp threaded on a skewer and brushed with olive oil seasoned with garlic, salt, and pepper; grilled over live coals; served immediately with lemon wedges and hot butter.

—, spiedini di Raw shrimp, ham slices, and fresh sage leaves alternately threaded on a skewer; brushed with olive oil seasoned with salt, pepper, and garlic; cooked in a frying pan or on a grill until shrimp is tender but not overcooked; drizzled with remaining olive oil.

— alla sorrentina Large shrimp and mozzarella cheese cubes alternately threaded on a skewer; arranged in a baking dish and covered with canned diced tomatoes, fresh herbs, and salt and pepper; baked until shrimp is just cooked; served immediately.

Scomberi Mackerel.

— grigliati a scottadito Whole gutted mackerel brushed with olive oil seasoned with garlic, parsley, and lemon juice; cooked over live coals.

— alla marinara Mackerel fillets dredged in seasoned flour and sautéed in olive oil with garlic and red pepper flakes; white wine, salt, pepper, and fresh herbs added and bought to a simmer; fish transferred to a serving plate and drizzled with the pan juices.

— *in tegame con rosmarino e aglio* Whole boned and gutted mackerel browned on both sides in olive oil; garlic, salt, pepper, and fresh rosemary added; pan covered and cooked over low heat until fish is tender; drizzled with lemon juice and served immediately.

Sogliole Sole.

— *alla panna* Butter, heavy cream, salt, and freshly ground white pepper heated to a simmer; sole fillets added and cooked until fish is cooked and sauce has thickened; sprinkled with chopped parsley and served immediately.

— *al pomodoro e funghi, filetti di* Onions, garlic, mushrooms, and fresh tomatoes sautéed in olive oil; white wine, fresh herbs, and seasonings added; poured over sole fillets which have been arranged in a greased ovenproof dish; baked in a hot oven.

— *alla salvia* Sole fillets dredged in flour, dipped in beaten eggs, and coated with bread crumbs; fried in oil with fresh sage leaves; served immediately.

— *al vino bianco* Onions and minced anchovies sautéed in butter; white wine added and brought to a boil; fresh sole fillets dredged in flour added and simmered until sole is tender; sauce finished with fresh lemon juice and whole butter.

Stoccafisso alla vicentina Onions, garlic, and chopped anchovies sautéed in olive oil; deglazed with white wine; cream added and simmered until slightly thickened; poured over reconstituted stockfish that has been coated lightly with seasoned flour; baked until fish is cooked.

Stoccafisso alla palermitana Soaked and rinsed stockfish sautéed in olive oil with onions, garlic, capers, olives, and diced potatoes; canned diced tomatoes and seasonings added and simmered until fish and potatoes are cooked.

Storione al cartoccio Sliced sturgeon fillets arranged on a greased sheet of wax paper; drizzled with olive oil, white wine, and butter; seasoned with minced onions, garlic, and fresh herbs; paper folded over and ends tucked in to prevent steam from escaping; baked in hot oven and served immediately.

Tinche alla piemontese Onions, fresh sage, and garlic sautéed in butter; deglazed with vinegar and grape juice; poured over fresh tench that has been dredged in flour and panfried in oil.

Tonno Tuna.

— *alla calabrese* Tuna steaks dredged in flour and browned in olive oil; removed from pan; pancetta, garlic, onions, and anchovy paste sautéed in remaining oil; canned diced tomatoes and fresh herbs added; tuna added to sauce and stewed until the fish is tender.

— *al cartoccio* Fresh tuna steak arranged on oiled waxed paper

Tonno al cartoccio (cont.)
and drizzled with olive oil and white wine; seasoned with salt, ground white pepper, and fresh herbs; covered loosely but securely and baked.

— *fresco al pomodoro* Fresh tuna steak dredged in seasoned flour and panfried in olive oil; in a separate pan, garlic and onions sautéed in olive oil; anchovy paste, white wine, tomato puree, and seasonings added and reduced until thick; tuna coated with sauce and served immediately.

— *con piselli* Onions, blanched fresh peas, and chopped parsley sautéed in olive oil; broth and fresh tuna added and simmered until fish is tender.

—, *salame di* Drained canned tuna combined with grated Parmesan cheese, eggs, milled boiled potatoes, and seasonings and wrapped in cheesecloth in the form of a sausage link; poached in court bouillon until firm; served cold, sliced, with fresh mayonnaise and sliced tomatoes.

Triglie alla livornese Red mullet dredged in seasoned flour and browned quickly in olive oil; arranged in an oiled baking dish and covered with tomato sauce; baked.

Trota Trout
— *con acciughe* Cleaned and trimmed trout dredged in seasoned flour and panfried in butter and olive oil; roughly chopped anchovies, sherry, fresh herbs, and salt and pepper added; covered and simmered until fish is cooked; served immediately drizzled with sauce.

— *bollita con maionese* Chilled poached trout boned and skinned and served with shredded lettuce, sliced tomatoes, and fresh mayonnaise.

— *alle olive* Onions, garlic, cubed potatoes, and fresh herbs sautéed in olive oil; canned diced tomatoes, green and black olives, and salt and pepper added; poured over panfried trout.

— *al piatto* Fresh boned and gutted trout arranged on a plate and drizzled with olive oil, white wine, minced onions, garlic, salt, and freshly ground black pepper; covered with aluminum foil and cooked on top of a pot containing boiling water; served immediately.

Trota salmonata con agliata alla ligure Poached salmon trout. Garlic mashed in a mortar with vinegar and bread crumbs; olive oil slowly incorporated into mixture and seasoned with salt and pepper; poured over hot poached fish and served with boiled potatoes.

Verde, in (*A method of preparing fish*) Chilled poached fish coated with *salsa verde* (see Part II, *Salsa verde*); served with lemon wedges and fresh parsley sprigs.

Vongole su pane abbrustolito Onions and garlic sautéed in olive oil; canned diced tomatoes, fresh herbs, salt and pepper added and simmered until thickened; cooked clams added and heated; served immediately over garlic toast.

Vongole alla siciliana Garlic and

fresh parsley sautéed in olive oil; water, salt, and pepper added and brought to a boil; cleaned live clams added and simmered, covered, until shells open; served immediately with broth.

Zuppa di frutti di mare Onions, garlic, celery, chopped parsley, and squid rings sautéed in olive oil; canned diced tomatoes, white wine, and broth added to pot and brought to a simmer; assorted shellfish added, various cooking times considered; seasoned with salt and pepper and served piping hot with crusty bread.

POLLAME — POULTRY

Anatra Duck.

— ***all'arancia*** Sugar caramelized in a sauce pan; fresh orange juice, lemon juice, and broth added and reduced; drizzled over roasted duck.

— ***al cognac*** Duck sections marinated in olive oil, cognac, red wine, garlic, fresh herbs, salt, and pepper; duck seared in oil until browned; marinade added and simmered, covered, until duck is tender.

— ***al porto*** Duck sections sautéed in butter with onions, carrots, celery, and mushrooms; port wine and stock added and simmered until duck is cooked tender; served with the pan juices.

— ***al sale*** Whole trimmed duckling placed in a baking pan over coarse salt; covered completely with more salt and baked to desired doneness; served at once.

Cappone Capon.

— ***al brunello*** Whole trimmed capon marinated in red wine *(Brunello di Montalcino)* with aromatic herbs and vegetables; seared in olive oil and bacon fat until nicely browned; chicken broth, marinade, and brandy added and simmered, covered, until capon is cooked tender.

— ***con noci alla lombarda*** Whole capon stuffed with softened butter, fresh bread crumbs, grated cheese, eggs, cream, salt, and pepper; trussed and simmered in seasoned water until cooked tender; served with broth.

— ***ripieno*** Whole trimmed capon stuffed with a mixture of crumbled stale bread moistened in milk, chopped ham, eggs, fresh herbs, salt, and pepper; trussed; braised in red wine and stock until tender; served with the pan juices.

Faraona arrosto Whole trimmed guinea hen marinated in olive oil, fresh lemon juice, and seasonings; covered with bacon strips and roasted in a moderate oven, basting frequently, until cooked; served hot, drizzled with pan juices.

Fegatini di pollo alla salvia Trimmed and halved chicken livers seasoned with salt, pepper, and fresh chopped sage; sautéed in butter with prosciutto; deglazed with white wine and served at once with grilled polenta.

Galletti allo spiedo Spring chicken rubbed with olive oil, salt, and

Galletti allo spiedo (cont.)
pepper; stuffed with fresh herbs, onions, and garlic; threaded on a skewer and roasted over live coals; basted as needed.

Galletti al vino Chicken sections dredged in seasoned flour and sautéed in butter with onions and garlic until nicely browned; red wine, brandy, broth, and seasonings added; covered and simmered until chicken is cooked tender.

Oca Goose.

— **ripiena, arrosto di** Whole trimmed goose sprinkled with salt and pepper; stuffed with a mixture of ground sausage, fresh bread crumbs, chopped goose giblets, raisins, and seasonings; trussed and roasted until tender.

— **con salsa di peperoni** Whole small goose browned in olive oil and butter and placed in the oven; goose transferred to a serving platter and pan juices deglazed with white wine; broth, chopped ham, sweet red peppers, and seasonings added and simmered until flavors have intensified; drizzled over bird.

— **al vino** Whole young goose rubbed with salt, pepper, and fresh herbs; placed in a hot oven until nicely browned; onions, carrots, and red wine added to roasting pan and covered, until tender; served with pan juices.

Pernice al forno Whole partridge rubbed with butter, salt, pepper, and sage; wrapped with bacon and roasted, basting occasionally, until tender; drizzled with pan juices.

Pollastrino alla griglia (*From Toscany*) Young squab butterflied and flattened and seasoned with salt and pepper; grilled over live coals, basting occasionally with olive oil if necessary.

Pollo Chicken.

— **arrosto al forno con rosmarino** Whole chicken rubbed with olive oil, salt, and pepper; the cavity stuffed with fresh rosemary and garlic cloves; roasted in a moderate oven, basting occasionally; served hot with pan juices.

— **arrosto in tegame** Chicken halves browned in olive oil and butter with garlic over moderate heat; white wine, fresh rosemary, salt, and pepper added and simmered, covered, until chicken is cooked tender; served hot with pan juices.

— **alla birra** Chicken sections dredged in seasoned flour and browned in butter; onions and beer added and brought to a simmer; covered and baked until chicken is tender; seasoned to taste and served with the reduced braising liquid.

— **alla boscaiola** Chicken sections dredged in seasoned flour and browned in olive oil with onions and garlic; white wine, fresh chopped tomatoes, mushrooms, broth, and seasonings added covered and simmered until chicken is tender.

— **alla cacciatora** Chicken sections seasoned with salt and pepper and browned in olive oil with onions; mushrooms, fresh herbs, salt, and pepper added and cooked, covered; white wine added and covered again, simmering until chicken is cooked; served very hot, drizzled with pan contents.

— *con carciofi e patate, petti di* Boneless and skinless chicken breasts seasoned with salt and pepper and sautéed in olive oil; deglazed with white wine and chicken broth and reduced to a syrupy consistency; chicken served with sauce and garnished with sautéed potato cubes and artichokes.

— *in casseruola alla sarda* Whole chicken rubbed with olive oil, salt, and pepper; stuffed with sautéed onions, tomato fillets, fresh bread crumbs, eggs, grated pecorino cheese, raisins, and cream; trussed and roasted, basted as needed.

— *cotto nel vino rosso* Chicken sections browned in olive oil; removed from pan and replaced with onions, garlic, mushrooms, and prosciutto; sautéed briefly and sprinkled with flour; red wine and fresh herbs added and simmered until thickened; chicken put back in pan and simmered, covered, until cooked.

— *alla diavola* Halved and flatted chicken rubbed with olive oil, salt, and red pepper flakes; roasted, basting occasionally, until cooked; chicken arranged on a serving platter and drizzled with pan juices that have been deglazed with white wine.

—, *fricassea di* Chicken sections, onions, carrots, garlic, celery, mushrooms, and fresh herbs sautéed in butter and olive oil;

sprinkled with flour and briefly cooked; chicken broth poured in and simmered until chicken is tender and sauce is nicely thickened; seasoned with salt and pepper.

— *fritti, petti di* Chicken breasts split in half and marinated in olive oil, salt, and fresh herbs; dipped in batter made of flour, milk, eggs, salt, and pepper; deep-fried in oil until cooked golden brown.

— *con funghi* Chicken sections seasoned with salt and pepper and browned in olive oil with onions and garlic; fresh mushrooms added and cooked over low to moderate heat, covered, until chicken is tender; deglazed with sherry and served immediately.

— *coi funghi secchi* Chicken sections, reconstituted dried wild mushrooms, onions, and garlic sautéed in olive oil and butter; deglazed with white wine; broth, canned diced tomatoes, and the strained water in which the mushrooms were soaked added to the pan; cooked, covered, until chicken is tender and the sauce has slightly thickened.

— *imbottito* Whole chicken rubbed with olive oil, salt, and pepper; stuffed with cooked rice, bread crumbs, eggs, grated Parmesan cheese, ground sausage, and fresh herbs; roasted in hot oven, basting frequently; heat reduced and cooked until tender.

— *al limone* Chicken quarters dredged in seasoned flour and browned in oil; arranged in a bak-

Pollo al limone (cont.)

ing dish with lemon juice, chicken broth, and seasonings; baked, covered, until chicken is cooked; sprinkled with chopped parsley and drizzled with pan juices.

— *al marsala* Chicken sections seasoned with salt and pepper and browned in butter; onions added and browned; stock and marsala poured in covered and simmered until tender; seasoned to taste and served with pan juices.

— *alle olive* Chicken sections seasoned with salt and pepper and browned in olive oil and butter; sprinkled with flour; chicken stock poured in and boiled until sauce has thickened; black pitted olives and fresh herbs added and simmered until chicken is cooked and tender.

— *all'origano* Chicken quarters seasoned with salt and pepper brushed with olive oil seasoned with fresh oregano, lemon juice, and minced garlic; broiled or roasted, basting occasionally, until cooked; drizzled with pan juices and served immediately.

— *in padella con le erbette* Chicken sections marinated in olive oil, lemon juice, garlic, fresh herbs (thyme, parsley, sage), salt, and pepper; seared in oil until nicely browned; marinade added and simmered uncovered over moderate heat until tender.

— *con peperoni* Chicken sections seasoned with salt and pepper and browned in olive oil with minced onions and garlic; white wine, chicken stock, tomato fillets, and roasted red peppers added; simmered, covered, until chicken is cooked tender.

— *piccante* Boneless, skinless chicken breast dredged in seasoned flour and browned in butter; excess fat drained from pan and chicken transferred to a baking dish; garlic and anchovies added to pan and mashed to a paste; vinegar, white wine, capers, fresh herbs, salt, and pepper added; chicken covered wtih liquid and baked until tender.

— *al prosciutto* Chicken sections dredged in seasoned flour and browned in olive oil with minced onions and prosciutto; chopped tomatoes and white wine added and simmered, covered, until chicken is tender.

— *ripieno al forno* Minced onions, garlic, and celery sautéed in olive oil; ground sausage added and cooked briefly; cooled mixture bound with fresh bread crumbs, eggs, and grated Parmesan cheese; stuffed into roasting chicken and trussed; bird rubbed with oil, salt, and pepper, and roasted, basting occasionally, until cooked tender.

—, *rollè di petto di* Minced garlic and onions sautéed in olive oil with ground pork; cooled and bound with a small amount of fresh bread crumbs; mixture spread on a boneless, skinless chicken breast and rolled, secured with string or toothpicks; stuffed breast panfried in butter until cooked and transferred to a serving dish; pan deglazed with white wine and juices poured over chicken.

— *con rosamarino* Chicken sections seasoned with salt and pepper and browned in butter with garlic and rosemary; water added; covered and simmered until tender.

— *in salsa tonnata* Chilled boiled chicken boned and skinned and arranged on a serving platter; drizzled with a sauce composed of canned tuna mashed with anchovies and seasonings and folded into mayonnaise; served with fresh herbs and greens.

— *alla senese, petti di* Boneless, skinless chicken breasts sautéed in butter; deglazed with lemon juice; sprinkled with fresh chopped parsley and whole butter swirled in; breasts transferred to a serving dish and coated with sauce.

— *in umido* Chicken sections or boneless chunks sautéed in olive oil with onions, garlic, and celery; canned diced tomatoes, chicken stock, fresh herbs, carrots, and potatoes added and simmered uncovered until chicken and vegetables are cooked and liquid has slightly thickened; seasoned with salt and pepper.

— *in umido col cavolo nero* Chicken sections, onions, garlic, and red cabbage sautéed in olive oil and butter; red wine added; chicken is covered and simmered until cooked tender; seasoned with salt and pepper.

— *in umido alla contadina* Chicken sections dredged in seasoned flour and sautéed in butter

with onions, garlic, carrots, and celery; canned diced tomatoes, red wine, stock, and mushrooms added; covered and simmered until tender; sauce enriched with cream and served over the chicken.

— *alla valdostana, petti di* Boned and skinned chicken breasts dredged in seasoned flour and panfried in butter; pan deglazed with white wine; fontina cheese melted over breasts and served immediately.

— *al vino bianco* Boneless, skinless chicken breasts dredged in seasoned flour and browned in butter and olive oil; white wine, fresh chives, and seasonings added; chicken covered and simmered until cooked; served immediately drizzled with pan juices.

— *e vitello, polpettone di* Freshly ground chicken and veal meat mixed with eggs, grated Parmesan cheese, flour, pistachios (optional), and seasonings; cylindrically shaped and wrapped in cheesecloth; poached in seasoned stock until firm; drained and chilled well; served cold with antipasti, salads, and so on.

Tacchinella tartufata Young turkey hen stuffed with ground sausage, chopped pork fat, minced truffles, and seasonings; bird studded with truffles and rubbed with olive oil and salt; roasted and basted as needed, until cooked tender.

Tacchino ripieno, arrosto di Whole trimmed turkey rubbed with olive oil, salt, and pepper; stuffed

Tacchino ripieno, arrosto di (cont.)
with fresh bread crumbs, chopped
turkey giblets, ground sausage,
eggs, minced onions, mushrooms,
and seasonings; trussed and
roasted.

Tacchino alla salvia Turkey breast
rubbed with salt, pepper, and
fresh chopped sage; barded with
bacon roasted and basted as
needed; garnished with fresh sage
leaves and drizzled with pan
juices.

AGNELLO E MONTONE
— LAMB AND MUTTON

Abbacchio Baby milk-fed lamb between the ages of one and two
months.

— **aglio e aceto** Lamb chunks sautéed in olive oil with garlic, onions, and fresh rosemary; water
or light broth and anchovy paste
thinned with vinegar added and
simmered until lamb is cooked to
desired doneness; sauce strained
and served separately.

— **arrosto** Whole baby lamb
rubbed with olive oil, salt, pepper, and garlic; roasted in oven
with quartered potatoes tossed in
oil; allowed to settle several minutes before carving.

— **brodettato** Lamb chunks seasoned with salt and pepper and
sautéed in olive oil with garlic,
onions, and bacon; pan contents
sprinkled with flour to make a
roux; white wine and water
added and simmered, covered,
until lamb is tender and sauce has
thickened; meat transferred to

serving platter; sauce enriched
with egg yolks and served immediately.

— **alla cacciatora** Baby lamb
chunks seasoned with salt and
pepper and browned in bacon fat
with onions and garlic; sprinkled
with flour to make a roux; white
wine, broth, and fresh rosemary
and sage added; simmered until
lamb is tender; anchovy paste
swirled in sauce immediately before serving.

— **e carciofi** (1) Lamb loin seasoned with salt, pepper, sage, and
rosemary and browned in butter
and olive oil; white wine added
and cooked to desired doneness,
more wine added as needed;
transferred to a serving platter
and surrounded with breaded
and fried artichokes. (2) Lamb
chunks seasoned with salt and
pepper and browned in olive oil
with onions, parsley, and garlic;
flour sprinkled on and incorporated into oil; white wine, broth,
and seasonings added; covered
and simmered until lamb is
nearly tender; fresh trimmed artichokes added and covered
again until artichokes and lamb
are tender.

— **al forno con patate alla romana**
Leg of baby lamb seasoned with
salt, pepper, fresh rosemary, and
garlic; placed in roasting pan with
peeled and quartered potatoes
that have been tossed in olive oil
and seasoned with salt and pepper; roasted until lamb has cooked
to desired doneness and potatoes
are tender.

— *con olive all'abruzzese* Leg of lamb cut into strips and dredged in seasoned flour; sautéed in olive oil until nicely browned; black olives, diced green peppers, and fresh herbs added; drizzled with fresh lemon juice and served very hot.

— *alla romana* Lamb chunks seasoned with salt and pepper and browned in lard with garlic and rosemary; flour sprinkled in to make a roux; white wine, wine vinegar, anchovy paste, and water added; lamb is covered and simmered until tender.

Agnello Lamb.

— *in agrodolce alla barese* Lamb chunks seasoned with salt and pepper and browned in olive oil; water, tomato paste, and garlic added and simmered; wine vinegar and sugar added when halfway cooked; continued cooking, covered, until lamb is tender.

— *in fricassea* Lamb chops seasoned with salt and pepper and browned in pork fat with onions, garlic, and pancetta; stock, white wine, and seasonings added and simmered, covered, until tender; chops transferred to a serving platter and sauce enriched with egg yolks and lemon juice; served immediately with sauce.

— *al limone* Lamb chunks (leg or shoulder) marinated in salt, lemon juice, and garlic; browned in olive oil; white wine, canned diced tomatoes, wine vinegar, and fresh herbs added and simmered until lamb is tender.

— *con le melanzane* Lamb chunks seasoned with salt and pepper and browned in olive oil with diced bacon, onions and garlic; pan contents sprinkled with flour; red wine and water added and simmered until lamb is tender and sauce has thickened; served over fried eggplant slices.

— *con patate al vino, costolette di* Lamb chops dredged in seasoned flour and browned in olive oil and butter; fresh rosemary, sage, garlic, and white wine added and simmered until chops are tender; served with diced panfried potatoes.

— *con riso all'americana* Lamb chunks seasoned with salt and pepper and browned in olive oil with onions and garlic; water and tomato paste added; covered and simmered until lamb is tender; seasoned and served over hot cooked rice.

— *con spaghetti alla foggiana* Boneless lamb chunks seasoned with salt and pepper and browned in olive oil with onions and garlic; water added and simmered until lamb is tender; seasoned and served over hot spaghetti; served at once.

— *in umido con cucuzza* Lamb chunks seasoned with salt and pepper and browned in olive oil with onions and garlic; canned diced tomatoes and fresh oregano added; covered and simmered until nearly cooked; squash added and covered again until lamb and squash are tender.

Animelle d'abbacchio Lamb's sweetbreads sautéed in butter with minced onions, garlic, and bacon;

Animelle d'abbacchio (cont.)
broth, salt, and pepper added and simmered until tender; whole butter swirled in and served immediately.

Arrosto di agnello al ginepro Small lamb leg placed in roasting pan with white wine, garlic, rosemary, juniper berries, and aromatic vegetables; simmered, covered, until almost half-cooked; lid removed and simmered, removing scum as needed, until lamb is tender.

Arrosto di agnello pasquale col vino bianco Spring lamb shoulder seasoned with salt and pepper and browned in olive oil and butter with garlic and rosemary; white wine added; covered and simmered until tender; served with strained pan juices.

Bracioline di agnello Lamb cutlets pounded thin; bacon, garlic, and onions placed in the center of each; cutlet rolled, securing with a toothpick; browned in olive oil; white wine added; lamb covered and simmered until tender; seasoned and served.

Coratella di abbacchio brodettato Diced lamb's lungs sautéed in bacon fat with onions and garlic; white wine and seasonings added and brought to a boil; lamb hearts and liver added, keeping in mind various cooking times; simmered until tender, wine added as needed; sauce enriched with egg yolks and lemon juice; served immediately.

Cosciotto di agnello arrosto Leg of lamb trimmed of excess fat and seasoned with salt, pepper, and rosemary; studded with pancetta and garlic cloves and rubbed with olive oil; roasted with quartered potatoes tossed in oil.

Costolettine Lamb chops.

— *di agnello alla calabrese* Lamb chops dredged in seasoned flour and panfried in lard; shingled on a serving plate and garnished with button mushrooms, anchovy fillets, poached artichoke hearts, and capers.

— *di agnello fritte* Baby lamb chops pounded flat and seasoned with salt and pepper; dipped in beaten eggs and coated with dried bread crumbs; panfried in oil until nicely browned and crispy.

— *di agnello al verde* Lamb chops seasoned with salt, pepper, and rosemary and browned in butter; white wine, capers, chopped green olives, and chopped parsley added and simmered until chops are tender; sauce reduced and finished with whole butter; served with lamb.

Montone all'abruzzese Boneless mutton shoulder cut into chunks and browned in olive oil; seasoned with salt, pepper, garlic, and fresh herbs; white wine and water added; covered and simmered until mutton is tender.

Montone del capraio Chunks of mutton shoulder browned in butter with onions and garlic; water and seasonings added; covered and simmered until mutton is tender; stewed meat served over sliced crusty bread.

Ragù d'agnello Lamb chunks sautéed in olive oil with onions, garlic, salt, and pepper; white wine, canned diced tomatoes, sweet peppers, and fresh herbs added; covered and simmered until lamb is tender.

Scottadito See Part II.

Spezzatino di agnello o capretto Lamb chunks sprinkled with marsala wine and allowed to marinate; patted dry, seasoned with salt and pepper, and browned in olive oil with onions and garlic; flour sprinkled in to make a roux; marsala wine and fresh herbs added and simmered, covered, until tender.

Stufatino di agnello con l'aceto Lamb chunks seasoned with salt and pepper and browned in olive oil with onions; wine vinegar and fresh green beans added; covered and simmered until lamb is tender.

Testina di abbacchio Lamb's head without the eyes, ears, and brain, brushed with olive oil and seasoned with salt and pepper; roasted, basted as needed.

Umido alla pugliese Lamb chunks seasoned with salt and pepper and browned in olive oil with onions and garlic; contents sprinkled with flour to make a roux; red wine, canned diced tomatoes, and seasonings added and simmered until lamb is tender and sauce has thickened; served over hot cooked pasta.

MANZO — BEEF

Arrosto di bue al sangue Boneless prime rib roast rubbed with olive oil, salt, and pepper and roasted until rare; garnished with baked tomato halves stuffed with bread crumbs, garlic, minced onions, parsley, olive oil, and seasonings.

Arrosto vecchio piemonte Sirloin seasoned with salt and pepper and pounded very thin; layered with sliced ham and *besciamella* and wrapped in pastry, well sealed; drizzled with melted butter and baked until pastry has become golden in color; allowed to settle before being cut.

Bistecca Beefsteak.

— *alla diavola* Beef steak panfried in olive oil to desired doneness; removed from pan; pan-deglazed with marsala and red wine; garlic, fennel seeds, minced onions, tomato paste, and seasonings added and simmered until thickened; drizzled over meat and served immediately.

— *di lombo con acciughe e olive* Beef steak brushed with butter and sprinkled with salt and pepper; grilled rare and garnished with sliced olives; served immediately topped with anchovy butter.

— *alla milanese* Beef steak panfried in butter and olive oil; transferred to a serving platter; garlic added to hot pan and toasted; steak seasoned with salt and pepper and drizzled with pan juices.

Bistecche alla piccantina Beef steak panfried in olive oil with black olives, tomato strips, anchovy fillets, and capers; white wine added and steak cooked to desired doneness; seasoned with salt and pepper and served immediately.

DISHES BY COURSE

Bistecche con uova alla contadina
Beef steak brushed with butter
and sprinkled with salt and pepper; grilled rare and topped with
a thin slice of prosciutto and a
fried egg.

Bistecchine alla cacciatora Beef
steaks pounded thin and dredged
in seasoned flour; browned in olive oil with onions and garlic; removed from pan; wild mushrooms, red wine, and canned
diced tomatoes added to pan and
simmered until sauce has thickened; steaks reheated in sauce
and served immediately.

Bocconcini di manzo piccante Beef
cubes seasoned with salt and pepper and browned in butter and
olive oil with onions; beef broth,
chopped tomatoes, potatoes, and
seasonings added and simmered
until beef is tender and potatoes
have become mush, thickening
the sauce.

Bollito misto Veal knuckle, beef brisket, veal brisket, beef tongue,
lamb's shoulder, and chicken
placed in a large pot and covered
with cold water; garlic, onions,
and fresh herbs added and simmered, each cut of meat removed
as it becomes tender; carrots, onions, celery, potatoes, cabbage,
canned diced tomatoes, and
cooked cotechino sausage added
and simmered until everything is
tender.

Braciolette di manzo Sirloin steak
pounded thin and layered with
bacon strips, sliced onions, garlic,
salt, and pepper; rolled tightly and
secured with a toothpick; broiled
or grilled to desired doneness and
served piping hot.

Brasato Braised; usually refers to
beef.

— **all'acciuga** Beef brisket
browned in pork fat with onions,
garlic, salt, and pepper; beef stock,
anchovy paste, and fresh parsley
added and simmered, covered,
until beef is tender.

— **di manzo con le cipolle** Bottom
round or brisket studded with
rolled strips of pancetta and seasoned with salt and pepper; arranged in a baking pan on a bed
of onions and covered securely;
roasted in the oven until tender;
served sliced with pan juices and
onions.

— **alle salsicce** Rump or bottom
round seasoned with salt and pepper and browned in butter; sausage links, onions, and garlic
added; water poured in and simmered, covered, until meat is tender; excess fat skimmed off prior
to serving.

— **ubriaco** Rump or bottom round
marinated in red wine, garlic, and
aromatic herbs and vegetables;
browned in olive oil and butter;
marinade added; covered and
simmered until tender, adding
more red wine if needed; seasoned and served with the
strained braising liquid.

Bue arrosto con legumi (From
Piemonte) Sirloin roast rubbed with
olive oil, salt, and pepper; cooked
in the oven, basted as needed;
sliced, arranged on a platter, and
surrounded with fresh cooked
string beans, peas, and carrots.

Carpaccio alla toscana Thinly sliced raw beef filet mignon drizzled with salt, ground black pepper, and freshly squeezed lemon juice; marinated for thirty minutes and served with chopped parsley and flakes of Parmesan cheese.

Costata di bue al cartoccio Prime rib roast seasoned with salt and pepper and browned in butter; wrapped loosely but securely in aluminum foil with fresh chopped tomatoes, carrots, celery, onions, garlic, and fresh herbs; roasted until rare.

Costata alla campagnola Boned and tied sirloin roast seasoned with salt and pepper and browned in butter and olive oil; garlic, onions, carrots, and celery added; white wine and stock added; covered and simmered until tender; served sliced with reduced cooking liquid.

Costata di manzo alla griglia Sirloin steak brushed with olive oil seasoned with salt, pepper, garlic, fresh sage, and oregano; grilled over live coals to desired doneness; served immediately drizzled with olive oil.

Costate alla pizzaiola Beef steak brushed with olive oil, salt, and pepper and grilled rare; removed from pan; garlic, onions, anchovy fillets, and fresh chopped tomatoes added and sautéed; seasoned with fresh oregano and served over steak.

Cotolette di trita alla milanese Ground beef mixed with fresh bread crumbs, eggs, grated Parmesan cheese, salt, pepper, and milk; formed into patties and dredged in seasoned flour, dipped in eggs, and coated with bread crumbs; panfried in butter until golden brown and crispy.

Farsumagru See Part II.

Fettine di manzo farcite Beef steak pounded thin and layered with sliced prosciutto, sliced cheese, salt, and pepper; dredged in seasoned flour, dipped in eggs, and coated with bread crumbs; panfried in olive oil until nicely browned; served immediately.

Fettine di manzo alla sorrentina Beef steak pounded thin and seared in hot oil; removed from pan and onions, garlic, canned chopped tomatoes, black olives, salt, and pepper added and brought to a simmer; steak reheated in sauce and served immediately.

Fettine in padella Small thin beef steaks drizzled with olive oil and allowed to sit for one hour; panfried in hot olive oil and served immediately, seasoned with salt, pepper, and pan juices.

Filetto al limone See *Carpaccio alla toscana*, this section.

Filetto alla siciliana Filet mignon panfried in butter with diced bacon and onions; deglazed with marsala wine and served at once, with strained pan juices.

Fiorentina, la T-bone steak sprinkled with cracked black peppercorns and salt and grilled over live flames until rare; drizzled with olive oil and served immediately.

Involtini di manzo Lean boneless

Involtini di manzo (cont.)
beef strips pounded thin and lay-ered with sliced prosciutto, fontina cheese, sliced tomatoes, and seasonings; rolled, tied, and browned in olive oil; white wine, stock, and chopped tomatoes added to pan and simmered, cov-ered, until tender.

Manzo Beef.

— *all'aceto* Bottom round roast browned in olive oil with minced onions; red wine vinegar, salt, pepper, and capers added; cov-ered and simmered until beef is tender.

— *brasato al barolo* Bottom round roast seasoned with salt and pep-per and browned in pork fat; red wine (Barolo), stock, onions, cel-ery, and garlic added; covered and simmered until nearly tender; carrots and potatoes added and covered again until done; sliced and served with braising liquid.

— *alla certosina* Beef bottom round browned in butter and ba-con fat; beef stock, anchovy fil-lets, nutmeg, parsley, salt, and pepper added; covered and sim-mered until meat is tender.

Polpettine Ground beef mixed with bread crumbs, minced onions, garlic, grated Parmesan cheese, eggs, milk, and seasonings; formed into balls and rolled in bread crumbs; panfried in oil, browning all sides; canned diced tomatoes, fresh herbs, salt, and pepper added; covered and sim-mered until sauce has thickened; served hot or cold.

— *ai capperi* Ground beef mixed with capers, bread crumbs, garlic, minced onions, grated Parmesan cheese, eggs, and seasonings; formed into balls; coated with sea-soned flour and nicely browned in oil; pan drizzled with white wine and served immediately with pan juices.

Polpettone Seasoned ground meat; meat loaf.

— *alla napoletana con pomodoro* Ground beef mixed with eggs, bread crumbs, grated Parmesan, milk, and seasonings; rolled thin and sprinkled with diced mozza-rella; meat wrapped around cheese and sealed; rolled in sea-soned flour and browned in oil; placed in a baking pan and coated with tomato sauce and red wine; baked, basted as needed.

— *in salsa verde* Ground beef mixed with minced sautéed on-ions, garlic, eggs, fresh bread crumbs, chopped parsley, ricotta, grated Parmesan, and milk; baked in casserole and served with *salsa verde* (see Part II).

— *alla toscana* Ground beef mixed with bread crumbs, onions, gar-lic, diced ham, grated Parmesan cheese, milk, eggs, and season-ings; formed into a loaf, rolled in bread crumbs, and browned in oil; white wine, wild mushrooms, and tomato puree added; covered and simmered until loaf is cooked and sauce has thickened.

Scaloppine di bue con capperi Beef fillets pounded thin into scallops and dredged in seasoned flour; panfried in olive oil; stock, wine vinegar, fresh parsley, and capers added and simmered briefly; served with boiled vegetables.

Scaloppine al marsala arricchite Beef scallops dredged in seasoned flour and panfried in butter; deglazed with marsala wine and enriched with heavy cream; scallops removed from pan; sauce reduced until it has thickened; sauce poured over meat and served immediately.

Scaloppine alla toscana Beef fillets pounded thin into scallops and dredged in seasoned flour; fried in butter and arranged on a serving platter; pan deglazed with marsala wine; chopped tomatoes, anchovies, and capers added and seasoned with salt and pepper; poured over scallops and served immediately.

Sciuscieddu siciliano Ground beef, eggs, fresh bread crumbs, milk, grated Parmesan, and chopped parsley mixed together and formed into balls; pre-cooked in boiling stock and arranged in a casserole layered with ricotta; broth added, covered and baked.

Spiedini alla romana Ground beef mixed with eggs, grated pecorino, bread crumbs, garlic, and parsley; formed into small ovals and gently threaded on a skewer alternating with cheese cubes and rolled ham; dredged in flour, dipped in eggs, and coated with bread crumbs; panfried in oil until golden brown.

Stracotto al barolo See *Manzo brasato al barolo*, this section.

Stufatino annegato Bottom round cut into cubes and sautéed in ol-

ive oil with onions; white wine, stock, cloves, curry powder, and salt and pepper added; covered and simmered until beef is tender.

Stufatino di manzo con i piselli Boneless beef chunks dredged in seasoned flour and browned in butter with onions, garlic, and celery; red wine, stock, and seasonings added; covered and simmered; carrots and fresh peas added; covered again and cooked until meat and vegetables are tender.

Stufato alla siciliana Boneless beef cubes dredged in seasoned flour and browned in olive oil with onions and garlic; red wine, beef broth, canned diced tomatoes, and fresh herbs added; covered and simmered; carrots, celery, more onions, and seasonings added, various cooking times considered; covered again and simmered until meat and vegetables are tender.

Umido alla trentina Beef cubes dredged in seasoned flour and browned in olive oil with onions, garlic, and parsley; beer, sliced sausage, and ham added; covered and simmered; carrots, celery, and potatoes added and covered again until beef and vegetables are tender.

MAIALE — PORK

Arista alla fiorentina Crown roast of pork (backbone should be severed at one-inch intervals so as to allow for carving chops easily) studded with garlic cloves and

Arista alla fiorentina (cont.)
rubbed with olive oil, rosemary, salt, and pepper; roasted to desired doneness, basted as needed. Boneless pork loin may be used and alternately can be roasted on a spit.

Arista di maiale Pork loin roast rubbed with olive oil and studded with garlic and rosemary; sprinkled with salt and pepper and roasted in the oven, basted as needed.

Arrosto di maiale Pork loin roast.

— *all'alloro* Boneless pork loin seasoned with salt and pepper and browned in butter; pan deglazed with vinegar; bay leaves added; cooked over low flame, covered, until tender, adding more water if needed.

— *di maiale all'arancia* Minced onions and garlic sautéed in olive oil; diced sweet peppers, orange juice, sugar, and salt added and simmered until slightly thickened; pork loin rubbed with oil, salt, and pepper and roasted, basted often with orange sauce; sliced and arranged on a serving platter, drizzled with sauce.

— *di maiale al latte* Pork loin roast seasoned with salt and pepper and browned in butter; milk added and simmered, covered, until meat is tender; served drizzled with pan gravy.

— *di maiale ubriaco* Pork loin roast dusted with seasoned flour and browned on all sides; brandy, red wine, and seasonings added; covered and simmered until tender.

Costatelle di maiale Pork chops marinated in vinegar for one hour; patted dry and seasoned with salt and pepper; dredged in flour, dipped in beaten eggs, and coated with bread crumbs; browned in olive oil and cooked on low flame, covered, to desired doneness.

— *con cavolo* Pork chops seasoned with salt and pepper and browned in olive oil with onions and garlic; shredded cabbage and canned diced tomatoes added; covered and cooked over low flame until chops are tender; pan deglazed with red wine; served at once with pan juices.

Coste di maiale con carciofi *(From Roma)* Pork chops browned in olive oil; sliced artichokes, onions, garlic, canned diced tomatoes, and seasonings added and simmered, covered, until tender.

Costine di maiale alla trevigiana Individual spareribs browned in olive oil with garlic and sage; white wine, salt, and pepper added; covered and simmered until tender.

Costolette di maiale Pork Chops.

— *ai due vini* Pork chops dredged in seasoned flour and browned in olive oil with minced onions and garlic; red wine, marsala wine, tomato paste, salt, pepper, and seasonings added; covered and simmered until tender.

— *con i funghi* Pork chops browned in oil with minced onions; white wine, canned diced tomatoes, reconstituted dried mushrooms, fresh mushrooms, and cream added; covered and simmered until tender.

— *alla modenese* Pork chops dredged in seasoned flour and browned in olive oil; fresh sage, salt, pepper, and canned diced tomatoes added; covered and simmered until tender.

— *alla napoletana* Pork chops dredged in seasoned flour and browned in olive oil; white wine, canned diced tomatoes, salt, and pepper added and simmered, covered, until tender. In a separate pan, sweet peppers and fresh mushrooms sautéed in olive oil; combined with the pan juices from the pork and served over the chops.

Filetto di maiale Boneless pork fillet cubes threaded on a skewer alternating with prosciutto, bay leaves, and bread cubes; grilled over live coals.

Filetto di maiale alle mele Pork loin rubbed with olive oil, salt, and pepper and roasted; in a separate pan, sliced apples, honey, and white wine simmered until a syrupy glaze has been obtained; pork loin served on a platter over the glazed apples and drizzled with the pan juices from the pork, which have been deglazed with stock.

Lonza profumata Pork loin sliced thin and panfried in butter with sage and rosemary; deglazed with brandy; stock added and simmered until syrupy; small pat of whole butter swirled in and served immediately.

Maiale alla bresciana Boned pork loin browned in olive oil with minced onions and garlic; red wine, stock, salt, and pepper added; covered and simmered; artichoke hearts, carrots, potatoes, celery, and fresh herbs added; covered again and cooked until meat and vegetables are tender.

Maiale alla ciociara Ground pork, ground sausage meat, eggs, grated Parmesan cheese, and seasonings mixed together and formed into small ovals; placed on a square of pastry dough; dough folded over and edges sealed; baked until golden brown and filling is cooked.

Maiale piccante Boned pork chops seasoned with salt, pepper, and powdered sage; browned in olive oil; vinegar and stock added; covered and simmered until tender; anchovy paste stirred into pan juices and served over chops.

Maialino arrostito Suckling pig stuffed with apple and orange quarters and sewed shut; pig rubbed with salt, pepper, and garlic and roasted until tender, basted as needed.

Porcellino allo spiedo Suckling pig brushed with pork fat and seasoned with salt, pepper, rosemary, and garlic; cavity brushed with oil; roasted on a spit over wood fire, basted as needed.

Porchetta See Part II.

Rosticcianna con polenta Pork ribs and sausage browned in oil with onions and celery; red wine and canned diced tomatoes added; covered and simmered; carrots,

Rosticcianna con polenta (cont.) potatoes, and fresh herbs added and covered again and cooked until meat and vegetables are tender; served over polenta mush.

Spezzatino di maiale al pomodoro Boneless pork chunks seasoned with salt and pepper and browned in olive oil with garlic; stock added; covered and simmered until partially cooked; canned diced tomatoes, onions, vinegar, and seasonings added; simmered uncovered until meat is tender and sauce has thickened.

Spezzatino tirolese Pork chunks marinated in olive oil, red wine, and seasonings; browned in olive oil and pork fat with onions and garlic; canned diced tomatoes, stock, cloves, bay leaves, and sausage links added; covered and simmered until nearly cooked; fat skimmed, potatoes, carrots, and seasonings added; covered once more and cooked until meat and vegetables are tender.

Spiedini in padella Cubed pork, sliced sausage, onions, sweet peppers, and sage leaves threaded on a skewer and panfried in pork fat; stock added and simmered gently until cooked; arranged on a serving platter and drizzled with pan juices.

Stufatino di maiale alla boscaiola Boneless pork chunks seasoned with salt and pepper and browned in olive oil with onions; white wine, wine vinegar, anchovy puree, wild mushrooms, juniper berries, and bay leaves added; covered and simmered until tender.

VITELLO — VEAL

Arrostino annegato Veal cutlets pounded thin and layered with sliced ham; rolled, secured with a toothpick, and browned in butter; white wine, vinegar, salt, and pepper added; covered and simmered until tender.

Arrosto di vitello Veal roast studded with garlic and rosemary and browned in butter; white wine, stock, salt, and pepper added; covered and simmered until veal is tender; served sliced with pan juices.

— farcito con prosciutto Boneless veal roast pounded thin and layered with a spinach frittata (see Part II), grated Parmesan cheese, prosciutto, minced onions, and garlic; rolled and tied; browned with olive oil, transferred to a baking pan, and roasted to desired doneness.

Bocconcini di vitello con funghi Boneless veal chunks browned in butter with onions and garlic; sprinkled with flour to make a roux; white wine, canned diced tomatoes, and seasonings added; covered and simmered; fresh quartered mushrooms added; covered again and cooked until meat and mushrooms are tender.

Costatelle di vitella alla cacciatora Veal chops pounded thin and seasoned with salt and pepper; browned in butter with onions, celery, garlic, carrots, and mushrooms; white wine and tomato paste added and simmered until veal is tender and sauce has thickened; seasoned with salt and pepper and served piping hot.

Cotolette Veal cutlets.

— *alla ghiottona* Veal cutlets pounded thin and dredged in seasoned flour, dipped in beaten eggs, and coated with bread crumbs; panfried in butter and arranged on a serving platter. In a separate pan, mushrooms, truffles, and diced ham sautéed in butter; stock added and bought to a simmer; served immediately with veal cutlets.

— *alla milanese* Veal cutlets pounded thin and dipped in beaten eggs; coated with bread crumbs and panfried in butter; seasoned with salt and pepper and served at once.

— *alla palermitana* Veal cutlets pounded thin and brushed with olive oil, salt, and pepper; coated with bread crumbs and grilled over live coals or on a *gratella* (see Part II) until crumbs become crispy, about three to four minutes.

— *alla parmigiana* Veal cutlets pounded thin and dipped in beaten eggs; coated with grated Parmesan cheese mixed with bread crumbs and browned in olive oil; topped with mozzarella cheese and baked briefly until cheese has melted; served piping hot with tomato sauce.

— *di vitella* Veal cutlets pounded thin and seasoned with salt and pepper; dipped in eggs, coated with bread crumbs mixed with grated cheese, and panfried in butter or olive oil; served piping hot with pan juices.

— *di vitello con bacon alla valdostana* Veal cutlets pounded thin and dipped in beaten eggs and coated with bread crumbs; panfried in butter and topped with pancetta and fontina cheese; placed under a broiler until cheese has melted; served at once.

Involtini alla sarda Veal cutlets pounded thin and layered with sliced ham and spread with a mixture of fresh bread crumbs, grated Parmesan, eggs, and sage; rolled and secured with a toothpick; coated with seasoned flour and browned in butter; marsala wine, stock, and fresh chopped tomatoes added and simmered, covered, until veal is tender.

Involtini di vitello Boneless veal cutlets pounded thin and layered with mozzarella cheese and anchovy fillets; rolled, fastened with a toothpick, and browned in butter; deglazed with white wine; seasoned served immediately.

Nodini di vitello alla salvia Veal chops pounded thin and dredged in seasoned flour; panfried in olive oil; transferred to a serving platter; pan deglazed with white wine and seasoned with salt, pepper, and sage; whole butter swirled in and sauce drizzled over chops.

Nodini di vitello con sughetto di acciughe Veal cutlets pounded thin and dredged in seasoned flour; panfried in butter and transferred to a warm serving platter; in a separate pan, garlic and chopped anchovy fillets sautéed in butter with salt, pepper, and parsley;

DISHES BY COURSE

Nodini di vitello con sughetto di acciughe (cont.)
drizzled over veal chops.

Oseleti scampai *(From Northern Italy)* Veal chunks, smoked pancetta pieces, pork livers, and sage leaves alternately threaded on a skewer and panfried in oil; drizzled with white wine and stock and served immediately with rice or polenta.

Ossibuchi Veal shanks.

— *in bianco* Veal shanks dredged in seasoned flour and browned in olive oil; white wine added; covered and simmered until tender; pan liquid seasoned and reduced; whole butter swirled in and drizzled over shanks.

— *della festa* Veal shanks dredged in seasoned flour and browned in butter; white wine, canned diced tomatoes, onions, and seasonings added; covered and simmered; cooked green peas and wild mushrooms added; lid replaced and cooked until mushrooms and veal are tender; served piping hot.

— *alla milanese* Veal shanks dredged in seasoned flour and browned in butter with minced onions and garlic; white wine and stock added; covered and simmered until veal is tender; sauce seasoned and served with veal.

Petto di vitello arrotolato Boneless veal breast pounded thin and seasoned with salt and pepper; layered with sliced pancetta, grated Parmesan cheese, and fresh herbs; rolled, tied, and browned in butter; white wine added; covered and simmered until tender.

Petto di vitello ripieno Boneless veal breast pounded thin and seasoned with salt and pepper; spread with a mixture of ground beef, eggs, grated Parmesan cheese, diced mortadella, and seasonings; rolled, tied, and placed in a pot of cold water with aromatic herbs and vegetables; brought to a simmer and cooked until tender.

Piccata di vitello Veal cutlets pounded thin and dredged in seasoned flour; panfried in butter and transferred to a warm serving platter; pan deglazed with white wine and flavored with fresh lemon juice; whole butter swirled in and poured over cutlets; served immediately.

Polpettone di vitello Ground veal combined with eggs, ricotta, grated Parmesan cheese, fresh bread crumbs, and seasonings; arranged in a loaf pan and brushed with olive oil; baked, basted as needed; served sliced with tomato sauce or *besciamella*.

Punta di vitello arrosto Veal loin roast browned in oil and pork fat with onions and garlic; stock added; loin covered with bacon strips and roasted to desired doneness; pan deglazed with white wine and drizzled over sliced meat; can be chilled and served cold.

Rollatini di vitello al pomodoro Veal scallops pounded thin and layered with sliced pancetta, grated Parmesan cheese, salt, and pepper; rolled, secured with a pick, and browned in butter; removed from pan; white wine and canned diced tomatoes added to pan and simmered until thickened; veal reheated in pan and served immediately.

Rotolo di vitello Rolled veal.

— ***alla forestiera*** Veal leg roast pounded flat and layered with bread crumbs, ground sausage meat, grated Parmesan cheese, eggs, milk, and seasonings; rolled to enclose filling and tied; browned in olive oil with garlic, onions, and bacon; white wine and stock added to pan and simmered, covered, until done.

— ***ripieno*** Veal leg roast pounded thin and layered with ground sausage meat combined with cooked rice, grated Parmesan cheese, eggs, minced onions, and seasonings; rolled and tied to enclose filling and browned in oil; placed in a baking pan and roasted to desired doneness.

— ***ripieno alla parmense*** Boneless veal roast pounded flat and layered with sliced ham, salt, and pepper; rolled, tied, and browned in butter; allow roast to rest before slicing.

— ***con spinaci*** Fresh chopped spinach sautéed in butter with minced onions and garlic; combined with chopped ham, grated Parmesan cheese, and seasonings; spread on a flattened piece of veal round, rolled tightly, and secured with string; browned in oil and butter; white wine added; covered and simmered until tender; served sliced, drizzled with pan juices.

Saltimbocca alla genovese Veal scallops pounded thin and sprinkled with salt and pepper; layered with fresh sage and sliced prosciutto; rolled, secured with a toothpick, and dredged in seasoned flour; browned in butter; marsala wine and stock added; covered and simmered until tender.

Saltimbocca alla romana Veal scallops pounded thin and topped with thinly sliced prosciutto and fresh sage; secured with a toothpick and panfried in butter until nicely browned and tender; drizzled with pan juices.

Scalloppe alla romana Veal scallops pounded thin and dredged in seasoned flour; panfried in butter; topped with sliced ham, Gruyère cheese, and fresh sage; white wine and cooked peas added; covered and simmered until meat is tender; served immediately with pan juices.

Scaloppine al marsala arricchite Veal scallops pounded thin and dredged in seasoned flour; panfried in butter; transferred to a warm serving platter; pan deglazed with marsala wine; cream added and simmered until sauce has thickened; poured over scallops and served at once.

Scaloppine di vitello Veal scallops.

— ***ammantate*** Veal scallops pounded thin and dredged in seasoned flour; panfried in butter; layered with sliced mozzarella and served immediately when cheese has melted; drizzled with pan juices.

— ***al limone*** Veal scallops pounded thin and dredged in seasoned flour; panfried in butter; drizzled with freshly squeezed lemon juice and served immediately.

— *al marsala* Veal scallops pounded thin and dredged in seasoned flour; panfried in butter; deglazed with marsala and broth and simmered until nearly evaporated; served immediately.

— *piccante* Veal scallops pounded thin and dredged in seasoned flour; panfried in butter and transferred to a warm serving platter; chopped anchovies, capers, and minced onions added to pan and sautéed; deglazed with brandy; cream added and reduced until thick; poured over veal scallops and served immediately.

— *alla pizzaiola* Veal scallops pounded thin and dredged in seasoned flour; panfried in olive oil; transferred to a warm platter; white wine, canned diced tomatoes and seasonings added and simmered until thickened; scallops reheated in sauce and served immediately.

Spezzatino di vitello Boneless veal chunks seasoned with salt and pepper and browned in olive oil with garlic and onions; white wine, canned diced tomatoes, and fresh herbs added; covered and simmered until meat is tender.

— *alla salvia* Boneless cubed veal shoulder dredged in seasoned flour and browned in butter; white wine, sage, salt, and pepper added; covered and simmered until tender; served in thickened sauce.

Spiedini all'uccelletto Boneless veal cubes, sliced sausage links, diced pancetta, and fresh sage leaves threaded on a skewer; browned in olive oil; white wine added to pan; covered and simmered until tender; pan juices reduced and drizzled over skewers.

Stufatino di vitello all'antica Boneless veal chunks browned in olive oil with onions, bacon, and garlic; white wine and broth added and brought to a simmer; carrots, potatoes, celery, leeks, and chopped tomatoes added, keeping in mind various cooking times of the vegetables; covered and stewed until meat and vegetables are tender.

Uccelletti alla golosa Eggs, grated Parmesan cheese, salt, and pepper beaten together and cooked into small omelets; placed in the center of a flattened slice of veal and topped with sliced mozzarella; rolled, secured with a toothpick, and dredged in seasoned flour; browned in butter; marsala wine and stock added and simmered, covered, until tender.

Vitello Veal.

— *alla milanese* Veal scallops pounded thin and dipped in beaten eggs; coated with seasoned bread crumbs and panfried in butter and olive oil; served immediately.

— *alla mozzarella* Veal scallops pounded thin and seasoned with salt and pepper; browned in olive oil and butter; sprinkled with lemon juice and topped with sliced prosciutto and sliced mozzarella cheese; pan covered until cheese has melted; served immediately.

— *in peperonata* Sliced sweet peppers, fresh chopped tomatoes, and salt sautéed in olive oil and slowly stewed, uncovered, until very soft; combined with tender veal chunks that have been stewed separately; served piping hot.

— *tonnato* Canned tuna pureed and combined with mayonnaise, capers, anchovy paste, lemon juice, and chopped parsley; served with sliced boiled veal, chilled and arranged on a platter.

SALSICCIA — SAUSAGE

Cotechino con le lenticchie Cotechino sausage, soaked in water overnight, placed in fresh cold water and brought to a simmer; cooked until done and cooled in water. In a separate pan, onions sautéed in olive oil; lentils and water added; simmered, covered, until lentils are tender; served with sliced sausage.

Cotechino di modena Cotechino sausage covered with cold water and brought to a boil; simmered gently until sausage is cooked; served sliced with lentils, mashed potatoes, or spinach.

Luganica coi crauti Chopped bacon and sauerkraut sautéed in pork fat; white wine and stock added and stewed slowly; diced apples and sliced sausage added and cooked until sausage is done; excess fat poured off before serving.

Luganica e riso See RISO E RISOTTO Section, *Luganega e,*.

Salsicce col cavolo nero Shredded cabbage and garlic sautéed in olive oil until wilted; cooked grilled

sausages added and stewed slowly until cabbage is very soft and tender; seasoned with salt and pepper and served at once.

Salsicce con cipolle Onions sautéed in olive oil until well caramelized; canned diced tomatoes and seasonings added and slightly reduced; parcooked sausages and green peppers added and slowly stewed until sausages are fully cooked.

Salsicce con funghi secchi Sweet Italian sausage links well browned in olive oil; excess fat poured off and red wine added; simmered, uncovered; reconstituted dried mushrooms and strained liquid added; reduced until sausage has cooked and liquid has nearly evaporated; served with mashed potatoes, polenta, vegetables, and so on.

Salsiccia alla griglia Italian sausage links pricked with a fork and placed under a broiler; cooked until well-done and served with sautéed onions and peppers.

Salsiccia con polenta Italian sausage links pricked with a fork and panfried until well browned; fat drained and tomato sauce added; simmered and covered until sausage has cooked; served piping hot with polenta and grated cheese.

Salsiccia con vino rosso Italian sausage links pricked with a fork and placed in cold water just to cover; brought to a boil and simmered until sausage is nearly cooked and water has evaporated (excess water poured off if necessary); red

Salsiccia con vino rosso (cont.)
wine added and simmered, covered, until sausage has completed cooking.

VERDURE —
VEGETABLES

Asparagi Asparagus.
— *al forno* Bundles of blanched asparagus spears wrapped in prosciutto and placed in a baking dish; drizzled with butter and baked until browned and tender.
— *fritti* Blanched asparagus spears dipped in beaten eggs and coated with seasoned bread crumbs; panfried in olive oil until nicely browned; seasoned with salt and served immediately.
— *e funghi al burro* Blanched asparagus tips and tiny whole mushrooms sautéed in butter until tender and dry; seasoned with salt and freshly ground black pepper and served immediately.
— *alla legnanese* Poached asparagus spears placed in a serving platter and drizzled with melted butter, grated Parmesan cheese, salt, and pepper; garnished with chopped hard-cooked eggs and served immediately.
— *alla milanese* Poached asparagus spears seasoned with salt and pepper and garnished with fried eggs; drizzled with melted butter and sprinkled with grated Parmesan cheese; browned quickly in the oven before serving.
— *alla parmigiana* Prepared as for *Asparagi alla milanese*, omitting the fried egg garnish.

— *alla parmigiana con uova fritte* Prepared as for *Asparagi alla milanese*.
—, *pasticcio di* Fresh asparagus spears blanched in salted water; placed in a casserole and coated with *besciamella* and sprinkled with grated Parmesan and mozzarella cheeses; baked until golden brown and bubbly.
—, *torta di* Blanched chopped asparagus placed in a shallow (precooked) pastry-lined pan and coated with *besciamella*; drizzled with melted butter and grated Parmesan cheese and baked until nicely browned; served hot.
Bietole all'aglio e pomodoro Diced blanched beetroot sautéed in olive oil with onions, garlic, and minced anchovies (optional); fresh chopped tomatoes added; covered and cooked until beets are tender; seasoned with salt and pepper and served hot.
Broccoli Broccoli.
— *all'aglio* Blanched broccoli cut into small pieces and sautéed in olive oil with garlic and chopped parsley; seasoned with salt and pepper and served piping hot.
— *all'agro* Blanched broccoli florets sautéed in olive oil with salt and pepper; drizzled with fresh lemon juice and served immediately.
— *al burro e formaggio* Blanched broccoli cut into small pieces sautéed in butter; seasoned with grated Parmesan cheese and served immediately.
— *fritti* Blanched broccoli florets dredged in seasoned flour; dipped

in beaten eggs and coated with bread crumbs; deep-fried or panfried in olive oil; drained well and served immediately.

— *con olive* Blanched broccoli sautéed in olive oil with garlic and Italian black olives; seasoned with salt and pepper.

— *alla siciliana* Blanched broccoli sautéed in olive oil with garlic and anchovies; drizzled with lemon juice, salt, and pepper and served immediately.

Caponata See *Melanzane*, this section.

Caponata alla siciliana Diced eggplant panfried in olive oil; removed from pan and replaced with diced onions, celery and garlic, sautéed; canned diced tomatoes added and simmered until slightly thickened; capers, pine nuts, sugar, wine vinegar, the eggplant, and seasonings added; covered and simmered until flavors meld; served hot or cold.

Carciofi Artichokes.

— *all'aglio* Trimmed and halved artichokes blanched in salted water; placed in an oiled casserole and stuffed with a mixture of garlic, minced anchovies, bread crumbs, olive oil, and seasonings; baked until nicely browned and tender.

— *arrostiti* Whole trimmed artichokes seasoned with salt, pepper, garlic, and chopped parsley; placed upright in a pan and fried in olive oil; broth added; covered and simmered until tender.

— *bolliti* Whole trimmed artichokes placed in boiling salted water with lemon slices and cooked until tender; served hot or cold.

— *fritti* Cooked chilled artichoke hearts dredged in seasoned flour, dipped in eggs, and coated with bread crumbs; fried in olive oil until golden brown.

— *alla giudia* Trimmed young artichokes, leaves spread open, fried in olive oil until nicely browned; seasoned with salt and pepper and served immediately.

— *gratinati* Trimmed quartered artichoke hearts blanched in salted water with lemon; sautéed in butter and transferred to a casserole; sprinkled with salt and grated Parmesan cheese and baked until golden brown and tender.

— *imbottiti alla siciliana* Whole trimmed artichokes, leaves spread open, stuffed with a mixture of fresh bread crumbs, grated cheese, chopped anchovies, garlic, and parsley; placed upright in a pan and fried lightly in olive oil; water added; covered and simmered until tender.

— *alla napoletana* Trimmed artichokes, leaves separated, stuffed with a mixture of shredded mozzarella cheese, grated Parmesan cheese, bread crumbs, parsley, eggs, salt, and pepper; placed in a baking pan with water and olive oil; simmered until liquid is reduced; covered and baked until tender.

— *e patate* Quartered artichoke hearts, sliced potatoes, garlic, and minced onions sautéed in olive

Carciofi e patate (cont.)
oil; stock or water added and simmered, covered, until tender; seasoned with salt and pepper and served hot.

— *e piselli stufati* Onions, garlic, and chopped parsley sautéed in olive oil; fresh peas, raw quartered artichoke hearts, and stock added; covered and simmered until peas and artichokes are tender; seasoned with salt and pepper and served piping hot.

— *e porri* Blanched quartered artichoke hearts and sliced leeks stewed in butter until tender; seasoned with salt and pepper and served immediately.

— *ripieni di mortadella* Trimmed whole artichokes stuffed with a mixture of bread crumbs, minced sautéed onions and garlic, grated Parmesan cheese, eggs, diced mortadella, and seasonings; carefully browned on all sides and arranged in a shallow pot; stock added and simmered, covered, until tender.

— *alla romana* Trimmed artichokes, leaves spread, stuffed with a mixture of fresh bread crumbs, chopped parsley, chopped mint, salt, and pepper; placed in a baking dish and drizzled with olive oil and water; covered and baked, until tender.

— *trifolati, fondi di* Trimmed artichoke bottoms sautéed in olive oil with garlic, salt, and pepper; stewed slowly until tender.

Carote Carrots.

— *al burro e formaggio* Sliced carrots combined with butter, salt, sugar, and cold water and simmered until liquid has been totally evaporated and carrots are tender (more liquid may be added during cooking as needed); tossed with grated Parmesan cheese and served immediately.

— *in fricassea* Sliced fresh carrots stewed slowly in butter with salt and sugar until tender; heavy cream mixed with egg yolks added and heated until sauce thickens; served immediately.

— *al marsala* Fresh sliced carrots sautéed in olive oil with salt and pepper; stock added covered and simmered until nearly tender; uncovered and sprinkled with sugar and marsala wine; reduced until carrots are tender and a syrupy glaze has formed.

—, *purea di* Carrots simmered in broth until tender; pureed and enriched with cream butter and grated Parmesan cheese; served hot.

Castagne e cavoletti Boiled chestnuts sautéed with fresh Brussels sprouts in butter; broth added, covered and simmered until tender; seasoned with salt and pepper and served piping hot.

Cavolfiore Cauliflower.

— *alla casalinga* Hot cooked cauliflower topped with a mixture of hard-cooked eggs, chopped parsley, toasted bread crumbs, salt, and pepper; served hot.

— *dorato* Blanched cauliflower florets dredged in seasoned flour and dipped in beaten eggs; panfried in butter and seasoned with salt and pepper; served immediately.

— *fritto* Cauliflower florets blanched in salted water; dipped in beaten eggs and coated with seasoned bread crumbs; panfried in olive oil or deep-fried until golden brown; served immediately.

— *gratinato* Blanched cauliflower sautéed in butter with salt and pepper; transferred to a casserole; coated with *besciamella* and sprinkled with grated Parmesan cheese; baked in the oven until golden brown and tender.

— *gratinato al burro e formaggio* Cauliflower cut into pieces and blanched in salted water; sautéed in butter and transferred to a casserole; sprinkled with salt, white pepper, and grated Parmesan cheese and browned in a hot oven; served piping hot.

— *al pomodoro* Cauliflower florets blanched in salted water; sautéed in olive oil with garlic, chopped parsley, and very ripe chopped tomatoes; covered and simmered until cauliflower is tender.

— *alla siracusana* Raw cauliflower florets tossed with olive oil, minced onions, leeks, sliced olives, minced anchovies, grated Parmesan cheese, salt, and pepper; placed in a baking dish and drizzled with red wine and more oil; covered and baked until tender.

Cavolini di bruxelles gratinati Blanched brussels sprouts seasoned with salt and pepper and placed in a casserole; topped with *besciamella*, melted butter, and fontina cheese; baked until golden brown and bubbly.

Cavolini di bruxelles stufati Blanched Brussels sprouts sautéed in butter with minced onions, salt, and pepper; heavy cream added and simmered until sauce has thickened and sprouts are tender; served immediately.

Cavolo imbottito Green cabbage blanched in boiling salted water until leaves soften and separate; leaves stuffed with a mixture of chopped cooked spinach, ground beef, grated cheese, eggs, and seasonings; browned on all sides in olive oil; water or stock added; covered and cooked until tender.

Cavolo rosso di Agrigento Shredded red cabbage sautéed in olive oil with salt and pepper; red wine vinegar and stock added and brought to a simmer; capers and black olives added; covered and stewed until tender.

Cicoria fina agliata Blanched dandelion greens sautéed in olive oil with garlic; seasoned with salt and pepper.

Cippole Onions.

—, *crostata di* Sliced onions stewed in butter until tender and placed in a pastry-lined tart pan; eggs, cream, and seasonings mixed together and poured into pan; baked until custard has set; allowed to settle before serving.

— *fritte* Sliced onions dipped in a batter of flour, milk, and egg; panfried in olive oil or deep-fried; drained well and seasoned with salt; served immediately.

— *alla sbirraglia* Peeled hollowed-out onions stuffed with a mixture of ground hot sausage

Cippole alla sbirraglia (cont.)
meat, bread crumbs, eggs, grated Parmesan cheese, garlic, and curry powder; drizzled with melted butter and baked until filling is cooked and onions are tender.

Cipolline Small onions.

— *in agrodolce* Small whole onions placed in a sauce pan with water, sugar, white vinegar, and salt; covered and simmered until tender; drained before being served.

— *e funghi* Fresh sliced wild mushrooms and sliced onions sautéed in olive oil with garlic, and chopped parsley; seasoned with salt, pepper, and red pepper flakes; drizzled with wine vinegar and served immediately.

— *al prosciutto e al rosmarino* Small boiling onions blanched in salted water with vinegar; combined with olive oil, butter, prosciutto, and rosemary; covered and stewed until onions are tender, shaking pan often; seasoned with salt and pepper.

Escarola imbottita Escarole leaves stuffed with a mixture of cooked ground beef, bread crumbs, raisins, minced anchovies, parsley, salt, and pepper; placed in a pan with olive oil; covered and stewed slowly until tender; turned occasionally to prevent burning.

Fagiolini String beans.

— *all'aglio e al pomodoro* Onions, garlic, and sage sautéed in olive oil; canned diced tomatoes and fresh string beans added; covered and simmered until beans are tender; seasoned with salt and pepper and served immediately.

— *al burro e formaggio* Fresh trimmed string beans blanched in salted water and sautéed in butter; sprinkled with grated Parmesan cheese and white pepper and served immediately.

— *dorati alla milanese* Blanched string bean bundles dipped in beaten egg and coated with seasoned flour; deep-fried in oil and seasoned with salt and pepper; served immediately.

— *con peperoni e pomodoro* Fresh trimmed string beans blanched in salted water; sautéed in olive oil with minced onions and sliced green peppers; canned diced tomatoes and seasonings added and simmered until tender.

— *al pomodoro (al forno)* Onions, garlic, parsley, pine nuts, and minced anchovies sautéed in olive oil; canned diced tomatoes added and brought to a simmer; blanched string beans added and poured into an oiled baking dish; baked until beans are tender; served immediately.

— *con prosciutto e crostini* Blanched string beans sautéed in butter with minced onions and thin strips of prosciutto; seasoned with salt and pepper and served piping hot.

Finocchi Fennel.

— *con burro e formaggio* Blanched sliced fennel sautéed in butter; stock added and simmered, uncovered, until liquid has been totally reduced and fennel is tender (more liquid may be added during cooking as needed); sprinkled with salt, ground black pepper, and grated Parmesan cheese; served piping hot.

— *alla casalinga* Fresh blanched fennel sautéed in olive oil with garlic and minced onions; white wine added; covered and simmered until tender; seasoned with salt and pepper and served piping hot.

— *fritti* Blanched fennel slices dipped in beaten eggs and coated with seasoned bread crumbs; panfried in oil until golden brown; seasoned with salt and served immediately.

— *gratinati* Fennel simmered in water with lemon until tender; placed in a casserole and coated with *besciamella* and grated Parmesan; baked until very hot and topping has nicely browned.

— *all'olio* Blanched sliced fennel slowly stewed in olive oil until tender; seasoned with salt and served immediately.

— *alla parmigiana* Thick fennel slices blanched in salted water; placed in a casserole and drizzled with melted butter and grated Parmesan cheese; baked until golden brown and tender.

— *in pizza* Sliced blanched fennel arranged in a single layer in a casserole; topped with tomato sauce, anchovy fillets, pitted olives, fresh herbs, mozzarella cheese, and grated Parmesan cheese; drizzled with olive oil and baked; allowed to settle briefly before serving.

— *alla valdostana* Boiled fennel placed in a casserole and topped with slices of fontina cheese; drizzled with melted butter and baked until topping is nicely browned.

Frittedda See Part II.

Funghi Mushrooms.

— *alla crema e tartufi* Sliced wild mushrooms sautéed briefly in butter with sliced truffles; heavy cream added and reduced until sauce has thickened; seasoned with salt and pepper and served immediately.

— *al funghetto* Fresh sliced mushrooms sautéed in olive oil with garlic, salt, pepper, and parsley; drizzled with freshly squeezed lemon juice and served piping hot.

— *imbottiti* Mushroom caps brushed with olive oil and stuffed with a mixture of bread crumbs, grated Parmesan cheese, garlic, minced onions, parsley, and melted butter; baked until tender; served piping hot.

— *all'italiana panati* Mushroom caps dipped in beaten eggs and coated with seasoned bread crumbs; panfried in butter and olive oil until golden brown; served piping hot with tomato sauce.

— *alla panna* Sliced white mushrooms and minced onions sautéed in butter and olive oil until dry; heavy cream added and simmered until sauce has thickened; seasoned with salt and freshly ground black pepper and served immediately.

— *alla parmigiana* Fresh white mushrooms tossed with olive oil, garlic, grated Parmesan cheese,

Funghi alla parmigiana (cont.)
chopped parsley, oregano, salt, and pepper; placed in a baking dish and sprinkled with bread crumbs; baked until tender.

— *con pomodoro* Sliced white mushrooms sautéed in olive oil with garlic and minced onions; fresh chopped tomatoes added and simmered until reduced and thickened; seasoned with salt, pepper, and fresh herbs; cooled and served chilled.

— *stufati* Small fresh mushrooms sautéed in olive oil with garlic and rosemary until nearly dry; fresh chopped tomatoes, salt, and pepper added; covered and stewed briefly until flavors meld.

— *al tegame* Sliced white mushrooms and garlic sautéed in butter and olive oil until the mixture is nearly dry; tomato strips, anchovy paste, and ground black pepper added and combined thoroughly; served very hot.

— *trifolati* Sliced white mushrooms sautéed briefly in hot olive oil with garlic, chopped parsley, and minced onions (optional); seasoned with salt and pepper and served piping hot.

Melanzane Eggplant; in most preparations, the eggplant is sliced, sprinkled with salt, and allowed to sit for about thirty minutes. This step rids the vegetable of excess moisture (which tends to be bitter) and permits better results when frying.

— *fritte* Sliced eggplant fried in olive oil until browned and tender; seasoned with salt, pepper, and grated Parmesan cheese; served immediately.

— *al funghetto* Cubed eggplant sautéed in olive oil with garlic, salt, and pepper; cooked, covered, until tender; served immediately.

— *alla griglia* Sliced eggplant marinated in olive oil, garlic, salt, and pepper; cooked under a broiler until browned and tender; seasoned with salt and pepper and drizzled with tomato sauce and grated cheese; served piping hot.

— *imbottite* Fresh eggplant halved lengthwise and cored; pulp sautéed in olive oil with minced onions, chopped tomatoes, and garlic; transferred to a mixing bowl and combined with bread crumbs, eggs, ricotta, cooked rice, and seasonings; stuffed in the eggplant and drizzled with oil; baked in a well-oiled casserole until nicely browned and tender.

— *all'italiana* Eggplant sliced lengthwise and browned in olive oil; spread with cooked ground beef mixed with bread crumbs, cheese, and seasonings; topped with another eggplant slice to enclose filling and dredged in seasoned flour; dipped in eggs and coated with bread crumbs; fried in olive oil until browned and finished cooking in the oven; served with tomato sauce.

— *alla parmigiana* Eggplant slices fried in olive oil until browned and tender; arranged in layers in a baking pan, seasoned bread crumbs and grated Parmesan between layers; topped with tomato sauce and mozzarella cheese;

baked until very hot.

— *ripiene di riso* Fresh eggplant cut into thick slices and panfried in olive oil; topped with a mixture of cooked rice, chopped ham, minced onions, garlic, and olive oil; layered with sliced mozzarella and baked until nicely browned and tender.

—, *tortino di* Fresh eggplant halved lengthwise and hollowed out; pulp sautéed with minced onions, garlic, and fresh basil; canned diced tomatoes added and simmered until sauce has thickened; eggplant brushed with olive oil and seasoned with salt and pepper; stuffed with tomato mixture and topped with mozzarella and Parmesan cheese; baked until eggplant is tender.

Misto ripieno Ground sausage mixed with bread crumbs, eggs, minced onions, garlic, grated Parmesan cheese, melted butter, and seasonings; stuffed into various hollowed-out vegetables, i.e., eggplant, peppers, onions, zucchini, and so on; baked until golden brown and tender, keeping in mind various cooking times.

Misto di verdure gratinate Various blanched vegetables, i.e., cauliflower, zucchini, broccoli, fennel, spinach, asparagus, and so on; placed in a casserole and coated with *besciamella*; sprinkled with grated Parmesan cheese and baked until golden brown and tender.

Patate Potatoes.

— *con le acciughe* Sliced potatoes cooked slowly in olive oil and butter until nicely browned and nearly soft; salt, pepper, garlic, parsley, and minced anchovies added and cooked until potatoes are tender.

— *arrosto* Blanched potato cubes seasoned with salt and pepper and tossed with olive oil, coating well; arranged in a single layer on a sheet pan and roasted until golden brown and tender; served immediately.

— *e peperoni in tegame* Parcooked potato slices sautéed in olive oil until nicely browned; sliced red peppers, which have been charred and skinned, added to potatoes and tossed to heat; seasoned with salt and pepper and served piping hot.

— *alla pizzaiola* Parcooked sliced potatoes sautéed in olive oil with minced onions, garlic, salt, and pepper; canned diced tomatoes added and simmered until potatoes are tender.

—, *puree di* Boiled potatoes pureed through a food mill or a ricer; hot milk, butter and grated Parmesan cheese added; seasoned with salt and pepper and served immediately.

— *trifolate* Sliced raw potatoes panfried in butter and olive oil; when nicely browned and tender, minced garlic and parsley added and cooked briefly; seasoned with salt and pepper and served immediately.

— *in umido* Cubed potatoes sautéed in butter with pancetta, garlic, and minced onions; canned

Patate in umido (cont.)
diced tomatoes and fresh basil added; covered and simmered until potatoes are tender; seasoned with salt and pepper.

Peperoni Peppers.

— *arrostiti* Sweet peppers charred under a broiler; skin removed and cut into thin slices; marinated in olive oil, salt, pepper, garlic, and vinegar; served cold.

— *fritti* Seeded sliced sweet peppers and garlic stewed in olive oil until limp; served hot with various meats.

— *imbottiti* Whole cored green peppers stuffed with a mixture of ground beef, rice, bread crumbs, grated cheese, garlic, minced onions, eggs, and seasonings; placed in a baking dish with olive oil and baked until tender; topped with tomato sauce and served piping hot.

— *della massaia* Sweet peppers halved and blanched in boiling salted water; stuffed with a mixture of bread crumbs, fresh herbs, minced onions and garlic, and olive oil; baked until nicely browned and tender.

Piselli Peas.

— *alla casalinga* Onions and pancetta sautéed in butter; stock added and brought to a simmer; fresh peas and aromatic herbs added; covered and simmered until tender; seasoned with salt and pepper.

— *alla fiorentina* Minced onions, garlic, and pancetta sautéed in olive oil, fresh peas and water added; covered and simmered until peas are tender; seasoned with salt and pepper and served immediately.

— *al prosciutto* Onions sautéed in olive oil; stock added and brought to a boil; fresh peas added and simmered until tender; diced prosciutto tossed in and seasoned with salt; served hot.

Pomodori Tomatoes.

— *ripieni alla casalinga* Halved, scooped out tomatoes stuffed with a mixture of fresh bread crumbs, grated Parmesan cheese, minced anchovy fillets, onions, olive oil, and seasonings; baked in a moderate oven until nicely browned but not overcooked.

— *al forno* Fresh halved tomatoes seasoned with salt and garlic and drizzled with olive oil; arranged in an oiled baking dish and roasted in a low to medium oven until very tender; seasonings adjusted and served immediately.

— *fritti* Ripe tomatoes cut into thick slices and shaken to remove seeds; dredged in seasoned flour, dipped in eggs, and coated with bread crumbs; panfried in olive oil until golden brown; drained well and served immediately.

— *al riso* Fresh tomatoes, tops sliced off and reserved, cored out and filled with raw rice, olive oil, chopped garlic, chopped basil, salt, pepper, and the tomato pulp mixed with tomato juice; covered with tomato tops and baked until rice is tender. Cool slightly before serving.

Porri Leeks.

— *alla besciamella* Sliced leeks

stewed in butter until tender and coated with *besciamella*; served piping hot with grated Parmesan cheese.

— *al burro e formaggio* Trimmed sliced leeks simmered in butter and water, covered, until nearly tender; uncovered and continued simmering until liquid has evaporated and leeks are tender and nicely browned; seasoned with grated Parmesan cheese.

— *in umido* Sliced leeks sautéed in olive oil with garlic, salt, and pepper; chopped fresh tomatoes, pitted black olives, salt, and pepper added; covered and simmered until leeks are tender.

Risi e bisi See RISO E RISOTTO Section, *Risi e bisi.*

Sedano alla parmigiana Blanched celery stalks cut into quarters and sautéed in butter with onions and prosciutto; stock added; covered and simmered until celery is tender and liquid has nearly evaporated; sprinkled with grated Parmesan cheese and browned in the oven.

Spinaci Spinach.

— *affogati* Fresh spinach cooked in hot olive oil with garlic, seasoned with salt and pepper and served piping hot.

—, *crocchette di* Chopped spinach sautéed in butter until dry; chilled and mixed with thick *besciamella*; formed into patties and coated with bread crumbs; panfried in butter and olive oil until golden brown and crispy; served immediately.

— *alla lombarda* Blanched spinach stewed in butter with salt and pepper; transferred to a serving platter and sprinkled with grated Parmesan cheese; garnished with a fried egg and served immediately.

— *alla romana* Spinach sautéed in pancetta with garlic, minced onions, bacon, pine nuts, and raisins; seasoned with salt and pepper and served immediately.

— *saltati* Blanched spinach and chopped garlic sautéed in olive oil; seasoned with salt and pepper and served piping hot.

Topinambur gratinati Cubed and blanched Jerusalem artichokes sautéed in butter with salt and pepper; placed in a casserole and sprinkled with grated Parmesan cheese; baked until nicely browned.

Verdure miste al forno Parcooked and quartered red potatoes, ripe tomato halves, onions, peppers, baby zucchini, and sliced eggplant generously coated with olive oil and sprinkled with salt and pepper; baked in the oven until golden brown and tender, keeping in mind various cooking times of the separate vegetables; served immediately.

Zucchine Zucchini.

— *con aglio e pomodoro* Sliced zucchini and garlic sautéed in olive oil; canned diced tomatoes and salt added; covered and simmered until zucchini are tender, being careful not to overcook; served immediately.

— *in agrodolce* Thick zucchini slices sautéed in vegetable oil; sea-

Zucchine in agrodolce (cont.)
soned with salt, pepper, sugar, and vinegar; served immediately or chilled and served cold; do not overcook.

— **alla crema** Thick zucchini slices sautéed briefly in butter with salt and pepper; fresh rosemary and heavy cream added and simmered until sauce has thickened and zucchini is tender.

— **fritte** (1) Zucchini slices panfried in vegetable oil until browned and tender; sprinkled with salt, pepper, parsley, and grated pecorino cheese; served piping hot. (2) Thinly sliced zucchini dredged in seasoned flour, dipped in eggs, and coated with bread crumbs; panfried in olive oil until golden brown and tender.

-, **fiori di** Fresh trimmed zucchini flowers dipped in a light batter and deep-fried or panfried in olive oil; drained well and seasoned with salt and pepper; served immediately.

— **gratinate** Sliced zucchini sautéed in olive oil with minced onions, salt, pepper, and garlic; alternately layered in a casserole with chopped sautéed tomatoes; sprinkled with grated Parmesan cheese and baked until nicely browned.

— **alla milanese** Blanched, halved zucchini scooped out and stuffed with bread crumbs mixed with grated Parmesan cheese, eggs, diced ham, and seasonings and bound with *besciamella*; baked in moderate oven until nicely browned and tender.

— **ripiene al forno** Fresh zucchini halved lengthwise and cored out; pulp sautéed in butter with minced onions and garlic; removed from heat and combined with bread crumbs, eggs, diced cooked ham, grated Parmesan cheese, *besciamella*, and seasonings; stuffed into zucchini halves and drizzled with butter; baked until golden brown and tender.

LEGUMI — LEGUMES

Cannellini con aglio, zuppa di Garlic, onions, parsley, carrots, and celery sautéed in olive oil; broth and cannellini beans added and simmered until beans are tender; seasoned with salt and pepper.

Cecina See Part II.

Ciaudedda See Part II.

Fagioli Beans.

— **bolliti** Beans soaked overnight in water; drained and rinsed and placed in a pot with clean cold water and salt; bought to a simmer and cooked gently until tender.

— **cotti nel fiasco** Pre-soaked cannellini beans placed in a wine bottle and filled with water, olive oil, garlic, salt, pepper, and minced onions; placed directly in live coals until beans are tender. The bottle may also be placed in a heavy pot and cooked in simmering water.

— **al forno** Cannellini beans, smoked ham hock, chopped tomatoes, onions, garlic, olive oil, salt, and pepper combined with water in a pot; heated to a simmer, covered and cooked until tender.

— *con sedano e carote* Diced pancetta sautéed in olive oil; carrots, celery, and cannellini beans added and covered with water; seasoned with salt and freshly ground black pepper; brought to a boil and simmered, covered, until tender.

— *al tonno* Cooked cannellini beans mixed with canned tuna, olive oil, raw onions, salt, and freshly ground black pepper; served chilled.

— *all'uccelletto* Cooked white cannellini beans sautéed with garlic, sage, and minced onions; chopped tomatoes added and simmered until flavors meld; seasoned with salt and pepper and served hot.

Fave Fava Beans.

— *alla romana* Fresh fava beans sautéed in olive oil with pancetta and onions; water, salt, and ground black pepper added; covered and simmered until tender.

— *stufate* Cleaned fava beans sautéed in olive oil with bacon, onions, and shredded lettuce; broth, salt and freshly ground black pepper added; covered and simmered until beans are tender.

— *alla toscana* Cooked fava beans sautéed in olive oil with prosciutto, minced onions, chopped parsley, salt, and ground black pepper; white wine added and simmered until nearly evaporated; served hot.

Jota See Part II.

Lenticchie Lentils.

— *e riso, zuppa di* Minced onions, celery, carrots, diced ham, rice, and lentils sautéed in butter and olive oil; chopped tomatoes and broth added and simmered until lentils and rice are tender; seasoned with salt and pepper.

— *in umido* Onions, sage, pancetta, and celery sautéed in olive oil; broth and lentils added; covered and simmered until lentils are tender; seasoned with salt and freshly ground black pepper.

Minestra di ceci alla contadina See under MINESTRA, BRODO, E ZUPPA Section.

Minestra di fagioli See under MINESTRA, BRODO, E ZUPPA Section.

Minestra di pasta e fagioli See under MINESTRA, BRODO, E ZUPPA.

'Ncapriata See Part II.

INSALATE — SALADS

Arance, insalata di Ripe oranges peeled and sliced, white pith removed; drizzled with olive oil, salt, and freshly ground black pepper; garnished with grated orange peel.

Arancio e limone, insalata di Fresh oranges and lemons peeled and sectioned, with pith removed; drizzled with olive oil, salt, ground black pepper, and fresh mint; served over shredded lettuce.

Asparagi, insalata di Fresh trimmed asparagus spears blanched in salted water; arranged on a platter and drizzled with olive oil, wine vinegar, salt, and freshly ground black pepper.

Buongustaia, insalata alla Tomatoes, celery, blanched string beans, cucumbers, sliced chicken meat, sliced prosciutto, grated cheese, and fresh herbs drizzled with olive oil, vinegar, salt, and pepper.

Calamari, insalata di Poached squid tossed with garlic, olive oil, fresh lemon juice, salt, ground black pepper, and chopped parsley; served with fresh sliced tomatoes and salad greens.

Carote, insalata di Fresh grated carrots mixed with olive oil, fresh lemon juice, salt, and freshly ground black pepper; served immediately.

Carote alla piacentina Sliced baby carrots marinated in olive oil, fresh lemon juice, salt, pepper, and garlic; garnished with fresh basil leaves and chopped hard-cooked eggs.

Cavolfiore, insalata di Poached cauliflower florets tossed with olive oil, white vinegar, chopped anchovies, olives, minced onions, capers, and fresh herbs; served over shredded greens.

Cavolfiore lesso in insalata Poached cauliflower florets dressed with olive oil, white vinegar, salt, and white pepper.

Ceci, insalata di Cooked chickpeas combined with minced onions, fresh tomatoes, olive oil, wine vinegar, salt, and ground black pepper.

Cicoria fina, insalata di Dandelion greens tossed with olive oil, wine vinegar, garlic, minced onions, olives, salt, and ground black pepper.

Cicoria al gorgonzola Trimmed and sliced endive drizzled with a mixture of olive oil, mustard, fresh lemon juice, salt, and pepper; sprinkled with crumbled Gorgonzola cheese and served with *crostini*.

Contadina, insalata alla Sliced cooked potatoes, cooked string beans, cooked chickpeas, sliced tomatoes, onions, and fresh herbs drizzled with olive oil, lemon juice, salt, and pepper.

Escarola, insalata di Escarole combined with fresh basil, olive oil, wine vinegar, salt, and pepper.

Fagiolini in insalata Blanched string beans drizzled with olive oil, freshly squeezed lemon juice, salt, and ground black pepper.

Finocchio in insalata Fresh fennel sliced very thin; dressed with olive oil, salt, and freshly ground black pepper.

Insalata mista Various mixed greens, e.g., romaine, bibb, arugula, chicory, and so on; combined with fresh garden vegetables; drizzled with olive oil, vinegar, salt, and pepper.

Lattuga romana e Gorgonzola, insalata di Romaine lettuce combined with olive oil, fresh lemon juice, salt, freshly ground black pepper, minced onions, and crumbled Gorgonzola cheese; served with *crostini*.

Lattuga romana, insalata di Chopped romaine lettuce and sliced red onions tossed with olive oil, wine vinegar, salt, and pepper.

Lenticchie, insalata di Cooked lentils combined with olive oil, wine vinegar, garlic, minced onions, parsley, salt, and ground black pepper.

Mare, insalata di Various poached seafood, e.g., shrimp, scallops, squid, clams, mussels, and so on combined with minced onions, sweet peppers, olives, capers, and fresh herbs; dressed with olive oil, fresh lemon juice, salt, and ground black pepper.

Panzanella See Part II.

Patate in insalata Sliced and cooked red potatoes dressed with olive oil, wine vinegar, salt, and freshly ground black pepper.

Patate e uova, insalata di Sliced boiled potatoes combined with chopped parsley, minced onions and celery, olive oil, wine vinegar, salt, and ground black pepper; garnished with chopped hard-cooked eggs.

Piemontese, insalata Sliced celery tossed with a mixture of olive oil, mustard, fresh lemon juice, chopped parsley, and fresh chervil; marinated for one hour; served chilled.

Pomodoro con oregano, insalata di Sliced ripe tomatoes sprinkled with fresh chopped oregano, salt, and ground black pepper; drizzled with olive oil.

Primavera, insalata Blanched and quartered artichoke hearts, shredded carrots, and shredded cheese tossed with olive oil, lemon, salt, and pepper.

Riso, insalata di Cooked rice combined with minced onions, sweet peppers, green peas, capers, poached asparagus tips, tomatoes, olives, olive oil, and white vinegar; seasoned with salt, pepper, and fresh herbs.

Riso con pollo, insalata di Finely shredded greens combined with cooked chicken slices, cooked rice, olives, onions, sweet peppers, and gherkins; dressed with olive oil, mustard, wine vinegar, salt, and pepper.

Riso alla romana, insalata di Cooked rice combined with cooked cannellini beans, diced prosciutto, anchovy fillets, pitted olives, and fresh herbs; drizzled with a dressing composed of olive oil, wine vinegar, garlic, salt, and pepper.

Rustica, insalata Cooked sliced potatoes and beetroot combined with blanched asparagus, string beans, broccoli, cauliflower, and diced mortadella; tossed with mayonnaise and lemon juice and seasoned with salt and pepper.

Sedano alla senape Sliced celery tossed with a mixture of olive oil, mustard, salt, pepper, and fresh lemon juice; marinated for one hour; served chilled.

Spinaci e funghi Fresh trimmed spinach leaves tossed with sliced white mushrooms, sliced onions, shredded pecorino cheese, and minced garlic; drizzled with olive oil, vinegar, salt, pepper, and parsley.

Spinaci alla senape Fresh trimmed spinach leaves drizzled with a dressing composed of olive oil, mustard, fresh lemon juice, salt, and pepper; garnished with chopped hard-cooked eggs.

DISHES BY COURSE

Tagliolini, insalata di Cooked egg noodles combined with olive oil, garlic, green peppers, diced gherkins, fresh basil, and grated Parmesan cheese.

Tonno e fagioli, insalata di Cooked white kidney beans combined with onions, canned tuna, olive oil, salt, ground black pepper, and wine vinegar.

Zucchine, insalata, di (1) Thinly sliced zucchini marinated in olive oil, fresh lemon juice, salt, pepper, and fresh basil; sprinkled with pine nuts and grated Parmesan cheese. (2) Blanched sliced zucchini tossed with garlic, chopped parsley, salt, freshly ground black pepper, olive oil, and wine vinegar.

I DOLCI — SWEETS

Amaretti alle mandorle Ground almonds and ground bitter almonds combined with sugar and bound with egg whites; spooned onto a greased and floured sheet pan and baked until lightly browned.

Anicini See Part II.

Arance al marsala Sliced ripe oranges, white pith removed, sprinkled with sugar and sweet marsala.

Bombolette di ricotta Creamed ricotta combined with beaten eggs, flour, lemon peel, and softened butter; panfried in oil until golden brown and puffy; drizzled with honey or powdered sugar and served immediately.

Budino di mascarpone e gorgonzola Creamed mascarpone and sweetened Gorgonzola cheeses combined with crushed walnuts and sugar; whipped cream folded in and poured into individual molds; served well chilled.

Budino di pane Crustless stale bread cubes placed in a greased baking pan; sprinkled with nuts and raisins; custard mixture (sugar, eggs, and milk) poured over just to cover; covered and baked until set; uncovered and placed back in the oven to brown the top; sprinkled with cinnamon sugar; cooled to room temperature before serving.

Budino di ricotta Creamed ricotta mixed with sugar, egg yolks, cocoa powder, and vanilla; poured into a mold lined with ladyfingers; served well chilled.

Cannoli alla siciliana Cannoli shells filled with a mixture of ricotta, sugar, Amaretto liqueur, diced candied fruit, chopped chocolate, and cocoa powder; served immediately after filling.

Cassata sicilana Sponge cake layered with sweetened ricotta flavored with chocolate and candied fruit; iced with white frosting.

Cassatella See Part II.

Castagnaccio See Part II.

Castagne al marsala Shelled parcooked chestnuts poached in red wine, marsala, and sugar; placed on a serving platter and drizzled with the reduced poaching syrup; served with sweetened whipped cream.

Certosino See Part II.

Ciliegie alla ricotta Fresh pitted cherries simmered in simple syrup until soft; served chilled with creamed ricotta mixed with milk and sugar;

Crema fredda di uva nera Puree of black grapes combined with flour and sugar and simmered over low heat until thickened; poured into small molds and chilled until set; topped with sweetened whipped cream just before serving.

Crema fritta Cooked sweet custard poured into a shallow baking pan and chilled until firm; cut into triangles and coated with bread crumbs; panfried in oil and sprinkled with powdered sugar.

Crostata di visciole Pitted Morello cherries combined with sugar, water, vanilla, and cinnamon; simmered until liquid has thickened and cherries are tender; poured into a pastry-lined pie pan and covered with pie dough; pinched to seal and baked; served chilled with sweetened whipped cream.

Crostoli See Part II.

Fave dei morti See Part II.

Fragole al vino Fresh ripe strawberries drizzled with sweet white wine and sprinkled with sugar; served well chilled.

Fritelle di mele Peeled and cored apples cut into one-fourth-inch slices and dipped in batter composed of flour, milk, and eggs; panfried in oil until golden brown; sprinkled with powdered sugar and served immediately.

Fritelle di riso Rice prepared with two to three times the amount of water so as to form a thick mush; once chilled, formed into balls and fried in oil until nicely browned and crispy; sprinkled with powdered sugar and served immediately.

Frutta sciroppata Peeled and sliced apples, pears, and peaches poached in simple syrup until soft; fruit removed and syrup reduced until thick; fruit served chilled in syrup and topped with sweetened whipped cream.

Gelatini di crema Raw egg yolks beaten with sugar until fluffy; cherry liqueur, vanilla, diced candied fruit (optional), and crushed macaroons stirred in; whipped cream folded in; whipped egg whites then folded in; poured into molds and frozen.

Granita di fragole Strawberry puree combined with simple syrup and placed in freezer; when ice crystals have begun to form, the mixture is stirred with a fork; process repeated every hour until frozen.

Granita di limone Granulated sugar stirred into freshly squeezed lemon juice until dissolved; poured over crushed ice and garnished with lemon slices; served immediately.

Meringhe al brandy Egg whites beaten stiff with powdered sugar and flavored with brandy; piped or spooned onto a greased and floured baking pan and baked in a very low oven (250 degrees Fahrenheit) until crunchy.

Meringhe con panna e castagna Egg whites beaten stiff with sugar; piped or spooned on a greased and floured baking pan and baked

Meringhe con panna e castagna (cont.)
until crunchy in an oven at 250 degrees Fahrenheit; served with sweetened whipped cream flavored with chestnut puree.

Monte bianco Shelled chestnuts poached in sweetened milk with vanilla until very tender; passed through a food mill and gently formed, with the aid of two forks, into the shape of a cone or "mountain"; topped with lightly whipped sweetened cream and garnished with glazed chestnuts.

Nepitelle See Part II.

Pallottole d'aranci Sugar cooked to the soft-ball stage with grated orange peel and vanilla; formed into balls and rolled in crushed almonds.

Pere ripiene alla milanese Fresh peeled pears hollowed out and stuffed with ground almonds, sugar, diced candied fruit, and vanilla; baked with sweet white wine until tender.

Pesca al vino rosso Ripe sweet peaches peeled and thinly sliced; fanned in a glass and sprinkled with chilled red wine.

Pesche imbottite alla mandorla Ripe peeled peaches hollowed out and filled with ground almonds mixed with sugar, candied orange peel, and vanilla; baked with sweet white wine until tender.

Piconi See Part II.

Ricotta con le pere Peeled and cored pear slices simmered in simple syrup until tender; removed from pan and remaining syrup reduced until thick; ricotta creamed until smooth and combined with sugar, cocoa powder, and the chilled syrup; poured over pears.

Semifreddo di crema Sweetened whipped cream combined with toasted almonds, chopped chocolate, and maraschino cherries; placed into molds and frozen.

Spuma di cioccolata Egg yolks beaten with sugar until fluffy; strong coffee, rum, and melted chocolate stirred in; whipped cream folded in, followed by whipped egg whites; poured into molds and chilled completely.

Spuma di fragole Strawberry puree sweetened with sugar and Maraschino liqueur; whipped cream folded in, followed by whipped egg whites; poured into a mold and chilled until set.

Susina al vino Whole plums poached in white wine, sugar, lemon peel, and cinnamon stick until tender; removed and liquid cooked down to a syrupy consistency; served hot or cold, drizzled with syrup and whipped cream on the side (optional).

Torrone d'Alba Sugar and honey cooked in water to the hard-crack stage; cooled slightly; stiffly beaten egg whites folded in, followed by the almonds; poured on an oiled marble surface and allowed to cool. (Can be broken into random fragments or scored with a knife while still warm and snapped off in even pieces.)

Torta di pistacchio Sweet custard flavored with ground pistachios; poured into a pastry-lined pie pan and baked until set.

Torta di ricotta Ricotta combined with eggs, almonds, candied citron, sugar, and vanilla; poured into a pastry-lined pie pan and baked until set.

Uova alla monacella Hard-cooked eggs halved and yolks removed; yolks mashed smooth and combined with sugar, cocoa powder, cinnamon, and raw egg yolks; stuffed inside the halved egg whites and dipped in beaten egg white; fried in oil until golden brown; sprinkled with powdered sugar and served hot.

Zabaglione Egg yolks and sugar whisked in a bowl over simmering water until light and fluffy, periodically sprinkling with marsala wine; poured into stemmed glasses and served immediately.

Zuccotto See Part II.

Zucotto con amaretti Egg yolks beaten with sugar until smooth and fluffy; crushed macaroons and creamed mascarpone cheese stirred in; whipped cream folded in, followed by whipped egg whites; poured in a ladyfinger-lined mold and chilled until set.

Zuppa all'emiliana Sponge cake rounds, custard, chocolate ganache, almonds, and fresh strawberries alternately layered in a wine glass; topped with sweetened whipped cream.

Zuppa inglese See Part II.

DISHES BY COURSE

Part II

Italian Food and
Beverage Vocabulary

ITALIAN PRONUNCIATION KEY

VOWELS

a ...... **ah** as in *mark*

è ...... **eh** as in *get*

e ...... **eh** as in *get*

i .... **ee** as in *feet*

o ...... has two sounds; **o** as in *front* and **oh** as in *soda*

u ...... **oo** as in *pool*

CONSONANTS

Most Italian consonants are pronounced as in English with the following exceptions:

c....... (before i or e) **ch** as in *cheese*

c....... (before a, o, and u) **k** as in *kite*

ch .... **k** as in *kite*

g ...... (before i or e) **j** as in *jelly*

g ...... (before a, o, and u) **gh** as in *gone*

gh .... **gh** as in *gone*

gli .... **ly** as in *million*

gn .... **ny** as in *canyon*

h ...... always silent

qu .... **qu** as in *queen*

s .... (between two vowels) **z** as in *rose*

sc ..... (before I and e) **sh** as in *ship*

z....... **ts** as in *pizza*

Abbacchio [ah-bAH-key-o] Baby milk-fed lamb between the ages of one and two months old.

Abbacchio arrosto [+ ahr-rO-sto] Roasted baby lamb.

Abboccato [ahb-bohk-kAH-to] Refers to semisweet wines.

Abbrustolire [ahb-broos-toh-lEE-reh] To broil or toast over an open flame.

Abruzzese, (all') [ah-broots-tsEH-zeh] Abruzzi style; denotes the use of red peppers, tomatoes, and sometimes ham in a preparation.

Abruzzi e Molise [ah-brOOts-tsee eh moh-lEE-zeh] Italian region located in east central Italy. Its cuisine, which is that of southern Italy, relies heavily upon fresh seafood, pork products, tomatoes, and red peppers. Figs are also an important food product of Abruzzi.

Abufaus [ah-boo-fah-oos] A type of spicy gingerbread from Sardinia often containing pine nuts, honey, and currants.

Accarrexiau [ahk-kahr-ray-ee-ah-oo] (*Sardinia*) A dramatic dish consisting of a whole sheep stuffed with a baby pig and spit-roasted slowly over a live flame.

Acciuga/Acciughe [ah-chee-OO-guh/ah-chee-OO-gheh] Anchovy/anchovies; also called *alice/alici*.

Acciugata [ah-chee-OO-gah-tah] See *Acciughe, salsa d'*.

Acciughe, salsa d' [sAHl-sah dee ah-chee-OO-gheh] A sauce composed of anchovy fillets crushed in a mortar with olive oil, and seasonings; also called *acciugata*.

Aceto [ah-chEH-to] Vinegar.

Aceto balsamico [+ bahl-sAHm-ee-ko] Balsamic vinegar; a concentrated vinegar made from cooked, unfermented grape juice. It can be aged up to eighty years in various kegs made of different aromatic woods (oak, chestnut, juniper, ash, mulberry, apple, and so on) throughout the aging process. The best balsamic vinegar comes from Modena.

Aceto balsamico di Modena [+ dee mO-deh-nah] Balsamic vinegar from Modena.

Aceto del duca [+ dehl dOO-kah] A commercial version of balsamic vinegar.

Aceto-dolce [ah-chEH-to–dOHl-cheh] Sour-sweet.

Aceto modenese [+ moh-deh-nEH-seh] A type of balsamic vinegar from Modena.

Acetosella [ah-cheh-toh-zEHl-luh] Sorell.

Acido [AH-chee-do] Sour.

Acini di pepe [AHh-chee-nee dee pEH-peh] Tiny peppercorn-sized pasta; used mainly in soups.

Acqua [AH-kwuh] Water.

Acqua acidulata [+ ah-chee-doo-lAH-tah] Water mixed with a small amount of lemon juice; used for poaching fish.

Acquacotta [ah-kwah-kOt-tah] A rustic Tuscan vegetable soup typically served over toasted bread.

Acquadella [ah-kwah-dEHl-lah] A variety of fish usually eaten fried in the Emilia-Romagna region.

Acqua di latte [+ dee lAHt-teh] Buttermilk.

Acqua gasosa [+ gah-sOH-sah] Carbonated water.

Acqua minerale [+ mee-neh-rAH-leh] Mineral water.

Acquavite [ah-kwah-vEE-teh] Brandy.

Adriatico, dell' [ahd-ree-AH-tee-ko] Describes foods marinated in olive oil and lemon and grilled over a live flame.

Affettati [ahf-feht-tAH-tee] Sliced; sliced cold meats, typically consisting of salami, prosciutto, coppa, and mortadella; generally served with bread as an antipasto.

Affogato [ahf-fohg-gAH-to] (1) Poached. (2) Braised.

Affumicato [ahf-foom-ee-kAH-to] Smoked.

Aglanico [ah-lyahn-ee-ko] A local wine grape from Campania.

Aglanico del vulture [+ dahl vool-tOO-reh] An excellent red sparkling wine from Basilicata.

Agliata [ah-lyAH-tuh] (1) (*Liguria*) A cold sauce prepared by pounding garlic, walnuts, and crustless bread cubes (dampened with vinegar) in a mortar and then slowly incorporating olive oil; served with fish. (2) (*Piedmont*) A thick condiment made from combining soft cheese with garlic, olive oil, lemon juice, and herbs; served with crusty bread or toast. (3) (*Tuscany*) A cold sauce composed of crustless bread cubes soaked in milk and combined with crushed garlic and walnuts; served with various dishes.

Agliata, risotto in bianco con [ree-zOHt-toh een bee-AHn-koh kohn +] Plain risotto tossed with *agliata* (Tuscan style) and grated Parmesan cheese.

Aglio [AH-lyee-o] Garlic.

Aglio e olio [AH-lyee-o eh OH-lee-o] Describes dishes (typically pasta) served with a sauce of garlic and olive oil.

Agnellino (di latte) [ah-nyehl-lEE-no dee lAHt-teh] Young milk-fed lamb. See *Abbacchio*.

Agnello [ahn-nyEHl-lo] Lamb.

Agnolotti [ah-nyoh-lOht-tee] (*Piedmont*) Small square pasta stuffed with various fillings; similar to ravioli. A specialty of Turin.

Agone/agoni [ah-gOH-neh/ah-gOH-nee] A freshwater fish found in Lake Como in northern Italy. Used in the preparation of *missoltit*.

Agresto [ah-grEHs-to] The juice of unripened grapes; used like vinegar.

Agresto, salsa d' [sAHl-sa dee +] A pureed sauce composed of unripened grape juice, walnuts, bread crumbs, broth, and seasonings; served cold.

Agrigento [Ah-gree-jEHn-to] A city and province in southern Sicily noted for almonds and *salsiccia al finocchio* (sausage flavored with fennel).

Agro [AHg-ro] Sour.

Agro, all' Describes vegetables seasoned with a dressing of lemon juice and olive oil.

Agrodolce [ahg-roh-dOl-cheh] Sweet and sour; a sauce composed of caramelized sugar, vinegar, garlic, and herbs; served with a variety of dishes.

Agrumi [ahg-rOO-mee] The Italian word for citrus fruits.

Aguglia [ah-gOO-lyah] A small saltwater fish related to the shark.

Considered a delicacy in Venice.

Aj [ahj] (*Milan*) Garlic.

Ajo e ojo [Ah-jo eh OH-jo] Describes spaghetti tossed with a sauce of olive oil, toasted garlic, salt, and pepper; from Rome.

Akragas bianco [ahk-rah-gahs bee-AHn-ko] A white Sicilian wine.

al [ahl] With; in the style of.

A.L.A. See *Antico Liquore Amarascato.*

Ala [AH-lah] Wing.

Ala di pollo [+ dee pOHl-lo] Chicken or poultry wing.

Alba [AHl-bah] A city in southern Piedmont famous for white truffles; some of the finest Italian wines are produced around Alba.

Albana [ahl-bAH-nah] A sweet white wine from Romagna of excellent quality.

Albanello di Siracusa [ahl-bah-nEHl-lo dee see-rah-kOO-sah] A white wine from Siracusa (Sicily).

Albarola [ahl-bah-rOH-lah] A small white wine grape grown in parts of Italy.

Albergo [ahl-bEHr-go] Hotel.

Albicocca/albicocche [ahl-bee-kOHk-kah/ahl-bee-kOHk-keh] Apricot.

Alborella [ahl-boh-rEHl-lah] Sprat; a variety of small lake fish common in Lombardy where it is eaten fried in olive oil.

Albume [ahl-bOO-meh] Egg white; also called *bianco d'uovo.*

Alchermes [ahl-kEHr-mehs] A deep red, herb-flavored liqueur.

Alcool [AHl-kohl] Alcohol.

Aleatico [ah-lay-AH-tee-ko] A type of grape used in parts of Italy to produce sweet dessert wines.

Ali [Ah-lee] Wings; see *Ala.*

Alice/alici [ah-lEE-cheh/ah-lEE-chee] Anchovy.

Alionza [ah-lee-OHn-tsah] A local wine from Emilia-Romagna.

All'/alla [ahl/AHl-lah] In the style of; with.

Allodola [ahl-lOH-doh-lah] Lark; a game bird of high esteem in parts of Italy.

Alloro [Ahl-lOH-ro] Bay leaf.

Alosa [ah-lOH-zah] A small river fish related to the sardine.

Alta cucina [AHl-tah koo-chEE-nah] Haute cuisine; food prepared with the finest ingredients in an elegant fashion.

Alto Adige [AHl-to AD-dee-jeh] An area of Trentino–Alto Adige in northern Italy. The cuisine of Alto Adige is clearly influenced by that of Austria; dumplings, fresh vegetables (cabbage, sauerkraut, potatoes), sour cream, and pork products—particularly smoked bacon (*speck*)—are typical of the region.

Alzavola/arzavola [ahl-tsAH-voh-lah/ahr-tsAH-voh-lah] Teal.

Amabile [ah-mAH-bee-leh] Describes semisweet wines.

Amarena [ah-mah-rEH-nah] Morello cherry; used to make desserts and maraschino liqueur; also called *marasca* and *marasche.*

Amaretti [ah-mah-rEHt-tee] Macaroons made with bitter almonds.

Amaretto di Saronno [ah-mah-rEHt-to dee sah-rOH-no] An Italian liqueur flavored with apricots and almonds.

Amaro [ah-mAH-ro] (1) Bitter. (2) A local liqueur from Piedmont similar to vermouth.

VOCABULARY

Amarone [ah-mah-rOH-neh] A strong, highly regarded dry red wine from Verona made only in small quantities; also known as *Recotot Amarone*.

Amaro Siciliano [+ see-chee-lee-AH-noh] A winelike liqueur from Sicily served as a digestive.

Amatriciana [ah-mah-tree-chee-AH-nah] (*Amatrice*) A pasta sauce composed of chopped onions and tomatoes, olive oil, bacon or *guanciale*, and chili peppers.

Amorini [ah-moh-rEE-nee] A type of pasta.

Ananas/ananasso [AH-nah-nahs/ah-nah-nAHs-so] Pineapple.

Anatra/Anitra [AH-nah-trah/AH-nee-trah] Duck.

Anchellini [ahn-kehl-lEE-nee] A pasta similar to ravioli; stuffed with meat and fried; a specialty of Sicily.

Anelletti [ah-nehl-lEHt-tee] Ring-shaped pasta.

Anelli [ah-nEHl-lee] Small ring-shaped pasta.

Anellini [ah-nehl-lEE-nee] Tiny ring-shaped pasta used in soups.

Aneto [ah-nEH-to] Dill.

Angiolottus [ahn-jee-oh-lOHt-toos] A stuffed pasta from Sardinia.

Anguilla [ahn-goo-EEl-lah] Eel.

Angulis [ahn-goo-lees] A ring-shaped sweet pastry decorated with colored sugar; a traditional Sardinian Easter pastry.

Anguria [ahn-gOO-ree-ah] Watermelon.

Anice [AH-nee-cheh] Anise.

Anicini [ah-nee-chEE-nee] Small anise-flavored cookies traditionally served with Vernaccia wine; a specialty of Sardinia.

Animelle [Ah-nee-mEHl-leh] Sweetbreads; the thymus glands of lamb, veal, and pork.

Anisetta [ah-nee-sEHt-tah] An Italian liqueur flavored with aniseed.

Anitra See *Anatra*.

Anitra selvatica [AH-nee-trah sehl-vAH-tee-kah] Wild duck.

Anolini [ah-noh-lEE-nee] Small ring or crescent-shaped pasta popular in Emilia-Romagna; typically stuffed with meat, bread crumbs, eggs, and grated cheese. Called *anvein* in Piacenza.

Antico Liquore Amarascato [ahn-tEE-ko lee-kwOH-reh ah-mah-rahs-kAH-to] A strong, sweet cherry-/grape-flavored wine from Sicily.

Antipasto (Antipasti) [ahn-tee-pAH-sto (ahn-tee-pAH-stee)] Literally "before the meal"; refers to the first course of a meal. Antipasti can be made up of smoked meats, cheeses, fish, vegetables, fruits, and so on, and can be served hot or cold.

Antipasti assortiti [+ ahs-sohr-tEE-tee] Assorted antipasti.

Antipasti misti [+ mEE-stee] Mixed antipasti.

Antipasti a piacere [+ ah pee-ah-chEH-reh] Antipasti chosen to one's liking.

Anvein [ahn-vay-een] See *Anolini*.

Aostin [ah-oos-tEHn] A rich, soft cheese from the Valle d'Aosta in northwestern Italy; sometimes called *Salmistra*.

Aperitivo [ah-peh-ree-tEE-voh] Aperitif.

Appetito [ahp-peh-tEE-toh] Appetite.

Arachide [ah-rah-kEY-deh] Peanut.

Aragona Canicattì [ah-rah-gOH-nah kah-nee-kAHt-tee] A dry red Sicilian wine from Agrigento; generally served before dinner.

Aragosta [ah-rah-gOs-tah] Spiny lobster.

Arancia [ah-rAHn-chee-ah] Orange.

Arancia amara [+ ah-mAH-rah] Bitter orange.

Arancia calabrese [+ kah-lah-brEH-seh] A variety of orange grown in Calabria.

Aranciata [ah-rahn-chee-AH-tah] Orangeade.

Aranciata di Nuoro [+ dee noo-OH-ro] A confection made from orange rind, honey, and almonds; a specialty of Sardinia.

Arancine [ah-rahn-chEE-neh] Fried rice croquettes seasoned with saffron and *caciocavallo* cheese and stuffed with various fillings.

Arbaia [ahr-bAH-ee-ah] A light red table wine from Sardinia.

Arbia [ahr-bee-ah] A dry white wine from the Chianti region of Tuscany.

Arborio [ahr-bOH-ree-o] An Italian short grained rice used in making risotto. *Arborio* is widely grown in northern Italy, particularly in the Po Valley.

Arezzo [ah-rEHts-tso] A city in eastern Tuscany where some of the finest cherries in Italy are grown.

Aringa [ah-rEEn-gah] Herring

Aringa affumicata [+ ahf-foom-ee-kAH-tah] Smoked herring, a common antipasto component.

Arista [AH-ree-stah] Loin roast of pork. In Tuscany, arista is roasted on a spit.

Aroma [ah-rOH-mah] Aroma.

Aromatico [ah-roh-mAH-tee-ko] Aromatic.

Arrabbiata, all' [ahr-rahb-bee-AH-tah] Denotes the presence of hot red chili peppers in a dish.

Arreganato [ahr-ray-gah-nAH-to] Describes dishes seasoned with oregano.

Arrostino annegato [ahr-roh-stEE-no ahn-neh-gAH-to] Skewered veal chunks seasoned with herbs and braised in white wine and stock.

Arrostire [ahr-roh-stEE-reh] To broil.

Arrosto [ahr-rOH-stah] Roasted.

Arsella [ahr-sEHl-lah] The name for clam in Genoa and Sardinia.

Arsumà [ahr-soo-mAH] A type of uncooked custard similar to zabaglione made with whole eggs, white wine, and sugar.

Arzavola [ahr-tsAH-voh-lah] See *Alzavola*.

Arzilla [ahr-tsEEl-lah] Skate or ray; a kite-shaped fish whose white, firm flesh is best prepared by broiling or poaching. Also called *razza*.

Asciutto [ah-shee-OOt-to] (1) Dry (2) Drained (*pasta*).

Ascoli Piceno [AHs-koh-lee pee-chEH-no] A province (and city) in Marche known throughout Italy for its hearty pizzas and stuffed olives.

Asiago [ah-see-AH-go] A sharp grating cheese made from partially skimmed cow's milk. Produced in the town of Asiago in the Veneto region. When young, *Asiago* makes a fine table cheese.

Asiago da taglio [+ dee tAH-lyee-o] *Asiago* aged less than two months.

Asin [AH-seen] A rich, soft cow's milk cheese from northern Italy.

Asparagi [ahs-pAH-rah-jee] Asparagus.

Asparagi, sugo di [sOO-go dee +] A sauce composed of *salsa bianca* flavored with asparagus puree.

Aspro [Ahs-pro] Sour.

Assaggiare [ahs-sahg-jee-AH-reh] Taste.

Assortimento pazzo [ahs-sohr-tee-mEHn-to pAH-tso] An elaborate assortment of meats, fish, vegetables, and so on.

Assortiti [ahs-sohr-tEE-tee] Mixed; assorted.

Astaco [AHs-tah-ko] Spiny lobster.

Asti [AHs-tee] A city in Piedmont famous for Asti Spumante wine.

Astice [AHs-tee-cheh] Lobster.

Asti spumante [AHs-tee spoo-mAHn-teh] A white sparkling wine from Asti (Piedmont).

Attorta [aht-tOHr-tah] A twisted cake filled with chocolate, ground almonds, and sometimes fruit; a specialty of Perugia (Umbria). Also called *serpe.*

Aurum [AH-oo-room] An orange-flavored liqueur from Pescara (Abruzzi).

Avanzi [ah-vAHn-tsee] Leftovers.

Avellane [ah-vayl-lAH-neh] Hazelnuts.

Avemarie [av-vay-mah-rEE-eh] A small, short soup noodle.

Avena [ah-vEH-nah] Oats.

Babà [bah-bUH] A Neapolitan dessert specialty consisting of sweet yeast dough baked with raisins; once baked, the cake is drizzled with rum and syrup and decorated with almonds.

Babà alla crema [+ AHl-luh krEH-muh] A layered *babà* filled with pastry cream.

Baccalà [bahk-kah-lUH] Dried, salted codfish.

Baci [bAH-chee] Kisses; a chocolate confection that is a Perugian specialty.

Baci di dama [+ dee dAH-muh] Delicate cookies from Tortona (Piedmont) made with almonds and layered with chocolate.

Backerbsensuppe [bAH-kuhr-bsen-sUHp-pah] Consommé seasoned with parsley and scallions and garnished with strands of egg. A specialty of Trentino–Alto Adige.

Bagna cauda [bAH-nyuh kah-OO-duh] A hot anchovy and garlic dip for raw vegetables; from Piedmont.

Bagnara [bah-nyAH-rah] A port town in Calabria and one of Italy's main suppliers of swordfish.

Bagnet d'tomatiche [bah-nyeht dee toh-mah-tee-keh] (*Piedmont*) The traditional tomato sauce served with *gran bui*; also known as *bagnet ross* and *salsa rossi*. See *Gran Bui.*

Bagnet ross [bah-nyeht rohs] See *Bagnet d'tomatiche.*

Bagnet verd [+ vehrd] See *Salsa verde.*

Bagno Maria [bAH-nyo mah-rEE-ah] Double boiler or water bath.

Bagoss [bah-gOHs] A strong-flavored, semihard cheese from Bagolino in the Lombardy region.

Bagozzo [bah-gOH-tso] A hard farmhouse cheese made from

cow's milk. Likened to *Grana*, Bagozzo is also called *Grana Bagozzo* and *Bresciano*.

Baicoli [bah-EE-koh-lee] Small, sweet, yeast biscuits flavored with orange from Veneto. Popularly dipped in coffee, milk, or chocolate.

Balsamella [bahl-sah-mEHl-luh] Béchamel sauce; see *Besciamella*.

Balsamella con parmigiano [+ kohn pahr-mee-jee-AH-noh] White cheese sauce; *besciamella* flavored with Parmesan cheese.

Banana [bah-nAH-nah] Banana.

Banchetto [bahn-kEHt-to] Banquet.

Barbabietola/bietola [bahr-bah-bee-EH-toh-lah/bee-EH-toh-lah] Beetroots.

Barbarano [bahr-bah-rAH-no] The name for certain red and white wines from the Veneto region.

Barbaresco [bahr-bah-rEHs-ko] A highly regarded red wine from Piedmont named after the town in which it is made.

Barbaroux, alla [bahr-bah-rOO] Describes pasta dishes, particularly cannelloni prepared with veal, cheese, and white sauce.

Barbera [bahr-bEH-rah] A red wine grape used in northern Italy.

Barbera di Anagni [+ dee an-nAH-nyee] A fine red wine from Lazio.

Barbera sardo [+ sAHr-do] A dry red wine from Sardinia.

Bardolino [bahr-doh-lEE-no] A light, red Venetian wine.

Barolo [bah-rOH-lo] One of the finest red wines of Piedmont produced in the town of Barolo.

Barolo chinato [+ key-nAH-to] A vermouth-like aperitif made with Barolo wine and infused with herbs.

Basilicata [bah-see-lee-kAH-tah] A small, mountainous region in southern Italy. Pork products, hot chili peppers, and sharp cheeses are characteristic of this region's cuisine.

Basilico [bah-sEE-lee-ko] Basil; Liguria is famous for its basil.

Bastardei [bahs-tahr-dEH-ee] A pork and beef sausage from Lombardy.

Bastarduna [bahs-tahr-dOO-nah] A variety of fig grown in Sicily.

Batsoa [baht-soh-ah] (*Piedmont*) Boiled pig's feet.

Batteria di cucina [baht-teh-rEE-ah dee koo-chEE-nah] Kitchen equipment, e.g., pots, pans, colanders, pasta roller, mortar and pestle, and so on.

Batticarne [baht-tee-kAHr-neh] A tool used to pound (flatten) meat (scaloppine, chicken, and so on).

Battuta [baht-tOO-tah] An Italian term for finely chopped vegetables and herbs that are browned in olive oil; used as a base for stocks, sauces, soups, etc. See *Soffritto*.

Battuta alla genovese [+ AHl-lah jeh-noh-vEH-seh] Another name for pesto.

Bauletto [bah-oo-lEHt-to] Stuffed, rolled veal.

Bava, alla [bAH-vah] Describes pasta dishes prepared with butter and fontina cheese.

Bavaresi [bah-vah-rEH-see] Bavarian cream; a custard cream made from cream, egg yolks, sugar, and gelatin.

Bavette [bah-vEHt-teh] Long flat pasta noodles.

Beccaccia [bayk-kAH-chee-ah] Woodcock.

Beccaccino [bayk-kah-chEE-no] Snipe.

Beccafico [behk-kah-fEE-ko] The Sicilian word for stuffed.

Becco [bEHk-ko] A local word for ram.

Belpaese [bel pah-EH-seh] Literally "beautiful country," Belpaese is a soft, mildly flavored cow's milk cheese from the Melzo area of Lombardy; one of Italy's famous cheeses.

Bel piano lombardo [bel pee-AH-no lohm-bAHr-do] A cow's milk cheese similar to Belpaese.

Bel Piemonte [bel pee-mOhn-teh] See *Fior d'Alpe.*

Ben cotto [ben kOHt-to] Well-done; refers to the doneness of cooked meats.

Bensone/benzone [behn-sOH-neh/ behn-tsOH-neh] A popular pastry from Modena (Emilia-Romagna) made with wheat flour, sugar, and eggs; baked in the shape of an *S.*

Bergamotto [bayr-gah-mOt-to] Bergamot; a small citrus fruit similar to the orange, grown in Calabria mainly for its essential oils.

Berlingozzo [behr-leen-gOts-tso] A small local Florentine cake.

Bernade [behr-nah-deh] A cheese made in northern Italy from cow's and goat's milk and flavored with saffron. Also called *Formagelle bernade.*

Besciamella [beh-shee-ah-mEHl-luh] Béchamel sauce; milk and/ or cream thickened with roux and seasoned with salt and white pepper. It is the base for several sauces; also called *balsamella.*

Besciamella, alla Describes dishes prepared or served with béchamel sauce.

Bianca piccante, salsa [sAHl-sah bee-AHn-kah peek-kAHn-teh] *Salsa bianca* seasoned with capers, lemon, and anchovy fillets.

Bianca, salsa White sauce; composed of a light chicken or veal stock thickened with butter and flour and seasoned with salt and white pepper.

Biancavilla [bee-ahn-kah-vEEl-lah] A full-bodied red wine from Sicily.

Bianchetti [bee-ahn-kEHt-tee] Very young, tiny fish; whitebait.

Bianco [bee-AHn-ko] White.

Bianco d'Arquata [+ dahr-qwAH-tah] A dry white wine of fine quality; from Umbria.

Bianco di Spagna [+ dee spAH-nyah] *Cannellini* beans.

Bianco d'uovo [+ dee oo-OH-vo] See *Albume.*

Bianco, in Refers to simply prepared or white dishes, i.e., pasta or rice that has no sauces or seasoning.

Bibita [bEE-bee-tah] Soft drink.

Bietola See *Barbabietola.*

Bignè [bee-nyEH] Term used to describe small, sweet pastries usually made with choux paste and filled with cream. In parts of Italy they are deep-fried and not necessarily filled.

Bigolaro [bee-goh-lAH-ro] An Italian kitchen tool used to make *bigoli* pasta.

Bigoli [bee-gOH-lee] The name for

thick spaghetti in Veneto.

Bionda [bee-OHn-dah] Blonde; refers to certain preparations possessing a light brown or blonde color.

Biova [bee-OH-vah] A type of Piedmontese bread; small loaves or rolls made from the same dough are referred to as *biovette*.

Biovette [bee-oh-vEHt-tuh] See *Biova*.

Biroldo [bee-rOl-do] A Tuscan blood sausage.

Birra [bEEr-ruh] Beer.

Birra alla spina [+ AHl-lah spEE-nah] Draught beer.

Birra chiara [+ key-AH-rah] Light beer.

Birra di barile [+ dee bah-rEE-leh] Draught beer.

Birra nera [+ nEH-rah] Dark beer.

Birreria [beer-reh-rEE-ah] Brewery.

Bisato [bee-sAH-to] The word for eel in Venice.

Bisato in tecia [+ een tEH-chee-uh] A Venetian specialty composed of marinated eel dipped in bread crumbs and fried in oil; served with tomato sauce.

Biscieùla [bee-shee-ay-OO-lah] A sweet yeast cake from Lombardy made with raisins and candied fruit; a lighter version of *panettone*.

Biscotti [bee-skOt-tee] Cookies; biscuits.

Biscotti del legaccio [+ dehl leh-gAH-chee-o] Sweet biscuits from Genoa flavored with fennel.

Biscotti di Prato [+ dee prAh-to] See *Cantucci di Prato*.

Biscottini [bee-skoht-tEE-nee] Small cookies.

Biscutin d'anis [bees-koo-tEEn dAH-nees] Anise-flavored cookies from Lombardy.

Biseghin [bee-seh-geen] The local word for snipe in parts of Veneto.

Bistecca [bee-stEHk-kah] Beefsteak.

Bistecca alla pizzaiola [+ AHl-lah pee-tsah-ee-OH-lah] (*Naples*) Beefsteak braised in *pizzaiola* sauce; also called *costata alla pizzaiola*. See *Pizzaiola*.

Bistecchina [bee-stay-kEY-nah] Thin slices of beef.

Bitto [bEEt-tol] A local goat's- or cow's-milk cheese from Sondrio (Lombardy). It can be used fresh as a table cheese or left to harden and grated.

Blanc de Morgex [blahnk deh mohr-gay] A dry white wine from the Valle d'Aosta.

Bocca di dama [bOHk-kah dee dAH-mah] Sponge cake.

Bocconcini [bohk-kohn-chEE-nee] (1) Veal stew; bite-sized version of *boccone*. Also called *olivette* because of the small oval shape of the veal. (2) Walnut-sized balls of mozzarella.

Bocconcini modenesi [+ moh-deh-nEH-see] Crustless bread stuffed with prosciutto, cheese, and sometimes white truffles; dipped in batter and fried. A specialty of Modena.

Boccone [bohk-kOHn-neh] Veal cooked in white wine sauce with herbs and sometimes tomatoes; a specialty of the Marche region.

Bocconotti [bohk-koh-nOHt-tee] A dessert tart featuring chocolate, candied fruit, and jam; a specialty of the Abruzzi region.

VOCABULARY

Bocconotti ripieni [+ ree-pee-EH-nee] A local favorite of Bologna consisting of little packets of pasta filled with chicken giblets, truffles, and bread crumbs.

Boeri [boh-eh-ree] Chocolate candies filled with cherries and cherry liqueur.

Bollire [bohl-lEE-reh] To boil.

Bollito [bohl-lEE-to] Boiled; boiled meat.

— **di gallina** [+ dee gahl-lEE-nuh] Boiled chicken.

— **di manzo** [+ dee mAHn-tso] Boiled beef.

— **misto** [+ mEE-sto] A dish of assorted boiled meats. *gran bollito misto* (grand mixed boiled dinner) typically consisting of beef, veal tongue, *guancia*, calf's head and foot, chicken, *zampone*, and *cotechino* and traditionally served with *salsa verde*; popular all over Italy.

Bologna [boh-lOH-nyah] One of northern Italy's great eating cities situated in Emilia-Romagna. Bologna is famous for its rich pasta dishes, mortadella sausage, and Bolognese sauce.

Bolognese, alla [boh-loh-nyEH-seh] Describes pasta dishes served with *salsa alla bolognese*.

Bolognese, salsa alla famous sauce from Bologna (Emilia-Romagna) composed of chopped tomatoes, tomato paste, *soffritto*, ground beef, olive oil, red wine, and seasonings.

Bomba [bOm-bah] The term for a stuffed, dome-shaped, sweet or savory dish. A *bomba* mold is used to prepare these dishes.

Bomba di mascarpone [+ dee mahs-kahr-pOH-neh] A dessert composed of a dome-shaped cake filled with mascarpone cheese, hazelnuts, chocolate, and candied fruit.

Bomba di riso [+ dee rEE-soh] A famous dish from Piacenza (Emilia) featuring boiled rice pressed in a *bomba* mold, stuffed with boned pigeon and mushrooms and then baked.

Bomba gelata [+ jeh-lAH-tah] The classic *bomba gelata* consists of ice cream lined in a *bomba* mold, filled with custard and sweetened whipped cream mixed with candied fruit, and garnished with almonds and shaved chocolate.

Bomboloni [bohm-boh-lOH-nee] (*Tuscany*) Doughnuts; brioche.

Bonarda [boh-nAH-dah] A grape grown in northen Italy and used in some of the local wines of Lombardy and Piedmont.

Bondiola/bondola [bohn-dee-OH-lah/bohn-dOH-lah] A farm sausage from northern Italy—notably Polesine (Veneto) and Sondrio (Lombardy)—made with a mixture of beef and pork.

Bônet [boh-nay] (*Piedmont*) A dessert pudding flavored with chocolate, rum, and amaretti crumbs.

Bonett di latimel [boh-neht dee lah-tee-mehl] A Milanese custard pudding flavored with vanilla.

Bongo [bOHn-go] An elaborate dessert from Florence featuring tiny cream puffs surrounding a mound of whipped cream. Additional cream puffs are arranged on the mound and melted chocolate is drizzled on the whole.

Bonissima [boh-nEEs-see-mah] Rich cake from Modena made with butter and eggs and flavored with lemon, walnuts, rum, and chocolate.

Bonnarelli [bohn-nah-rEHl-lee] The name in Rome for a type of thin flat pasta.

Boraggine [boh-rAH-jee-neh] Borage; also called *borrana*.

Bordatino [boh-dah-tEE-no] (*Tuscany*) A red bean and cabbage soup.

Borgogno bianco [bohr-gOH-nyo bee-AHn-ko] A white wine from Bolzano (Trentino-Alto Adige).

Borlengo [bohr-lEHn-gho] A large pancake topped with pork fat, garlic, grated cheese and rosemary; a specialty of Modena.

Borlotti [bohr-lOHt-tee] A type of dried red kidney bean.

Borrana [bohr-rAH-nuh] See *Boraggine*.

Bortellina della nonna [bohr-tehl-lEE-nah dEHl-la nOHn-nah] A savory pancake stuffed with prosciutto; a local dish of Bettola (the Emilia-Romagna region).

Bosco eliceo [bOHs-ko eh-lee-chEH-o] A full-bodied red wine from Romagna.

Bottaggio [boht-tAH-jee-o] See *Cassoeula*.

Bottarga [boht-tAHr-guh] Tuna roe; typically seasoned with olive oil and lemon juice and served as an antipasto or used in pasta sauces. Also known as *bottarga di tonno*.

Bottiglia [boht-tEE-lyah] Bottle.

Bovoletti [boh-voh-lEHt-tee] See *Bovolo*.

Bovolo [boh-voh-lo] (1) The name in parts of northern Italy for a large sea snail; traditionally poached or cooked directly on hot coals and served with a garlic and olive oil sauce. Small *bovoli* are called *bovoletti*. (2) A local Venetian bread baked in the shape of a snail.

Bovoloni [bohv-oh-lOH-nee] The name for *bovolo* in parts of Italy. See *Bovolo*.

Bozzoli [bohts-tsOH-lee] Cocoon-shaped pasta.

Bra [brah] A hard, sharp cow's-milk cheese produced in the town of Bra in Piedmont.

Bracciatelli [brah-chee-ah-tEHl-lee] Small doughnutlike pastries traditionally prepared for the Easter celebration in Romagna.

Brace, alla [brAH-cheh] Braised.

Brachetto [brah-kEHt-to] A sparkling red wine from the Asti area of Piedmont.

Braciato [brah-chee-AH-to] Beef braised in wine, stock, and aromatic vegetables; also called *brasato*.

Braciola/braciuola [brah-chee-OH-lah/brah-chee-OO-lah] (1) Meat chop; typically refers to pork or mutton, often stuffed and grilled. (2) Long thin cuts of beef, lamb, or pork stuffed, rolled, and grilled.

Braciola di montone [+ dee mohn-tOH-neh] Mutton chop.

Braciolette [brah-chee-oh-lEHt-teh] Small chops or cuts of meat.

Braciolette alla scottadito [+ AHl+ lah skoht-tah-dEE-to] The name in Lazio for grilled lamb chops served piping hot and eaten with the fingers.

Braciolettine [brah-chee-OH-layt-tEE-neh] Small slices of meat; also known as *braciolone.*

Braciolone [brah-chee-oh-lOH-neh] See *Braciolettine.*

Braciuola [brah-chee-OO-lah] See *Braciola/braciuola.*

Bransi/branzi [brAHn-see/brAHn-tsee] A soft cow's-milk cheese from Bergamo (Lombardy).

Branzia [brahn-tsEE-ah] The Venetian word for sea bass. See *Branzino, Spigola.*

Branzino [brahn-tsEE-no] Sea bass; also called *spigola.*

Brasato [brah-sAH-to]). Braised; often referring to beef. See *Braciato.* (2) A local Italian word for stew.

Brassadela [brahs-sah-dEH-lah] A sweet pastry cake flavored with *grappa;* from Verona (Veneto).

Brazadèl [brah-tsah-dEHl] A dark barley bread from Lombardy.

Brendola [brayn-doh-lah] A local white Venetian wine.

Bresaola [breh-sAH-oh-lah] A dried, salted beef product from the Valtellina valley (Lombardy); traditionally sliced thin and served as an antipasto.

Bresciano [brays-chee-AH-no] See *Bagozzo.*

Bricco manzoni [brEEk-ko mahn-tsOH-nee] A red Piedmontese wine.

Briciolata [bree-chee-oh-lAH-tuh] A simple pasta sauce composed of bread crumbs toasted in olive oil and seasoned with salt and pepper. From northern Italy.

Brigidini [Bree-jee-dEE-nee] Sweet (usually) or savory fried wafers.

Also known as *pizzelle* or *cialde.*

Brigidini alla Franca [+ AHl-lah frAHn-kuh] Fried anise-flavored wafers.

Brigidini salati [+ sah-lAH-tee] Salted wafers made with potato flour and fried.

Broade [broh-AH-deh] See *Brovada.*

Brocca [brOHk-kuh] Jug; pitcher.

Broccoletti [brohk-koh-lEHt-tee] Broccoli.

Broccoli [brOHk-koh-lee] Broccoli; also *broccoletti.*

Brochat [broh-kaht] A custard like dessert from the Valle d'Aosta made with eggs, sugar, and wine and traditionally accompanied with black bread. Similar to *zabaglione.*

Brocotta [broh-kOHt-tuh] The name sometimes used in parts of Italy for ricotta cheese.

Brodettato [broh-dayt-tAH-to] Term describing meat cooked in white wine and enriched with egg yolks and lemon juice.

Brodetto [broh-dEHt-to] A fish stew popular throughout Italy; several variations.

Brodo [brOH-do] Stock; broth.

Brodo di carne [+ dee kAHr-neh] Meat stock; usually refers to beef stock.

Brodo di manzo [+ mAHn-tso] Beef Stock.

Brodo di pesce [+ dee pEH-sheh] Fish stock.

Brodo di pollo [+ dee pOHl-lo] Chicken stock.

Brodo vegetale [+ veh-jeh-tAH-leh] Vegetable stock.

Brodo di verdura [+ vayr-dOO-ruh] Vegetable stock.

Broèto [broh-EH-to] The name for *brodetto* in Veneto.

Brolio [brOH-lee-o] An area in Tuscany producing some of Italy's finest Chianti wines.

Brovada [broh-vAH-duh] (*Friuli-Venezia Giulia*); marinated turnips sautéed in olive oil with garlic and onions and seasoned with caraway seeds. Traditionally served with *musett.*

Brunello di Montalcino [broo-nEL-lo dee mohn-tahl-chEE-no] One of Italy's great red wines produced in the town of Montalcino in Tuscany.

Brus [broos](*Piedmont*) A mixture of various cheeses fermented with alochol.

Bruscandoli [broos-kAHn-doh-lee] Hops.

Bruschetta [broos-kEHt-tuh] Thick slices of bread drizzled with olive oil and garlic and grilled over a charcoal grill. Particularly popular in Abruzzi and Apulia.

Brüscitt [broo-sheet] A dish from Milan featuring chunks of beef simmered with red wine and pancetta; served with polenta.

Brustolà [broos-toh-lUH] Sweetened polenta traditionally served at the end of the meal; from Veneto.

Bucatini [boo-kah-tEE-nee] Thick, hollow spaghetti. Also called *perciatelli.*

Buccellato [boo-chehl-lAH-to] A ring-shaped yeast cake featuring raisins and aniseed and served with strawberries; a specialty of Lucca (Tuscany).

Budino [boo-dEE-no] Term referring to sweet or savory puddings or mousses.

Bue [bOO-eh] Beef.

Buji [bOO-jee] A local Piedmontese word for *gran bollito misto*; see *Gran bollito misto.*

Buongustaio [boo-ohn-goo-stAH-ee-oh] A connoisseur of fine food and wine; gourmet.

Buono [boo-OHn-o] Good.

Buricchi [boo-rEE-keh] (*Emilia-Romagna*) Large ravioli stuffed with ground chicken and herbs; a specialty of Ferrara.

Buridda [boo-rEEd-dah] The Sardinian version of *burrida* made with rayfish.

Buridda/Burrida [boo-rEEd-dah/ boor-rEE-dah] A fish stew originating in Liguria featuring a variety of fresh local seafood.

Buriello [boo-ree-EHl-lo] See *Manteca.*

Burischio, il [eel boo-rEEs-kee-o] The name for blood pudding in parts of Italy.

Burrata [boor-rAH-tah] Another name for *manteca* cheese.

Burrida See *Buridda/Burrida.*

Burriello [boor-ree-EHl-lo] See *manteca.*

Burrino [boor-rEE-no] Another name for *manteca* cheese.

Burro [bOOr-ro] (1) Butter. (2) Another name for *manteca* cheese.

Burro, al Cooked in butter.

Burro composto [+ kohm-pOH-sto] Compound butter; creamed butter combined with various ingredients, e.g. herbs, shrimp, nuts, garlic, and so on.

Burro di acciuga [+ dee ah-chee-OO-gah] Anchovy butter.

Burro di panna [bOOr-ro dee pAHn-nah] Creamy, high-quality butter; some of Italy's finest comes from Emilia-Romagna.

Burro fuso [+ fOO-so] Melted butter.

Burro maneggiato [+ mah-neh-jee-AH-to] Softened whole butter kneaded with flour; used to enrich and slightly thicken various sauces.

Burtleina [boort-leh-ee-nuh] A type of savory pancake from Piacenza (Emilia-Romagna); similar to *borlengo*.

Büsecca [boo-sEHk-kah] The word in Milan for tripe.

Busecca, la [lah boo-sEHk-kah] A substantial tripe and vegetable soup from Milan (Lombardy).

Busecchin, el [ehl boo-seh-kEEn] The word for blood pudding in Milan and parts of Lombardy.

Busecchin de corada [+ dee kohr-AH-dah] A dish from Milan featuring lungs simmered in stock with olive oil and tomatoes.

Busecchio [boo-sEHk-kee-oh] A type of pork sausage from Milan.

Bussolai [boos-sohl-AH-ee] See *Buzolai*.

Bussolano [boos-sohl-AH-no] (*Veneto*) A sweet cake flavored with marsala wine.

Butirro [boo-tEEr-ro] See *Manteca*.

Buttafuoco [boot-tah-foo-OH-ko] A sparkling red wine from Lombardy.

Buttarga di tonno [boot-tAHr-gah dee tOHn-no] See *Bottarga*.

Buttariga [boot-tah-rEE-gah] See *Bottarga*.

Buzolai [boo-tsoh-lAH-ee] Rich

cookies made with flour, butter, sugar, and eggs; a specialty of Friuli.

Cacao [kah-kAH-oh] Cocoa.

Cacciagione [kah-cheeah-jeeOH-neh] Game.

Caccialepre [kah-chee-ah-lEH-preh] A type of plant used as a vegetable in southern Italy.

Cacciatora, alla [kah-chee-ah-tO-rah] Describes meat dishes cooked in a sauce composed of mushrooms, garlic, peppers, onions, herbs, tomatoes, and wine.

Cacciatori [kah-chee-ah-tO-ree] A type of salami from northern Italy.

Cacio [kAH-chee-o] The name for cheese in Tuscany.

Cacio bianco [+ bee-AHn-kah] Cottage cheese.

Caciocavallo [kah-chee-oh-kah-vAHl-lo] A mild cow's-milk cheese from southern Italy similar to Provolone. *Caciocavallo* can be eaten fresh or aged and used as a grating cheese.

Caciofiore [kah-chee-oh-fee-OH-reh] A soft farm cheese made from ewe's or goat's milk. Made in several parts of Italy.

Cacio grattato [+ graht-tAH-to] Grated cheese.

Cacio magro [+ mAHg-ro] A type of dried cottage cheese.

Cacio pecorino di montagna [+ pEH-koh-ree-no dee mohn-tAH-nyah] A ewe's-milk cheese from Tuscany.

Cacio ricotta [+ ree-kOHt-tah] A custardlike dessert from Abruzzi made from milk and rennet and flavored with citron.

Caciotta [kah-chee-OHt-tah] Various small ewe's- or goat's-milk farm cheeses produced in several parts of Italy.

Caciotta norcia [+ nOHr-chee-ah] A ewe's-milk cheese from central Italy.

Caciucco [kah-chee-OOk-ko] A fish soup from Livorno, containing a variety of fish and seasoned with garlic and tomatoes.

Caciucco alla livornese [+ AHl-lah lee-vohr-nEH-zeh] A hearty fish stew; a Livorno (Tuscany) specialty.

Caciunitti [kah-chee-oon-EEt-tee] (*Marche*) Small chocolate stuffed pastries.

Caduta di formaggio [kah-dOO-tah dee fohr-mAH-jee-oh] A pasta dish from Veneto featuring vermicelli tossed with a sauce composed of Gorgonzola cheese, butter, and brandy.

Caffè [kahf-fEH] Coffee.

Caffè borgia [+ bOHr-jee-ah] Coffee fortified with apricot brandy.

Caffè cappuccino [+ kahp-poo-chEE-no] *Caffè espresso* mixed with steamed milk; topped with whipped cream and sprinkled with cinnamon, chocolate, and/or powdered orange rind.

Caffè con panna [+ kohn pAHn-nah] A mild cup of coffee mixed with steamed milk and topped with whipped cream.

Caffè corretto [+ kohr-rEHt-to] *Caffè espresso* laced with brandy.

Caffè e latte [+ eh lAHt-teh] Hot coffee mixed with hot milk.

Caffè espresso [+ ehs-prEHs-soh] Strong black coffee.

Caffè freddo [+ frEHd-do] Iced coffee.

Caffè macchiato [+ mAH-key-ah-to] *Caffè espresso* with cold milk or cream.

Caffè nero [+ nEH-ro] Black coffee.

Caffè ristretto [+ rees-trEHt-to] Very strong black coffee.

Caffettiera [kahf-feht-tee-EH-rah] Coffeepot.

Caglio [kAH-lyo] Rennet.

Cagnina [kah-nyEE-nah] Sweet local wine from Emilia-Romagna.

Calabria [kahl-AH-bree-ah] A coastal, mountainous region located in southern Italy. Swordfish, eggplant, and citrus fruits play an important role in the Calabrian diet.

Calamaretti [kah-lah-mah-rEHt-tee] Baby squid.

Calamari [kahl-ah-mAH-ree] Squid; popular throughout Italy.

Calascioni [kah-lah-shee-OH-nee] Large ravioli stuffed with spinach and cheese; from Rome.

Calcagno [kahl-kAH-nyo] A hard ewe's-milk cheese from Sicily.

Calcinello [kahl-chee-nEHl-lo] The name for littleneck clams in parts of Emilia-Romagna.

Calcioni [kahl-chee-OH-nee] Large, sweet ravioli.

Caldariello [kahl-dah-ree-EHl-lo] Lamb chunks cooked in olive oil with onions, fennel, and sheep's milk; a specialty of Apulia.

Caldo [kAHl-do] Warm. *Molto caldo* means hot.

Caldo gallego [+ gahl-EH-go] A soup made with chicken and white beans.

Caldo gallina [+ gahl-lEE-nah] Chicken soup.

Calice [kAH-lee-cheh] Goblet.

Calore [kah-lOH-reh] Heat.

Calzagatti [kahl-tsah-gAHt-tee] A type of cornmeal mush served with pork and beans; a specialty of Emilia-Romagna.

Calzone [kahl-tsOH-neh] Stuffed pizza.

Calzonei [kahl-tsoh-nEH-ee] (*Veneto*) Pasta stuffed with squash and cheese; similar to ravioli.

Calzone Napoletano [+ nah-poh-leh-tAH-no] Bread dough stuffed with salami, mozzarella, and Parmesan cheese.

Calzone pugliese [+ poo-lyEH-seh] Dough stuffed with vegetables or cheese; meatless.

Calzonetti [kahl-tsoh-nEHt-tee] A type of omelette.

Calzonetti con pomodoro [+ kohn poh-moh-dOH-ro] A cheese omelette served with tomato sauce; from Abruzzi.

Calzuneddi [kahl-tsoo-nEHd-dee] Small, fried *calzone*.

Cam [kahm] A fermented barley drink.

Cameriere [kah-meh-ree-EH-reh] Waiter.

Camoscio [kah-mOH-shee-o] Chamois; a type of mountain goat found in parts of Italy.

Camoscio alla valdierese [+ AHl-lah vahl-dee-ay-rEH-seh] Braised chamois with white truffles; a specialty of Piedmont.

Campagnola, alla [kahm-pah-nyOH-lah] Country style; describes dishes prepared with tomatoes, onions, and mushrooms.

Campania [kahm-pAH-nee-ah] Making up Italy's "shin," Campania boasts the finest fruits and vegetables in Italy. This region is also well known for its hearty pizza and pasta dishes.

Campari [kahm-pAH-ree] An Italian spirit made from herbs and bitter orange peel.

Canaiolo [kah-nah-ee-OH-lo] A sweet red grape used in wine making.

Canapiglia [kah-nah-pEE-lyah] A local name in parts of Veneto for a type of duck.

Candelaus [kahn-deh-lAH-oos] An orange/almond-flavored pastry from Sardinia.

Candito [kahn-dEE-to] Candied.

Canederli [kah-neh-dehr-lee] Small dumplings served with soup or as a small meal.

Canederli tirolesi [+ tee-roh-lEH-zeh] Small dumplings served with *speck* (smoked ham) and sausage.

Canestrato [kah-neh-strAH-to] A popular Sicilian cheese made from ewe's milk; also known as *Pecorino Siciliano*.

Canestrelli [kah-neh-strEHl-lee] A type of Ligurian breakfast pastry.

Canestrello [kah-neh-strEHl-lo] A variety of shellfish related to the scallop.

Canestrino [kah-neh-strEE-no] A type of small sea scallop.

Cannariculi [kahn-nah-rEE-koo-lee] Sweet fritters glazed with honey; a specialty of Calabria.

Cannarozzetti [kahn-nah-roh-tsEHt-tee] Short, ribbed pasta.

Cannella [kahn-nEHl-lah] Cinnamon.

Cannellini [kahn-nehl-lEE-nee] White Italian kidney beans.

Cannellino [kahn-nehl-lEE-no] A

sweet variety of Frascati wine.

Cannelloni [kahn-nehl-lOH-nee] Large pasta tubes stuffed with meat or cheese filling.

Cannellotti [kahn-nehl-lOHt-tee] A pasta shape.

Cannelo [kahn-nEH-lo] A local name for *cannolicchio* in parts of Emilia-Romagna.

Cannocchia [kahn-nOH-kee-ah] Squill; A variety of crustacean related to the shrimp; also called *cicala.*

Cannocchie fritte [kahn-nOH-kee-eh frEEt-teh] Fried squill.

Cannoli [kahn-nOH-lee] Tubular pastry, fried or baked and stuffed with a variety of fillings.

Cannoli alla siciliana [+ AHl-la see-chee-lee-AH-nah] Fried pastry tubes filled with sweetened ricotta mixed with candied fruit or chocolate chunks.

Cannolicchi [kahn-noh-lEE-kee] Very short tubed pasta similar to *ditali.*

Cannolicchio [kahn-noh-lEE-kee-o] A type of shellfish used mainly in fish stews.

Cantarello [kahn-tah-rEHl-lo] Chanterelle; a variety of wild mushroom.

Cantina [kahn-tEE-nah] Wine cellar; wine shop.

Cantucci di Prato [kanh-tOO-chee dee prAH-to] Anise-flavored cookies from Prato (Tuscany).

Capa tonda [kAH-pah tOHn-dah] (*Veneto*) Small cuttlefish sautéed with garlic and onions in olive oil.

Capelli d'angelo [kah-pEHl-lee dee AHn-jeh-lo] Literally "angel hair"; long, very thin noodles;

best served with a light sauce or in broth.

Capellini [kah-pehl-lEE-nee] Angel hair pasta; see *Capelli d'angelo.*

Capillari [kah-peel-lAH-ree] Baby eels.

Capitone [kah-pee-tOH-neh] A large eel.

Capocello [kah-poh-chEHl-lo] A sausage from Apulia.

Capocollo [kah-poh-kOHl-lo] Cured pork shoulder.

Capo cuoco [kAH-po koo-OH-ko] Chef in charge.

Capo d'anno [kAH-po dAHn-no] New Year's day

Caponata [kah-poh-nAH-tah] A Sicilian dish featuring eggplant sautéed with capers, olives, celery, and often tuna roe and crayfish tails; served in a sweet and sour tomato sauce

Caponata alla marinara [+ AHl-lah mah-ree-nAH-rah] Crusty bread flavored with garlic and herbs and served with crushed olives and anchovies.

Caponatina [kah-poh-nah-tEE-nah] The name for *caponata* in parts of Sicily; see *Caponata.*

Capone [kah-pOH-neh] A type of fish used in soups and stews.

Capote [kah-pOH-teh] A large caper.

Capozzella [kah-poh-tsEHl-lah] In Naples, *capozzella* is roasted lamb's head.

Cappa [kAHp-pah] A local Italian name for a type of shellfish similar to the scallop.

Cappasanta [kahp-pah-sAHn-tah] Bay scallop.

Cappellacci [kahp-pehl-lAH-chee] A type of stuffed pasta; from Ferrara.

Cappellacci con la zucca alla Ferarrese [+ khon lah tsOO-kah AHl-lah feh-rah-rEH-seh] A specialty of Ferrara (Emilia-Romagna) featuring pasta stuffed with pureed pumpkin and Parmesan cheese; drizzled with melted butter and grated Parmesan.

Cappelletti [kahp-peh-lEHt-tee] "Little hats"; pasta stuffed with a mixture of ground chicken, sausage, Parmesan cheese, and seasonings; from Romagna.

Cappelli da prete [kahp-pEHl-lee dah prEH-teh] "Priest's hats"; a pork sausage from Emilia-Romagna formed in the shape of a priest's hat.

Cappelli di turchi [+ dee tOOr-key] A now obsolete name for *cannoli*.

Capperi [kahp-pEH-ree] Capers; some of the finest capers in the world are grown in Pantelleria, a Mediterranean island off the southwest coast of Sicily.

Capperozzoli [kahp-peh-rOH-tsoh-lee] A Venetian name for a variety of clam.

Capponcella [kahp-pohn-chEHl-lah] A hen whose ovaries have been removed.

Cappone [kahp-pOH-neh] A young castrated cock.

Cappon magro [kAHp-pon mAHg-ro] A famous salad dish from Genoa featuring boiled fish, garlic, olives, root vegetables, hard-cooked eggs, capers, and anchovies.

Cappuccino See *Caffè cappuccino*.

Capra [kAH-prah] Goat.

Capretto [kah-prEHt-to] Kid; young goat.

Caprettu o forno [kah-prEHt-too oh fOHr-no] (*Palermo*) Young roasted goat.

Capri [kAH-pree] An island off the coast of Campania recognized for its seafood dishes, particularly those featuring crayfish.

Capriata [kah-pree-AH-tah] A common Italian dish composed of beans seasoned and mashed with olive oil; typically served with endive.

Caprino [kah-prEE-no] The collective name for various goats'-milk cheeses.

Caprino romano [+ roh-mAH-no] (*Lazio*) Romano cheese made from goat's milk.

Capriolo [kah-pree-OH-lah] Roebuck.

Capuzedde [kah-poo-tsEHd-deh] (*Basilicata*) Lamb's head roasted over hot coals.

Carabaccia [kah-rah-bAH-chee-ah] (*Tuscany*) Onion soup lightly seasoned with cinnamon.

Carabazada [kah-rah-bah-tsAH-dah] (*Tuscany*) Onion soup.

Caraffa [kah-rAHf-fah] Carafe.

Caramello [kah-rah-mEHl-lo] Caramel.

Carasau [kah-rah-sah-oo] (*Sardinia*) A crisp, very thin unleavened bread. Also called *carta di musica* or *foglio di musica*.

Carassai [kah-rahs-sAH-ee] A cow's-milk cheese from Carassi (Ascoli Piceno).

Caraxiu [kah-rah-syoo] (*Sardinia*) A method of cooking meat in which a pit is filled with myrtle branches and stones and lit. When the stones are hot, the meat (often a small whole pig or kid) is placed upon them and covered with more hot stones.

Carbonade [kahr-boh-nAH-deh] (*Valle d'Aosta*) A hearty stew made with preserved beef, vegetables and wine; traditionally served with polenta.

Carbonara, alla [kahr-boh-nAH-rah] (1) Describes dishes prepared with pancetta or smoked ham and eggs. (2) Describes foods cooked over a charcoal fire.

Carbonara, spaghetti alla [spah-ghEHt-tee AHl-lah +] A famous dish featuring spaghetti cooked al dente and immediately tossed with chopped pancetta, raw beaten egg, and grated Parmesan cheese; from Lazio.

Carbonata [kahr-boh-nAH-tah] Beef braised in red wine.

Carcassa [kahr-kAHs-sah] Carcass.

Carciofi [kahr-chee-OH-fee] Artichoke; used heavily in the Italian kitchen, particularly in Rome.

Carciofini [kahr-chee-oh-fEE-nee] Baby artichokes.

Cardi [kAHr-dee] Cardoons; a Mediterranean vegetable similar in taste and appearance to celery.

Cardi alla perugia [+ AHl-lah peh-rOO-jee-nah] Batter-fried cardoons from Perugia (Umbria).

Carnaroli [kahn-nahr-OH-lee] A variety of Italian rice used in risotto and other dishes.

Carne [kAHr-neh] Meat.

Carne a carrargiu [+ kahr-rAHr-jee-oo] See *Caraxiu.*

Carne pastizzada [+ pahs-tee-tsAH-dah] (*Veneto*) Beef braised in wine vinegar.

Carne, salsa di Tomato-meat sauce. Se also *Ragú.*

Carnesecca [kahr-neh sEH-kah] The Tuscan word for pancetta.

Carne tritata [+ tree-tAH-tah] Beef hash.

Carnevale [kahr-neh-vAH-leh] Carnival; a festival in Italy taking place four weeks before Lent and lasting until Ash Wednesday.

Carota [kah-rOH-tah] Carrot.

Carpa [kAHr-puh] Carp; also spelled *carpione.*

Carpaccio (filetto al) [fee-lEHt-toh ahl kahr-pAH-chee-o] Thinly sliced raw beef fillet drizzled with olive oil, salt, and pepper; served with various cold sauces.

Carpio [kAHr-pee-o] Carp.

Carpione [kahr-pee-OH-neh] (1) A variety of trout; salmon trout. (2) Marinated fish; made in several parts of Italy.

Carrettiera, alla [kahr-reht-tii-EH-rah] Describes certain dished prepared with mushrooms and tuna.

Carrozza, in [kahr-rOH-tsah] "In a carriage"; see *Carrozza, mozzarella in.*

Carrozza, mozzarella in [mohts-tsah-rEHl-lah een +] A famous Neapolitan specialty consisting of mozzarella cheese placed between slices of bread, dipped in a thin batter, and fried.

Carta da giuco [+ dah jee-OO-koh] See *Stracci.*

Carta da musica [+ dah mOO-see-kah] See *Carasau.*

Carta del giorno [kAHr-tah dehl jee-OHr-no] Bill of fare.

Carteddate [kahr-dehd-dAH-teh] See *Cartellate.*

Cartellate [kahr-tehl-lAH-teh] A type of fritter from Apulia sweetened with honey. Also spelled *carteddate*.

Cartilagine [kahr-tee-lAH-jee-neh] Cartilage.

Cartoccio, al [kahr-tOH-chee-o] Describes foods—particularly fish—wrapped in parchment with oil and wine and baked.

Casa, della [dEHl-lah kAH-sah] Specialty of the chef.

Casadello [kah-sah-dEHl-lo] A sweet, simple cake from Emilia-Romagna.

Casalinga, (alla) [kah-sah-lEEn-gah] Home cooking; homemade.

Casalini [kah-sah-lEE-nee] A variety of small tomato used in sauces.

Casarecal [kah-sah-ree-kAHl] (*Marche*) A sweet pastry bun.

Casarecci [kah-sah-rEH-chee] A sweet pastry from the Marche region.

Casareccio [kah-sah-rEH-chee-o] A type of unkneaded bread from Sicily.

Caschettas [kahs-kEHt-tahs] An almond pastry from Sardinia.

Caseggioni [kah-seh-jee-OH-nee] A cow's-milk cheese from Sardinia.

Casiddi [kah-sEEd-dee] A hard, local cheese from Basilicata; made from goat's- or ewe's milk.

Casigliolo [kah-see-lyee-OH-lo] A cow's-milk cheese from Sicily similar to *Caciocavallo*; also known as *casigiolo*, *panella*, *padella*, and *peradivacca*.

Casizzolos [[kah-seets-tsOH-los] A mild-flavored cow's-milk cheese produced in Sardinia.

Casizzolu [kah-seets-tsOH-loo] See *Casizzolos*.

Casônèi [kah-soh-nEH-ee] Pasta stuffed with salami, sausage, Parmesan cheese, and sometimes raisins and served with sage butter; a specialty of Bergamo and Bresica.

Cassata gelata [+ jay-lAH-tah] A dessert composed of sweetened ricotta mixed with candied fruit and poured into an ice cream–lined mold; frozen and unmolded before serving.

Cassata siciliana [kahs-sAH-tah see-chee-lee-AH-nah] A specialty of Sicily; a famous dessert featuring pound cake filled or layered with a creamy mixture of ricotta, candied fruit, and chocolate chips; decorated with chocolate frosting.

Cassatella [kahs-sah-tEHl-lah] (*Emilia-Romagna*) An uncooked cake made with cookie crumbs, beaten egg yolks and whites, chocolate, and butter.

Casseruola, in [een kahs-seh-roo-OH-lah] Cooked and/or served in a casserole.

Cassoeula [kahs-soh-eh-oo-lah] (*Lombardy*) Pork cooked with vegetables, cabbage, and *lugànega* sausage in stock; served with polenta. Also called *cazzoeula* and *bottaggio*.

Cassola [kahs-sOH-lah] A fish stew from Sardinia.

Cassoni [kahs-sOH-nee] (1) A small fried savory turnover, usually filled with sautéed greens. (2) Fried *consum*; see *Consum*.

Castagnaccio [kahs-tah-nyAH-chee-o] A Florentine pastry made with chestnut flour, raisins, pine nuts, fennel, and oil.

Castagne [kahs-tAH-nyeh] Small chestnuts; popular in northern Italy; see *Marroni*.

Castagnoli [kahs-tah-nyOH-lee] Anise-flavored fritters.

Castegneti [kahs-tay-nyEH-tee] Small almond pastries from Apulia.

Castelluccio [kahs-tehl-lOO-chee-o] A town in Umbria noted for lentils of superb quality.

Castelmagno [kahs-tEHl-mAH-nyo] A blue-veined cheese produced in Piedmont; similar to Gorgonzola.

Castrato [kahs-trAH-to] A young castrated sheep.

Casu becciu [kah-soo beh-chee-oo] A strong cheese from the Gallura region of Sardinia made from cow's or goat's milk; also referred to as *Casu iscaldidu* and *Casu marzu*.

Casu cotto [kAH-soo kOHt-to] A dish from parts of Sardinia featuring grilled fresh cheese.

Casu iscaldidu [+ ees-kahl-dEE-doo] See *Casu becciu*.

Casu marzu [kAH-soo mAHr-tsoo] See *Casu becciu*.

Catino [kah-tEE-no] A large earthenware bowl typically used to soak or wash foods.

Cauciunitti [kahoo-cheeoo-nEEt-tee] A traditional Christmas pastry made by filling sweet dough with almond paste and deep-frying; from Abruzzi.

Cavallo [kah-vAHl-lo] Horse; horse meat.

Caval pist [kAH-vahl peest] (*Emilia-Romagna*) Ground spiced horse meat.

Cavatappi [kah-vah-tAHp-pee] Literally "corkscrew." Short twisted pasta, usually ridged.

Cavatieddi [kah-vah-tee-EHd-dee] (*Apulia*) A shell-shaped pasta made from hard-wheat flour. Traditionally served tossed with arugula, olive oil, hot pepper, and garlic.

Cavatoni [kah-vah-tOH-nee] A short, tubed, slightly curved pasta.

Cavatoni incannati [+ een-kahn-nAH-tee] A type of pasta from Sicily usually served with meat or tuna.

Cavatoni rigati [+ ree-gAH-tee] Ribbed *cavatoni*.

Cavaturaccioli [kah-vah-too-rAH-chee-oh-lee] Corkscrew. See also *Cavatappi*.

Caviale [kah-vee-AH-leh] Caviar; fish roe.

Cavolata [kah-voh-lAH-tah] A Sardinian specialty of cabbage cooked with potatoes and cracklings.

Cavolfiore [kah-vohl-fee-OH-reh] Cauliflower.

Cavoli-cappucci in agrodolce [kah-vOH-lee-kahp-pOO-chee een ahg-roh-dOHl-cheh] (*Veneto*) Brussels sprouts seasoned with caraway and served in sweet-and-sour sauce.

Cavoli imbottiti [kah-vOH-lee eem-boht-tEE-tee] Stuffed cabbage.

Cavolino di bruxelles [cah-voh-lEE-no dee brook-sEHl-leh] Brussels sprouts.

Cavollat [kah-vohl-laht] (*Lombardy*) A kind of sweet custard served as a dessert.

Cavolo [kAH-voh-loh] Cabbage.

Cavolo di bruxelles [+ dee brook-sEHl-leh] Brussels sprouts.

Cavolo nero [+ nEH-ro] A type of dark green cabbage.

Cavolo riccio [+ rEE-chee-o] Kale.

Cavolo rosso [+ rOHs-so] Red cabbage.

Cavolo verza [+ vEH-tsah] Savoy cabbage.

Cavolrapa [kah-vohl-rAH-lah] Kohlrabi.

Cazzilli [kahts-tsEEl-lee] (*Sicily*) Potato-cheese fritters.

Cazzoeula [cahts-tsoh-eh-oo-lah] See *Cassoeula*.

Cazzottini [kah-tsoht-tEE-nee] (*Emilia-Romagna*) Small simple bread rolls.

Cazzuda di montone alla fiorentina [kah-tsOO-duh dee mohn-tOH-neh AHl-ah fee-oh-rehn-tEE-nah] (*Tuscany*) A mutton stew made with white beans, tomatoes, herbs, and bread crumbs.

Ceci [chEH-chee] Chickpea.

Cecina [cheh-chEE-nah] (*Tuscany*) A type of chickpea "cake" made from pureed chickpeas mixed with oil and seasonings and baked in a pie tin.

Cedro [chEHd-ro] Citron; grown in Calabria and Sicily, the citron is thought to be the first citrus fruit introduced to Italy.

Cee [chEH-eh] A local Tuscan word for *cieche*; see *Cieche*.

Cefaleti in padella [cheh-fahl-EH-tee een pah-dEH-lah] Small mullet fried in olive oil with garlic, parsley, and lemon juice; a specialty of Veneto.

Cefali in gratella [chEH-fah-lee een grah-tEHl-lah] Grilled mullet.

Cefalo [chEH-fah-lo] Gray mullet.

Cefalo reale [+ reh-AH-leh] A name sometimes used in Umbria for mullet.

Cena [chEH-nah] Dinner.

Cenci [chEHn-chee] (*Tuscany*) Sweet pastry strips tied in a loose decorative knot and fried.

Ceneri [chEH-neh-ree] Ashes.

Centerbe [chehn-tEHr-beh] An Italian liqueur flavored with a "hundred herbs"; from Pescara (Abruzzi).

Ceppatella [chehp-pah-tEHl-lah] A type of mushroom.

Cerase [cheh-rAH-seh] The name for cherries in parts of Italy.

Cerasella [cheh-rah-sEHl-lah] A cherry liqueur.

Cereali [cheh-reh-AH-lee] Cereals.

Cerfoglio [chehr-fOH-lyo] Chervil.

Cernia [chEHr-nee-ah] Grouper.

Certosa [chehr-tOH-zah] An herb liqueur; similar to Chartreuse.

Certosino [chehr-toh-zEE-no] A spiced fruit cake traditionally prepared for the Christmas feast in parts of Italy.

Cervella [chehr-vEHl-lo] Brains.

Cervellàa [chehr-vayl-luh] The local Milanese name for *cervellada*.

Cervellada [cheh-vehl-lAH-dah] A Milanese sausage made from pork meat, pork fat, marrow, cheese, and originally pig's brains; also spelled *cervellata*.

Cervellata [chehr-vehl-lAH-tah] See *Cervellàa*.

Cervo [chEHr-vo] Deer; venison.

Cetriolini [cheh-tree-oh-lEE-nee] Gherkin.

Cetriolo [cheh-tree-OH-lo] Cucumber.

Cevrin di caozze [cheh-vrEEn dee kah-OH-tseh] A goat's-milk cheese from Piedmont.

Charlotte di farina gialla [kahr-lOHt-teh dee fah-rEE-nah gee-AHl-lah] An apple tart from Lombardy.

Cheppia [kEHp-pee-ah] Shad.

Chiacchiere [kee-AH-kee-eh-reh] A popular Carnival pastry composed of fried sweet dough.

Chiaccia reale [kee-AH-chee-ah reh-AH-leh] Icing.

Chiama vinu [kee-AH-mah vEE-noo] A local Sicilian specialty featuring pasta dusted with bread crumbs and fried in olive oil.

Chianchiarelli [kee-AHn-kee-ah-rEHl-lee] Tiny *orecchiette*; see *Orecchiette*.

Chianti [kee-AHn-tee] Italy's most famous wine produced in the Chianti region of Tuscany. This red wine is made from the Sangiovese, Canaiolo, Trebbiano, and Malvasia grapes.

Chianti classico [+ klAHs-see-ko] Term for dry red Chianti wines of fine quality.

Chianti, tipo [tEE-po +] A term referring to wines similar to Chianti.

Chiara [kee-AH-rah] Egg white.

Chiavari [kee-ah-vah-ree] A Ligurian cheese made from cow's milk.

Chifel [kee-fehl] A cumin-flavored bun.

Chiocciole [kee-OH-chee-oh-leh] (1) Snails. (2) A snail-shaped pasta noodle.

Chiocciole di maremma [+ dee mah-rEHm-mah] A Tuscan word for snails.

Chiòdi di garofano [key-OH-dee dee gah-roh-fAH-no] Cloves.

Chiodini [key-oh-dEE-nee] A wild, edible fungus.

Chisciòo [kees-chee-OH-wo] See *Cicc.*

Chitarra [kee-tAHr-rah] "Guitar"; an instrument used to cut pasta (*maccheroni alla chitarra*) into noodles; a sheet of pasta sits on a bed of wire strings and is pressed through with the aid of a rolling pin; popular in Abruzzi and Marche.

Chiurletto [kee-oor-lEH-to] A game bird similar to the curlew; see *Chiurlo.*

Chiurlo [kee-OOr-lo] Curlew; a shore bird consumed in parts of northern Italy.

Chizze [kee-tseh] Fried stuffed dough.

Chnolle [knohl-leh] (*Piedmont*) Cornmeal dumplings; typically served in soup.

Ciabatta [chee-ah-bAHt-tah] A type of bread formed in the shape of a certain shoe (*ciabatta*).

Ciacci montanari [chee-AH-chee mohn-tah-nAH-ree] A type of gnocchi from the mountainous regions of Emilia-Romagna. It is made from a dough composed of flour, cheese, oil, and water; fried on a hot griddle.

Cialde [chee-AHl-deh] A thin wafer used in various sweet preparations; also called *cialdoni*.

Cialdoni [chee-ahl-dOH-nee] See *Cialde.*

Cialledda [chee-ahl-lEHd-dah] A peasant soup composed of olive oil, tomatoes, cucumbers, and seasonings; eaten cold.

Cialzòn [chee-ahl-tsOHn] (*Venezia Giulia*) A stuffed pasta filled with fresh local cheese and usually served in broth. Also spelled *cjalsòn*.

Ciambella [chee-ahm-bEHl-lah] A ring-shaped sweet cake having several versions; made in parts of northern Italy, particularly Emilia-Romagna.

Ciambotto [chee-ahm-bOHt-to] A fish sauce for pasta popular in Apulia.

Ciaudedda [chee-ah-oo-dEHd-dah] (*Basilicata*) A hearty fava bean soup.

Cibo della miseria, il [eel chEE-bo dEHl-lah mee-sEH-ree-ah] "The food of poverty"; in earlier times, this phrase referred to polenta.

Cibreo [chee-brEH-o] *Salsa bianca* prepared with chicken livers, chicken wattles (the fleshy growth dangling from the chin), and unlaid eggs.

Cicala [chee-AH-lah] See *Cannocchia*.

Cicc [cheek] A savory cheese tart from Lombardy; also called *chisciòo*.

Ciccioli [chEE-chee-oh-lee] Pork cracklings.

Ciceri e tria [chEE-cheh-ree eh trEE-ah] A pasta and chickpea soup from Apulia.

Cicero [chEE-cheh-ro] A local Italian name for the chickpea.

Ciciones [chee-chee-OH-nehs] (*Sardinia*) Small cornmeal dumplings.

Cicoria [chee-kOH-ree-ah] Chicory.

Cicorie e favette [chee-kOH-ree-eh eh fah-vEHt-teh] A white bean and endive puree; used as a bread spread.

Cieche [chee-EH-keh] Tiny baby eels.

Ciliegia [chee-lee-EH-jee-ah] Cherry.

Cilindrati [chee-leen-drAH-tee] Bread rolls made by rolling thin sheets of dough into small cylinders.

Cima alla genovese [chEE-mah AHl-lah jeh-noh-vEH-seh] A traditional Ligurian dish composed of breast or shoulder of veal stuffed with ground veal, sweetbreads, brains, pistachio nuts, Parmesan cheese, and bread crumbs; served cold.

Cime di rappa [chEE-meh dee rAHp-pah] Turnip greens.

Cinestrata [chee-neh-strAH-tah] (*Tuscany*) A light soup flavored with marsala wine, nutmeg, and cinnamon.

Cinghiale [cheen-ghee-AH-leh] Wild boar.

Cinghialetto [cheen-ghee-ah-lEHt-to] Young wild boar.

Cioccolata [chee-oh-koh-lAH-ta] Chocolate.

Cioccolata calda [+ kAHl-dah] Hot chocolate (beverage).

Cioccolatini [chee-oh-koh-lah-tEE-nee] The name for various chocolate candies.

Ciccolato [chee-oh-koh-lAH-to] Hot chocolate (beverage).

Ciliege [chee-lee-EH-jeh] Cherries.

Cimino [chee-mEE-no] Cumin.

Ciopa [chee-oh-pah] A crusty bread from Veneto.

Cipolla [chee-pOHl-lah] Onion.

Cipollacci [chee-pohl-lAH-chee] Small bitter onions.

Cipollata [chee-pohl-lAH-tah]

(*Tuscany*) Onion soup seasoned with pancetta and Parmesan cheese.

Cipolline [chee-pohl-lEE-neh] The Italian name for pearl onions or chives.

Cipolline sott'aceto [+ soht ah-chEH-to] Pearl onions marinated in vinegar and herbs.

Ciriola [chee-ree-OH-lah] A small crusty bread roll.

Ciriole ternane [chee-ree-OH-leh tehr-nAH-neh] (*Umbria*) Fresh pasta tossed with a wild mushrooms, garlic, and olive oil sauce.

Cirioli [chee-ree-OH-lee] Baby eels.

Ciufulitti [chee-oo-foo-lEEt-tee] A tubed pasta from Abruzzi.

Ciupeta [chee-oo-pEH-tah] A round, crown-shaped loaf of bread; from Ferrara (Emilia-Romagna).

Ciuppin [chee-oop-pEEn] (*Liguria*) A fish stew containing various types of fish (whatever is in the day's catch). The stew is often pureed and used as a sauce for pasta.

Civet [chee-veht] See *Sivet*.

Civraxiu [cheev-rahy-ee-oo] A Sardinian semolina bread.

Cjalsòn [kjahl-sOHn] See *Cialzòn*.

Classico [klAHs-see-co] A term on a wine bottle indicating good quality.

Clastidium [klahs-tEE-dee-oom] A dry white wine from Lombardy.

Clinton [klEEn-tohn] The name of a red wine from Veneto; also the name of the grape from which it is made.

Clustrum [kloos-troom] See *Crustulum*.

Coagulato [koh-ah-goo-lAH-to] Coagulated.

Coari [koh-ah-ree] A type of bread made with bacon pieces; from Veneto.

Còcciule [kOH-chee-oo-leh] The word for a variety of clam in Sardinia.

Cocco [kOH-ko] Coconut.

Coccone [koh-kOH-neh] The word for mushroom in parts of Piedmont.

Cocomero [koh-kOH-meh-ro] Watermelon.

Coda [kOH-dah] Tail.

Coda di bue [+ dee bOO-eh] Oxtail.

Coda di rospo [+ dee rOHs-po] Monkfish.

Coda (alla) vaccinara [+ vah-chee-nAH-tah] Oxtail braised in red wine and tomato sauce; a specialty of Lazio.

Codone [koh-dOH-neh] A local word in Veneto for a variety of wild duck.

Colapasta [koh-lah-pAH-stah] Colander.

Colazione [koh-lah-tsee-OH-neh] Breakfast.

Colla di pesce [kOHl-lah dee pEH-sheh] Gelatin derived from the dried bladder of sturgeon.

Colomba di pavullo [koh-lOHm-bah dee pah-vOOl-lo] A yeast cake layered with fruit, jam, and pine nuts; from Emilia-Romagna.

Colomba pasquale [+ pahs-kwAH-leh] (*Milan and Pavia*) A traditional Easter cake made from a yeast dough and decorated with almonds; formed in the shape of a dove.

Coltassala [kohl-tahs-sAH-lah] A dry red Tuscan wine.

Coltello [kohl-tEHl-lo] Knife.

Compantico [kohm-pAHn-tee-ko] Term refering to any sandwich filling.

Completo [kohm-plEH-toh] Complete; whole.

Composta di frutta [kohm-pOHs-tah dee frOOt-tah] Fruit compote; chunks of fruit slowly stewed in syrup, often with liqueur; served cold.

Compreso [kohm-prEH-so] Included.

Con [kohn] With.

Concentrato di pomodoro [kohn-chayn-trAH-to dee poh-moh-dOH-ro] Tomato concentrate; tomato paste.

Conchiglie [kohn-kEY-lyeh] Shell-shaped pasta.

Conchiglie di San Giacomo [+ dee sahn jee-ah-kOH-mo] An Italian word for scallop.

Conchiglie di San Giacomo fritte [+ frEEt-teh] Fried scallops.

Conchiglie piccole rigate [kohn-kEE-lyeh peek-kOH-leh ree-gAH-tee] Small ridged sea shell pasta.

Conchiglie rigati. [+ ree-gAH-tee] Ridged, shell-shaped pasta.

Conchigliette [kohn-key-lyEHt-teh] Small shell-shaped pasta.

Condimento [kohn-dee-mEHn-to] Condiment.

Confetteria [kohn-feht-teh-rEE-ah] Candies, confections, and so on.

Confetti [kohn-fEHt-tee] Sugar-coated almonds; traditionally presented at special occasions.

Confettura [kon-feht-tOO-rah] Jam.

Congelare [kohn-geh-lAH-reh] Freeze.

Conghiaccio [kohn ghee-AH-chee-o] On the rocks.

Coniglio [koh-nEE-lyo] Rabbit.

Coniglio salvatico [+ sahl-vah-tEE-ko] Wild hare.

Coniglio salvatico in salmì [+ een-sah-lAH-mee] Marinated hare roasted and then braised in the marinade; the reduced, seasoned marinade is served with the hare.

Conserva [kohn-sEHr-vah] (1) Jam. (2) Term often referred to preserved tomatoes.

Conserve [kohn-sEHr-veh] Preserves.

Consum [kohn-soom] Small dumplings stuffed with sautéed greens and cooked on a griddle; see *Cassoni*.

Contadina, alla [AHl-lah kohn-tah-dEE-nah] Peasant style; describes dishes prepared with mushrooms, bacon, Parmesan cheese, and butter.

Contorno [kohn-tOHr-no] A vegetable side dish.

Controfiletto [kohn-troh-fee-lEHt-to] A flavorful cut of beef from the sirloin.

Conza [kOHn-tsah] The stuffing, usually made up of ground beef and cheese, for *sfinciuni*; see *Sfinciuni*.

Copate [koh-pAH-teh] A type of thin wafer flavored with honey and nuts; from Tuscany.

Copero [koh-pEH-ro] Cover.

Coppa [kOHp-pah] Cured pork from the high back of the pig; similar to pancetta.

Coppa arrosta [+ ahr-rOHs-tah] Marinated, roasted *Coppa*.

Coppa di testa [+ dee tEHs-tah] A

sausage made from pig's head.

Coppietta [kohp-pee-EHt-tah] (*Emilia-Romagna*) A local bread from Ferrara.

Coppiette [kohp-pee-EHt-teh] Meat balls; ground beef.

Corarelle [koh-rah-rEHl-leh] Small pasta squares; used in soups.

Coratella [koh-rah-tEHl-lah] (*Lazio*) A dish featuring the heart, lungs, liver, and spleen of lamb sautéed in olive oil and pork fat and seasoned with pepper.

Corbuglione [kohr-boo-lyee-OH-neh] Court bouillon; a seasoned stock used to poach fish.

Corda [kOHr-dah] (*Sardinia*) Strips of tripe slowly cooked on a spit.

Coregoni [koh-reh-gOH-nee] A freshwater fish related to the trout.

Cornetti [kohr-nEHt-tee] A chocolate candy filled with candied fruit.

Cornetti cilindrati [+ chee-leen-drAH-tee] Crescent-shaped *cilandrati*; see *Cilindrati*.

Cornetto [kohr-nEHt-to] (1) Breadstick. (2) Stuffed breakfast pastry.

Coronata [koh-roh-nAH-tah] A local white wine from Liguria.

Corvina veronese [kohr-vEE-nah vay-roh-nEH-seh] A local wine grape from Veneto.

Corzetti (alla polceverasca) [kohr-tsEHt-tee AHl-lah pOHl-cheh-veh-rAHs-kah] Spiral-shaped egg pasta; from Genoa (Liguria).

Coscette [kohs-chEHt-teh] Thighs.

Còscia [kOH-shee-ah] Haunch; hindquarter.

Còscia di capriolo [+ dee kahp-ree-OH-lah] Haunch of venison.

Cosciotto [kOHs-chee-oht-to] Leg.

Costa [kOHs-tah] Rib; also spelled *costole*.

Costada alla pizzaiola [AHl-lah pee-tsah-ee-OH-lah] See *Bistecca alla pizzaiola*.

Costata [kohs-tAH-tah] A rib or T-bone steak.

Costata alla fiorentina [+ AHl-lah fee-oh-rehn-tEE-nah] A thick T-bone steak brushed with olive oil and seasoned with salt and pepper; grilled rare.

Costata di manzo [een-tehr-kohs-tAH-tah dee mAHn-tso] A steak cut from the rib section.

Coste [kOHs-teh] Swiss chard.

Costole [kOHs-tohleh] Ribs; also spelled *costa*.

Costolette [kohs-toh-lEHt-teh] Veal rib chop; sometimes refers to cutlets of veal.

Costolette alla milanese [+ AHl-lah mee-lah-nEH-seh] (*Milan*) A famous dish featuring veal rib chops dipped in egg and bread crumbs and fried in butter.

Costolette di maiale [dee mah-ee-AH-leh] Pork chop.

Costolette di maiale alla modenese [+ AHl-lah moh-deh-nEH-seh] Seasoned pork chops boiled then sautéed in lard; finished with white wine.

Costotelle [kohs-toh-tEHl-leh] Chops.

Cotechino [koh-teh-kEY-no] A large spicy pork sausage from northern Italy; traditionally served with lentils.

Cotechino in galera [+ een gah-lEH-rah] Sausage wrapped in bacon and thinly sliced beef and braised in stock and white wine.

V O C A B U L A R Y

Cotenna [koh-tEHn-nah] Prosciutto rind; used to flavor soups, sauces, and so on.

Cotica [kOH-tee-kah] Pork rind.

Cotichelle [koh-tee-kEHl-leh] A type of pork sausage made with eggs and cheese; from Liguria.

Cotogna [koh-tOH-nyah] Quince.

Cotognate [koh-toh-nyAH-tah] A confection made from quinces and sugar.

Cotoletta [koh-toh-lEH-tah] Cutlet.

Cotolette alla bolognese [koh-toh-lEHt-teh AHl-lah boh-loh-nyEH-seh] Describes chops panfried with prosciutto and topped with cheese.

Cotolette alla milanese [+ mee-lah-nEH-seh] Describes chops dipped in egg and bread crumbs and and panfried.

Cotronese [koh-troh-nEH-seh] Ewe's-milk cheese from Cotrone (Calabria).

Cotto [kOHt-to] Cooked.

Cotto a vapore [+ ah vah-pOH-reh] Steamed.

Cozza pelosa [kOH-tsah peh-lOH-sah] A type of mussel having a shell covered with a hairlike substance.

Cozze [kOH-tseh] Mussels.

Crauti [krAH-oo-tee] Sauerkraut.

Crema [krEH-mah] A term used to describe smooth and creamy preparations that may or may not include cream, i.e., custards, sauces, soups, dessert creams, and so on.

Crema cotta [+ kOHt-tah] Sweetened cream combined with gelatin and poured into molds to set.

Crema della mia nonna [+ dAYl-lah mEE-ah nOHn-nah] A dessert custard made from caramelized sugar, egg yolks, milk, and flavored with citron.

Crema di legumi con crostini al burro [+ dee leh-gOO-mee kohn krohs-tEE-nee ahl bOOr-ro] (*Piedmont*) Cream of vegetable soup garnished with croutons.

Crema d'orzo [+ dee-OHr-tso] A type of barley gruel from Veneto.

Crema d'uova [+ dee-oo-OH-vah] Sweetened egg custard; served as a dessert.

Crema fritta (Veneziana) [+ frEEt-tah veh-neh-tsee-AH-nah] Chilled custard cut into diamonds and dipped in egg whites and then bread crumbs and fried in olive oil; from northern Italy.

Crema inglese [+ een-glEH-seh] A custard sauce made from egg yolks, milk, and sugar.

Crema pasticcera [+ pahs-tee-chEH-rah] Pastry cream; a custard-like preparation made from egg yolks, milk, sugar, and corn or potato starch. It is used as a pastry filling, as a dessert sauce, and as the base for gelato and zuppa inglese.

Crema romana [+ roh-mAH-nah] A mixture of melted chocolate and cream; used as a cake icing or filling.

Creme al burro [krEH-meh ahl bOOr-ro] Buttercream.

Cremino [kreh-mEE-no] Cream cheese.

Creopolion [kreh-oh-poh-lee-ohn] A butcher shop in ancient Rome.

Crescentina [kray-shayn-tEE-nah] (*Emilia-Romagna*) A type of pancake, often prepared with bits of prosciutto or cracklings in the dough; also called *piedone*.

Crescenza [krEH-shehn-tsah] A soft, mild cow's-milk cheese from northern Italy.

Crescia [krEH-shee-ah] A flat cheese bread from Marche; also called *Pizza al Formaggio*.

Crescione [kray-shee-OH-neh] Watercress.

Crespe [krEHs-peh] Crepes.

Crespelle [krehs-pEHl-leh] (1) Crepes. (2) Sweet or savory fritters.

Crespelle alla fiorentina [AHl-lah fee-oh-rehn-tEE-nah] A famous Florentine dish featuring crepes stuffed with spinach, ricotta, and Parmesan cheese; topped with *besciamella* and tomato sauce and baked.

Crespolini al formaggio [krEHs-poh-lee-nee ahl fohr-mAH-jee-o] Cheese and spinach filled crepes.

Crespone [krehs-pOH-neh] A local sausage from Mantua (Lombardy) made from pork, pork fat, beef, and seasoned with garlic.

Creste di gallo [krEHs-teh dee gAHl-lo] Cockscombs.

Cresti di gallo [krEHs-tee dee gAHl-lo] Ridged elbow macaroni featuring a curly mane or "cock's comb" along its convex side.

Creta [krEH-tah] Clay; see *alla Creta*.

Creta, alla Describes foods cooked in a clay pot.

Crispeddi [krees-pEHd-dee] A type of fritter from Sicily.

Crispelle 'mbusse [krees-pEHl-leh eem-bOOs-seh] (*Abruzzi*) Savory crepes seasoned with parsley and nutmeg and served in chicken broth; sometimes stuffed with diced chicken. Also called *scripelle*.

Crispigne [krees-pEE-nyee] A local plant from southern Italy used as a vegetable.

Croccante [kroh-kAHn-teh] Crisp.

Croccante di mandorle [+ dee mAHn-dohr-leh] A crisp confection made from caramelized sugar and almonds; almond brittle.

Crocche [krOH-keh] Croquette.

Crocchette [kroh-kEHt-teh] Croquettes.

Crocette [kroh-chEHt-teh] (1) Baked stuffed figs; served as a dessert in Calabria. (2) (*Marche*) Snails cooked in herb sauce.

Crosetti [kroh-sEHt-tee] A type of pasta from Liguria.

Crosta [krOHs-tah] Crust.

Crostacei [krohs-tAH-cheh-ee] Crustaceans.

Crostata [krohs-tAH-tah] Tart; flan.

Crostata alla napoletana [+ AHl-lah nah-poh-leh-tAH-nah] (*Naples*) A chocolate-apricot tart.

Crostata alla siciliana [+ AHl-lah see-chee-lee-AH-nah] (*Sicily*) A pistachio custard tart.

Crostata di pere alla milanese [+ dee pEH-reh AHl-lah mee-lah-nEH-seh] (*Milan*) A pear tart.

Crostini [krohs-tEE-nee] Small toasted bread pieces topped with various garnishes and served as an appetizer; grilled polenta rounds can also be used in place of the toast.

Crostini alla napoletana [+ AHl-lah nah-poh-leh-tAH-nah] Tiny pizza bites.

Crostini alla provatura [+ AHl-lah proh-vah-tOO-rah] Bread slices

Crostini alla provatura (cont.) dipped in egg and layered with *Provatura* cheese; baked.

Crostini con mozzarella e acciughe [+ kohn moh-tsah-rEHl-lah eh ah-chee-OO-gheh] Small fried sandwiches filled with mozzarella cheese.

Crostini di fegatini [+ dee feh-gah-tEE-nee] Small toasted bread squares spread with chicken livers; served as a garnish or an appetizer.

Crostini di mare [+ dee mAH-reh] Stuffed hollowed-out bread.

Crostini di midollo [+ dee mee-dOHl-lo] Toasted bread spread with ground bone marrow.

Crostini en brodo [+ eh brOH-do] Broth or consommé garnished with croutons.

Crostoli [krohs-tOH-lee] A simple fried cookie from Veneto.

Crotonese [kroh-toh-nEH-seh] A cheese from Crotone (Calabria) similar to pecorino; made from a combination of goat's and ewe's milk.

Crudo [krOO-do] Raw.

Crumiri [kroo-mEE-ree] A specialty cookie of Casale (Piedmont).

Crustulum/clustrum [kroos-too-loom/kloos-troom] A former name for *bruscetta*.

Cucchiaio/cucchiaino [koo-key-AH-ee-o/coo-key-ah-EE-no] Spoon.

Cucciddata [koo-cheed-dAH-tah] A local Sicilian dessert featuring chocolate, nuts, and cream.

Cucculli [koo-kOOl-lee] A fried potato dumpling.

Cucina [koo-chEE-nah] Kitchen; cooking.

Cucina alla graticola [+ AHl-lah grah-tEE-koh-lah] Grill cooking.

Cucina casalinga, la [lah + kah-sah-lEEn-gah] Home cooking.

Cucina, farda [fAHr-dah +] Cook.

Cucina, libro di [lEEb-ro dee +] Cookbook.

Cucina povera, la [+ pOH-veh-rah] Peasant cooking.

Cucinare [koo-cheen-AH-ree] To cook.

Cucuzza [koo-kOO-tsah] A variety of green Italian squash.

Cu'irgionis [koo-eer-jee-oh-nees] Stuffed pasta with spinach and fresh cheese; from Sardinia.

Culatello [koo-lah-tEHl-loh] An excellent pork sausage made from cured pork shoulder and stuffed in pig's bladder; a specialty of Castelmaggiore and Monticello (Emilia-Romagna) and parts of Lombardy..

Culingiones [koo-leen-jee-OH-nehs] (*Sardinia*) Pasta stuffed with spinach and cheese.

Culuriones de patate [koo-loo-ree-OH-nehs dee pah-tAH-tah] A Sardinian specialty featuring large ravioli made from potato dough stuffed with pecorino and spinach; served with tomato sauce.

Culurzones [koo-loor-tsOH-nehs] See *Culurjones de patate*.

Culusciones [koo-loo-shee-oh-nehs] Dough stuffed with vegetables and cheese.

Cumino [koo-mEE-no] Caraway seeds.

Cuocere [koo-OH-cheh-reh] Bake.

Cuore [koo-OH-reh] Heart.

Cupeta [koo-peh-tah] A type of pastry flavored with honey and walnuts; from Lombardy.

Curzié [koor-tsee-EH] (*Emilia-Romagna*) Thin, broad noodles served in broth.

Cuscinetti [koo-zee-nEHt-tee] Literally "small cushions"; typically refers to small bite-sized sandwiches breaded and fried.

Cuscinetti al prosciutto [+ ahl proh-shee-OOt-to] *Cuscinetti* made with prosciutto and cheese.

Cuscinetti di vitello [+ dee vee-tEHl-lo] Roast of veal.

Cuscusu [koos-kOO-soo] Couscous; semolina flakes.

Cuscusu di trapani [+ dee trAH-pah-nee] A specialty of Trapani (Sicily) featuring couscous topped with poached seafood.

Dado [dAH-do] Bouillon cubes; soup base.

Dattero [dAHt-teh-ro] Date.

Dattero (di mare) [+ dee mAH-reh] A type of shellfish; typically used in soups.

Defrutum [deh-frOO-toom] A type of grape syrup used as a sweetener in ancient Rome.

Delicato [day-lee-kAH-to] Fine.

Dente, al [ahl dEHn-teh] "To the tooth"; refers to pasta (originally) and vegetables cooked until just done.

Dente di leone [dEHn-teh dee lee-OH-neh] Dandelion.

Dente, molto al [al mOHl-to +] Describes pasta and vegetables cooked slightly underdone; these foods are usually exposed to more cooking.

Dentice [dEHn-tee-cheh] Dentex; a saltwater fish of high repute.

Denti di cavallo [+ dee kah-vAHl-lo] See *Rigatoni*.

Desinare [deh-zee-nAH-reh] Dinner.

Diamanti [dee-ah-mAHn-tee] Diamond-shaped pasta.

Diavolicchio [dee-ah-voh-lEE-kee-o] The word for chili peppers in parts of southern Italy; also called *diavolillo*.

Diavolilli [dee-ah-voh-lEEl-lee] (1) Small hot red peppers. (2) A sweet almond confection.

Diavolo, alla [AHl-lah dee-AH-voh-lah] Describes highly spiced grilled meats.

Digestivi [dee-jehs-tEE-vee] A liqueur or brandy drunk after a meal.

Dindo [dEEn-do] Turkey.

Dindo alla schiavona [+ AHl-lah skey-ah-vOH-nah] (*Veneto*) Roasted turkey stuffed with a chestnut-prune dressing.

Dita di apostoli [dEE-tah dee ah-pOHs-toh-lee] A dessert crepe filled with sweetened ricotta.

Ditali [dee-tAH-lee] Short, tubed pasta.

Ditalini [dee-tah-lEE-nee] Short, tubed pasta; smaller than *ditali*.

Ditalini rigati [+ ree-gAH-tee] Ridged *ditalini*.

Diverso [dee-vEHr-so] Assorted.

Dolce [dOHl-cheh] Sweet.

Dolce e forte, salsa [sAHl-sah + eh fOHr-teh] A type of sweet and sour sauce made with raisins, cherries, garlic and vinegar; served with game.

Dolce, il Dessert.

Dolce latte [+ lAHt-teh] A cow's-milk cheese similar to Gorgonzola.

Dolce sardo [+ sAHr-do] A soft goat's- or ewe's-milk cheese; from Sardinia.

Dolcetti [dohl-chEHt-tee] Petit fours.

Dolci di riposto [+ dee ree-pOHs-to] (*Sicily*) A small almond paste confection.

Dolci, i [ee dOHl-chee] The Italian word for sweets.

Doppio burro [dOHp-pee-o bOOr-ro] Cream sauce; a rich sauce made by reducing heavy cream and butter until the desired consistency is attained.

Dorata [doh-rAH-tah] John Dory; a firm-fleshed sea fish best cooked by grilling or poaching; also used in fish stews.

Dorato [doh-rAH-to] Describes foods achieving a golden brown color through frying.

Doria, alla [AHl-lah dOH-ree-ah] Describes dishes prepared with cucumbers.

Dose [dOH-seh] A term referring to the amount of a given ingredient.

Dragoncello [drah-gOHn-chehl-lo] Tarragon.

Drogheria [dro-gheh-rEE-ah] Grocery.

Duja [dOO-jah] A clay pot.

Dunderet di patate [doon-deh-reht dee pah-tAH-tah] A type of potato gnocchi from Piedmont.

Duro [dOO-ro] Hard; tough.

E [ay/eh] And.

Echino [eh-kEE-no] Sea urchin.

Einbrennsuppe [ahyn-bren-sOO-peh] A type of porridge made from flour, potatoes, and wine; from Trentino–Alto Adige.

Elegante [ay-lay-gAHn-teh] Elegant.

Elicoidali [eh-lee-koh-ee-dAH-lee] A tubed, ridged pasta similar to *rigatoni*.

Elisir china [ay-lee-sEEr kEY-nah] A local aperitif from Piedmont flavored with quinine.

Elisir d'oropa [+ dee-oo-rOH-pah] (*Piedmont*) An aperitif similar to vermouth.

Emiliano [ay-mEE-lee-ah-no] A hard, grana-like cheese made from cow's milk; from Emilia.

Emilia-Romagna [ay-mee-lEE-ah-roh-mAH-nyah] Perhaps the finest Italian cuisine can be found in this northern province. Prosciutto, *coppa*, pancetta, and mortadella are examples of the region's fine sausages; numerous pasta dishes, seafood specialties, and grana cheese play an important role in the cookery of Emilia-Romagna.

Endiva [ehn-dEE-vah] Chicory; endive.

Epouvantable [eh-poh-oo-vahn-tah-bleh] A Milanese dessert featuring chocolate custard sandwiched between ladyfingers.

Erba luce [EHr-bah lOO-cheh] A local wine grape from Piedmont.

Erbazzone [ehr-bah-tsOH-neh] See *Scarpazzone*.

Erbazzone dolce [+ dOHl-cheh] (*Emilia-Romagna*) An interesting dessert tart utilizing beet greens, ricotta cheese, sugar, and almonds.

Erbe [EHr-beh] Herbs.

Erbette [ehr-bEHt-teh] The name for greens—i.e., chard—in parts of Italy.

Erbivendolo [ehr-bee-vEHn-doh-lo] Produce vendor.

Erdbeertorte [EHrd-behr-tOR-teh] A type of raspberry tart from Veneto.

Espresso [ehs-prEHs-so] See *Caffè espresso*.

Essenza [ehs-sEHn-tsah] Essence.

Est! Est! Est! [ehst ehst ehst] A famous white wine from Lazio.

Estragone [ehs-trah-gOH-neh] The word for tarragon in parts of Italy.

Estratto [Ehs-trAHt-to] Extract; typically refers to tomato or meat extract.

Faggio [fAH-jee-o] The name for mushroom in Florence.

Fagiani al vino di neive [fah-jee-AH-nee ahl vEE-no dee neh-ee-veh] (*Piedmont*) Pheasant braised with white truffles in wine.

Fagiano [fah-jee-AH-no] Pheasant.

Fagiano alla norcina [+ AHl-lah nohr-chEE-nah] Roasted pheasant stuffed with truffles; from Umbria.

Fagioli [fah-jee-OH-lee] Beans.

Fagioli al corallo [+ ahl-koh-rAHl-lo] Green beans.

Fagioli all'uccelletto [+ ahl-oo-chehl-lEHt-to] Beans cooked with tomato, garlic, and sage.

Fagioli con le cotiche [+ kohn leh kOH-tee-keh] Beans slowly cooked with pork in tomato sauce.

Fagioli e cavoli alla gallurese [+ eh kah-vOH-lee AHl-lah gahl-oo-rEH-seh] (*Sardinia*) Red beans cooked with garlic, pork, and greens.

Fagioliera [fah-jee-oh-lee-EH-rah] A plump two-handled clay pot used to bake beans in the oven.

Fagioli in salsa [+ een sAHl-sah] Cold, cooked beans tossed with oil, vinegar, garlic, and anchovies.

Fagiolini [fah-jee-oh-lEE-nee] Green beans.

Fagottini [fah-goht-tEE-nee] "Little bundles"; various doughs stuffed with sweet or savory fillings and served as an antipasto.

Fagottini di Venezia [+ dee veh-nEH-tsee-ah] (*Veneto*) Thin crepes stuffed with raisins and candied fruit.

Falanghina [fah-lahn-ghEE-nah] A white wine grape.

Falso [fAHl-so] False; mock.

Fantasia [fahn-tah-sEE-ah] A word used to describe a variety of aromatic, flavorful dishes.

Far [fahr] A type of grain common in ancient Rome.

Faraona [fah-rah-OH-nah] Guinea hen.

Faraona al vino rosso [+ ahl vEE-noh rOHz-zo] Guinea hen braised in red wine.

Farcia [fAHr-chee-ah] Forcemeat; stuffing.

Farcito [fahr-chEE-to] Stuffed.

Farfalle [fahr-fAHl-leh] "Butterfly"; butterfly-shaped pasta.

Farfalline [fahr-fahl-lEE-neh] Small *farfalle*.

Farfelletta [fahr-fehl-lEHt-tah] See *Farfelle*.

Farina [fah-rEE-nah] Flour.

Farina di grano turco [+ dee grAH-no tOOr-ko] Corn starch; corn flour.

Farina dolce [+ dOHl-cheh] Chestnut flour.

Farina gialla [+ jee-AHl-lah] Cornmeal.

Farinata di ceci [fah-ree-nAH-tah dee chEH-chee] (*Liguria*) A type of polenta made from chickpea flour.

Farro [fAHr-ro] A barley porridge.

Farsumagru [fahr-soo-mAH-groo] (*Sicily*) Braised veal stuffed with a variety of ingredients, including salami, bread, cheese, eggs and herbs; also spelled *farsumauru*.

Faso al fùrn [fAH-so ahl foorn] Baked beans with bacon, garlic, and spices; from Piedmont.

Fatto in casa [fAHt-to een kAH-zah] Homemade; home style.

Fava [fAH-vah] Broad bean.

Fava e lardu [+ eh lAHr-doo] See *Favata*.

Favata [fah-vAH-tah] (*Sardinia*) Fava beans cooked with cabbage, tomatoes, sausage, and salt pork; also called *fava e lardu*.

Fave [fAH-veh] Fava bean.

Fave dei morti [+ dEH-ee mOHr-tee] A small almond confection in the shape of a fava bean; traditionally served on All Soul's Day.

Favette [fah-vEHt-teh] Sweet fritters from Venice.

Favonio [fah-vOH-nee-o] Dry red and white wines from Apulia.

Fazzoletti [fah-tsoh-lEHt-tee] Literally "handkerchiefs." Crepes stuffed with ground meat and cheese.

Fecola di patate [feh-kOH-lah dee pah-tAH-tah] Potato flour.

Fedeli [feh-dEH-lee] Long, fine round pasta noodles slightly thicker than *fedelini*.

Fedelini [feh-deh-lEE-nee] Long, very fine pasta noodles; served in soup. Also known as *tagliolini*,

taglierini, and *tarliarini*.

Fegatelli [feh-gah-tEHl-lee] (*Tuscany*) Pork liver stuffed in caul or crepes and grilled on a spit or fried.

Fegati dolci [fEH-gah-tee dOHl-chee] A sausage made from pork liver and honey.

Fegatini [feh-gah-tEE-nee] Chicken livers.

Fegatini, salsa di [sAHl-sah dee +] *Salsa bianca* flavored with chopped chicken livers.

Fegati pazzi [fEH-gah-tee pAH-tsee] A spicy sausage made from pork liver and hot peppers; from Abruzzi.

Fegato [fEH-gah-to] Liver.

Fegato alla veneziana [+ AHl-lah veh-neh-tsee-AH-nah] (*Veneto*) Liver fried in oil and smothered with caramelized onions.

Fegato di vitello [+ dee vee-tEHl-lo] Calf's liver.

Fegato di vitello alla milanese [+ AHl-lah mee-lah-nEH-seh] Fried, breaded calf's liver.

Fenescecchie [feh-neh-shEH-kee-eh] (*Apulia*) Long tubed pasta noodles.

Ferittus [feh-reet-tOOs] Pasta with tomato and meat sauce; from Sardinia.

Ferri [fEHr-ree] The grill.

Ferri, ai Grilled.

Fesa [fEH-sah] Beef thigh.

Fesa di spalla [+ dee spAHl-lah] A cut of veal from the shoulder area.

Festa [fEHs-tuh] Feast.

Festa di San Giuseppe [+ dee sahn jee-oo-sEHp-peh] Saint Joseph's Day; a traditional spring holiday.

Festonati [fehs-toh-nAH-tee] A

type of pasta resembling a festoon.

Fetta [fEHt-tah] Slice.

Fetta A Sardinian ewe's-milk cheese.

Fettine [feht-tEE-neh] Thin slices of meat.

Fettucce [feht-tOO-cheh] A type of pasta noodle.

Fettuccelle [feht-too-chEHl-leh] A type of pasta noodle.

Fettuccine [feht-too-chEE-nee] A flat noodle about $^3/_8$-inch wide.

Fettuccine al Burro [+ ahl bOOr-ro] Fettuccine tossed with butter.

Fettuccine alla papalina [+ AHl-lah pah-pah-lee-nah] Pasta served with chopped pork and mushrooms.

Fettuccine alla romana [+ AHl-lah roh-mAH-nah] Fettuccine tossed with butter and Parmesan cheese.

Fettunta [fayt-tOOn-tah] (*Tuscany*) Grilled bread slices rubbed with garlic and olive oil; the Tuscan name for *bruschetta*.

Fiamifferi [fee-ah-mEEf-feh-ree] Matches.

Fiandolein [fee-ahn-doh-leh-een] A type of bread pudding popular in parts of northern Italy.

Fiasco [fee-AHs-ko] A straw-covered bottle.

Fichi [fEE-kee] Figs.

Fichi d'India [+ dEEn-dee-ah] "Indian figs"; the nickname for the prickly pear in parts of southern Italy.

Fichi secchi [+ sEH-kee] Dried figs.

Fico [fEE-ko] Fig.

Filetti di tacchino alla bolognese [fee-lEHt-tee dee tah-kEE-no AHl-lah boh-loh-nyEE-seh] Tur-key breast roasted with ham.

Filetto [fee-lEHt-to] Fillet.

Filetto di bue [+ dee bOO-eh] Fillet of beef.

Filone [fee-lOH-neh] See *Schienali*.

Finanziera [fee-nahn-tsee-EH-rah] A rich mixture of porcini mushrooms, truffles, cockscombs, and chicken livers in a marsala wine sauce; used as a garnish or pasta sauce.

Finferlo [fEEn-fayr-lo] Chanterelle mushroom.

Fino [fEE-no] Fine.

Finocchio [fee-nOH-key-o] Fennel.

Finocchiona [fee-noh-key-OH-nah] (*Tuscany*) A type of mortadella flavored with fennel.

Fiocchetto [fee-oh-kEHt-to] (1) Pork shoulder. (2) A spicy ham enclosed in sausage casing.

Fiocci [fee-OH-chee] Bowtie pasta; *farfalle*.

Fiocco [fee-OHk-ko] A cut of veal from the breast.

Fiochetti [fee-oh-kEHt-tee] Short rolled bow tie-shaped pasta.

Fior d'Alpe [fEE-ohr dAHl-peh] A cow's-milk cheese from Lombardy similar to Belpaese.

Fior d'Alpi [fEE-ohr dAHl-pee] A sweet liqueur flavored with herbs.

Fior di latte [+ dee lAHt-teh] (1) (*Campania*) The name for mozzarella cheese when it is made from cow's milk; also known as *Scamorze*. (2) A caramel-custard dessert.

Fiorentina, (alla) [fee-oh-rehn-tEE-nah] "In the style of Florence"; refers to dishes cooked with olive oil, garlic, and herbs.

Fiorentina, la An Italian word for T-bone steak.

Fiore sardo [fee-OH-reh sAHr-do] A Sardinian grating cheese made from ewe's milk.

Fiori [fee-OH-ree] Flowers; blossoms.

Fiori di zucca [+ dee tsOOk-kah] Zucchini blossoms.

Fiori di zucca alla padovana [+ AHl-lah pah-doh-vAH-nah] Fritters made from zucchini blossoms.

Firenze [fee-rEHn-tseh] Florence; one of Italy's great culinary cities situated in northern Tuscany. Regional specialties include *Bistecca alla fiorentina, Pollo alla diavola, Minestrone alla fiorentina, Fritto misto, Fagioli all'uccelletto,* and *Acquacotta*.

Firriettu, a [feer-ree-EHt-too] Describes tubed noodles made by wrapping fresh pasta sheets around a wire.

Fischietti [fees-key-EHt-tee] Very small tubed noodles.

Focacce [foh-kAH-cheh] (*Veneto*) A traditional holiday sweet pastry.

Focaccette [foh-kah-chEHt-teh] Small fried turnovers stuffed with cheese and herbs.

Focaccia [foh-kAH-chee-ah] flat, round bread often seasoned with rosemary.

Focaccia di vitello [+ dee vee-tEHl-lo] Ground veal pattie.

Focaccia castelnovese [+ kahs-tEHl-noh-vEH-seh] A Ligurian pastry made with cornmeal and pine nuts.

Focaccia vicentina [+ vee-chehn-tEE-nah] A special cookie made in Vicenza (Veneto) during Easter.

Focolare [foh-koh-lAH-reh] Fireplace; stove.

Foggiano [fOH-jee-ah-no] A local ewe's-milk cheese from Sardinia.

Fogher [foh-ghEHr] A type of stove.

Fogli di musica [fOH-lyee dee mOO-see-kah] (*Sardinia*) A flat, crisp bread made from hard wheat. Also called *Carasau* and *Carte di musica*.

Foglie di alloro [fOH-lyeh dee ahl-lOH-ro] Bay leaves.

Foijoeu de Spagna [[foh-ee-joh-eh-oo de spAH-nyah] Tripe cooked with beans; from Lombardy.

Foiolo [foh-ee-OH-lo] Tripe.

Fondi di carciofo [fOHn-dee dee kahr-chee-OH-fo] Artichoke hearts.

Fonduta [fohn-dOO-tah] (*Piedmont*) A cheese fondue made with butter, egg yolks, and fontina cheese; served with *crostini* or crusty bread.

Fongadina [fohn-gah-dEE-nah] (*Veneto*) A rich stew made with lamb's, or calf's, offal.

Fontal [fohn-tAHl] A cow's-milk cheese from northeast Italy similar to fontina.

Fontina (*Val d'Aosta*) [fohn-tEE-nah vahl dah-OHs-tah] A mild, delicate, cow's-milk cheese produced in the Val d'Aosta; considered one of Italy's great cheeses.

Forchetta [fohr-kEHt-tah] Fork.

Forma [fOHr-mah] Mold.

Formagella [fohr-mah-jEHl-lah] A cow's-milk cheese from Brescia (Lombardy).

Formaggino [fohr-mAH-jee-no] Processed cheese.

Formaggio [fohr-mAH-jee-o] The Italian word for cheese.

Formaggio di crema [+ dee krEH-mah] Cream cheese.

Formato [fohr-mAH-to] Loaf.

Formato di carne [+ dee kAHr-neh] Meatloaf.

Fornaio [fohr-nAH-ee-o] Baker.

Forno [fOHr-no] (1) Oven. (2) Bakery.

Forno, al Baked.

Forte [fOHr-teh] Strong.

Fracassare [frah-kahs-sAH-reh] To cut or break meat in small pieces.

Fracosta di bue [frahs-kOH-tah dee bOO-eh] Boneless rib steak.

Fra diavolo [frah dee-AH-voh-lo] Describes foods (usually lobster) cooked or served with a spicy tomato sauce.

Fragile [frAH-jee-leh] See *Pasta frolla fragile*.

Fragole [frAH-goh-leh] Strawberries.

Fragole di bosco [+ dee bOHs-ko] Wild strawberries.

Fragoline [frAH-goh-lee-neh] Small wild strawberries.

Fragoline di mare [+ dee mAH-reh] "Sea strawberry"; the Italian name for a variety of small squid.

Francesina [frahn-cheh-sEE-nah] Breadstick.

Frantoiana [frahn-toh-ee-AH-nah] Bean soup.

Frascati [frahs-kAH-tee] A highly regarded white wine from Frascati (Lazio).

Frattaglie [fraht-tAH-lyeh] Giblets.

Freddo [frEHd-do] Cold.

Fregnacce [fray-nyAH-cheh] Crepes (*crespelle*) served with fresh cheese; from Lazio.

Fregolata [fray-goh-lAH-tah] (*Venice*) Rich almond cookies.

Frègula [frEH-goo-lah] (*Sardinia*) Small semolina dumplings flavored with saffron; served in soups.

Frègula cun còcciule [+ koon kOH-chee-oo-leh] (*Sardinia*) A clam and dumpling soup; see *Frègula*.

Freisa [frEH-ee-sah] A red wine from Piedmont.

Fresa [frEH-sah] A Sardinian cow's-milk cheese.

Fresco [frEHs-ko] Fresh; cool.

Fricando/fricandeau [free-kahn-dOH/free-kahn-doo] Veal braised in white wine with bacon and marsala wine.

Fricassata [free-kahs-sAH-tah] Stewed sheep offal.

Fricassea [free-kahs-sEH-ah] (*Liguria*) Chicken and vegetables stewed in butter, lemon juice, and stock and enriched with egg yolks; lamb is sometimes substituted for the chicken.

Frico [frEE-ko] Hard *grana*-type cheese sliced and fried in olive oil until crisp.

Frienno magnanno [free-EHn-no mah-nyAHn-no] The Neapolitan name for *fritto misto*.

Friggere [frEE-jeh-reh] Fry.

Friggere in padella [+ een pah-dEHl-lah] To fry in a frying pan.

Friggitore [free-jee-tOH-reh] A café specializing in fried foods.

Frisa [frEE-sah] A local Apulian bread.

Frisceu [free-shEE-oo] Vegetable fritters.

Friscieù [free-shee-eh-OO] An apple fritter.

Frisedda [free-sEHd-dah] A crusty roll popular in southern Italy.

Frìtole [frEE-toh-leh] Small sweet fritters.

Frittata [freet-tAH-tah] A flat, round omelet.

Frittata genovese [+ jeh-noh-vEH-seh] A flat omelet seasoned with basil, fresh spinach, and cheese.

Frittatine [freet-tah-tEE-neh] Thin, fine omelets; typically stuffed.

Frittatine di patate [+ dee pah-tAH-tah] Potato pancakes.

Frittedda alla palermitana [freet-tEHd-dah AHl-lah pah-lEHr-mee-tah-nah] A Sicilian dish of young, fresh artichokes, peas, and fava beans slowly cooked in olive oil and seasoned with fennel.

Frittella [freet-tEHl-lah] Fritter; pancake.

Frittelle [freet-tEHl-leh] A type of pasta.

Frittelle di polenta [+ dee poh-lEHn-tah] Cornmeal fritters.

Frittelloni di Cervia [freet-tehl-lOH-nee dee chEHr-vee-ah] Spinach and cheese fritters.

Fritto [frEEt-to] Fried; fried food.

Fritto alla pescatora [+ AHl-lah pehs-kah-tOH-rah] Whole fish dredged in flour and fried.

Fritto allo stecco [+ AHl-lo stEHk-ko] Skewers of small meat chunks breaded and fried; from Liguria.

Fritto del così [+ dehl koh-zEE] (*Abruzzi*) A small cheese sandwich which is dipped in batter and fried; typically made with *scamorza* cheese.

Fritto di pesce [+ dee pEH-sheh] Fried fish.

Frittole [frEEt-toh-leh] (1) (*Calabria*) A dish of slowly cooked pork fat and meat. (2) (*Venice*) Fritter.

Fritto misto [+ mEEs-to] Mixed fried foods. *Il grande fritto misto*

consists of an entire meal based on fried foods, from the antipasto to the dessert.

Fritto misto di pesce [+ dee pEH-sheh] Assorted fried fish.

Frittura [freet-tOO-ruh] Fried dish.

Frittura di mitili [+ dee mEE-tee-lee] Fried mussels.

Frittura di rane [+ dee rAH-neh] Fried frog's legs.

Frittura mista [+ mEEs-tuh] The name for *fritto misto* in parts of Italy.

Frittura secca [+ sEHk-kah] Fried meat and cheese fritters.

Friuli [free-OO-lee] See *Venezia Giulia*.

Frizzante [freets-tsAHn-teh] Sparkling.

Frullare [frool-lAH-reh] To whisk.

Frullato [frool-AH-to] Whipped.

Frullato di frutta [+ dee frOO-tah] A fruited milk shake.

Frullato di latte [+ dee lAHt-teh] Milk shake.

Frullino [frool-lEE-no] A special wooden spoon used to whip various preparations.

Frumento [froo-mEHm-to] Wheat.

Frutta [frOOt-tah] Fruit.

Frutta candita [+ kahn-dEE-tah] Candied fruit.

Frutta cotta [+ kOHt-tah] Cooked or stewed fruit.

Frutta dei morti [+ dEH-ee mOHr-tee] A Sicilian pastry flavored with almonds and candied fruit.

Frutta di stagione [+ dee stah-jee-OH-neh] Fruit in season.

Frutta fresca [+ frEHs-kah] Fresh fruit.

Frutta sciroppata [+ shee-rohp-pAH-tah] Fruit cooked in syrup.

Frutta secca [+ sEHk-kah] Dried fruit.

Frutti alla marturana [frOOt-tee AHl-lah mahr-too-rAH-nah] Almond paste candies resembling miniture fruits.

Frutti di mare [frOOt-tee dee mAH-reh] Seafood.

Frutti misti [+ mEEs-tee] Mixed fruit.

Fruttivendolo [+ vEHn-doh-lo] Produce vendor.

Fugassa [foo-gAHs-sah] A local name for *focaccia* in parts of Italy.

Fugazza [foo-gAH-tsah] *Focaccia.*

Fumare [foo-mAH-reh] Smoke.

Funghetti [foon-ghEHt-tee] A mushroom-shaped sweet pastry from Marche.

Funghetto [foon-ghEHt-to] See *Trifolati.*

Funghi [fOOn-ghee] Mushrooms.

Funghi fritti [+ frEEt-tee] Fried mushrooms.

Funghi porcini [+ pohr-chEE-nee] Boletus.

Funghi ripieni [+ ree-pee-EH-nee] Stuffed mushrooms.

Funghi secchi [+ sEH-chee] Dried mushrooms.

Funghi sott'olio ed aceto [+ soht-OH-lee-oh ehd ah-chEH-to] Marinated mushrooms.

Fuoco [foo-OH-ko] Fire.

Furmai [foo-mAH-ee] A cow's-milk cheese produced in the Val Chiavenna in Lombardy.

Fusilli [foo-sEE-lee] Thin spiral-shaped pasta.

Fusilli bucati [+ boo-kAH-tee] Short, tightly wound pasta springs.

Fuso [fOO-so] Melted.

Gabana [gah-bAH-nah] (*Friuli*) A holiday pastry composed of rolled puff pastry filled with chocolate chips, dried fruits, and nuts.

Galani [gah-lAH-nee] (*Venice*) A sweet fried pastry.

Galantina [gah-lahn-tEE-nah] A dish featuring whole boneless fish or poultry (usually) stuffed with layers of lean meat strips; it is then wrapped in cheesecloth and poached in stock. The *galantina* is chilled and sliced prior to serving.

Galantina tartufata [+ tahr-too-fAH-tah] Truffles coated with aspic.

Galinella [gah-lee-nEHl-lah] Guinea fowl.

Gallette [gahl-lEHt-teh] A type of crispy peasant bread.

Galletti [gahl-lEHt-tee] Rock cornish hens.

Gallina [gahl-lEE-nah] Hen.

Gallinaccio [gahl-lee-nAH-chee-o] An Italian name for the chanterelle mushroom.

Gallina faraona [+ fah-rah-OH-nah] Guinea hen.

Gallina regina [+ ray-gEE-nah] Hazel hen.

Gallinella [gahl-lee-nEHl-lah] Spring chicken.

Gallo [gAHl-lo] Stewing chicken.

Gallo di montagna [+ dee mohn-tAH-nyah] Grouse.

Gamba [gAHm-bah] Leg.

Gamberello [gahm-beh-rEHl-lo] Prawn.

Gamberetto [gahm-beh-rEHt-to] Shrimp.

Gamberi [gAHm-beh-ree] Crayfish.

Gamberi imperiali [+ eem-peh-ree-AH-lee] Prawn.

Gambero rosso [gahm-bEH-ro rOHs-so] A large, reddish shrimp.

Gambette di rana [gahm-bEHt-teh dee rAH-nah] Frog's legs.

Gambon [gAHm-bohn] A type of ham from northern Italy.

Garetto [gah-rEHt-to] Shin; knuckle.

Garganelli [gahr-gahn-EHl-lee] A pasta shape resembling ridged *penne*.

Garibaldi, salsa [sAHl-sah gah-ree-bAHl-dee] Brown sauce seasoned with capers, anchovies, and curry.

Garmugia [gahr-moo-jee-ah] A Tuscan dish featuring beef fried in olive oil with fresh artichokes.

Garofolato [gah-roh-foh-lAH-to] Beef stew seasoned with cloves.

Garum [gAH-room] A spice mix used in ancient Rome.

Gasse [gAHs-seh] Small bow-tie pasta.

Gattinara [gaht-tee-nAH-rah] A fine red wine from Piedmont.

Gattuccio [gaht-tOO-chee-o] Dog-fish.

Gelateria [jeh-lah-teh-rEE-ah] Ice cream shop.

Gelatina [jeh-lah-tEE-nah] Aspic jelly.

Gelatina di frutta [+ dee frOOt-tah] Fruit jelly.

Gelatina di maiale [+ dee mah-ee-AH-leh] Cold aspic-coated pork.

Gelato [jeh-lAH-to] Custard-based (egg yolks and milk) ice cream.

Genepì [jeh-neh-pEE] A local herb liqueur from Abruzzi.

Génery [jEH-neh-ree] A type of *grappa* flavored with herbs.

Génova [jEH-noh-vah] Genoa. A port city located in Liguria famous for fine dining. Ravioli, gnocchi,

basil, pine nuts, and pesto are characteristic of Genoese cooking.

Genovese, alla [AHl-lah jeh-noh-vEH-seh] Refers to dishes prepared with basil, garlic, olive oil, and sometimes pine nuts.

Germano reale [jehr-mAH-no reh-AH-leh] A variety of wild duck.

Gesmini [jehs-mEE-nee] (*Sardinia*) A sweet almond-flavored pastry.

Ghiacciato [ghee-ah-chee-AH-to] (1) Iced; well chilled. (2) A drink made of fruit juice mixed with crushed ice.

Ghiaccio [ghee-AH-chee-o] Ice.

Ghiaie della furba [ghee-AH-ee-eh] A dry red wine from Tuscany.

Ghianda [ghee-AHn-dah] Acorn.

Ghiotta [ghee-OHt-tah] (1) Gravy. (2) A spicy fish soup from Sicily.

Ghiozzo [ghee-OH-tso] Gudgeon; a small freshwater fish best eaten fried.

Gialletti/giallettini [jee-ahl-lEHt-tee/jee-ahl-leht-tEE-nee] A sweet Venetian cookie flavored with pine nuts, raisins, and lemon; also called *zaletti*.

Giallino [jee-ahl-lEE-no] Chanterelle mushroom.

Giallo [jee-AHl-lo] Yellow.

Gianchetti [jee-ahn-kEHt-tee] Freshly hatched fish; commonly used in fritters and omelets. Also called *nunnate*.

Gianduia [jee-ahn-dOO-ee-ah] (*Piedmont*) A chocolate-hazelnut custard served as a dessert.

Gianduiotti/giandujotti [jee-ahn-dOO-ee-oht-tee/jee-ahn-doo-joht-tee] A chocolate confection flavored with hazelnuts; from Turin (Piedmont).

Giardiniera di Sottaceti [jee-ahr-dee-nee-EH-rah dee soht-tah-chEH-tee] Pickled vegetables.

Ginepro [jee-nEH-pro] Juniper.

Ginestrata [jee-nEH-strah-tah] An ancient soup composed of chicken broth enriched with egg yolks and seasoned with cinnamon and nutmeg.

Gioddu [jee-OHd-doo] Junket; a sweet, custard-like dessert made with rennet.

Giorno, del [dehl jee-OHr-no] Of the day.

Giovane [jee-OH-vah-neh] Young.

Girasole [jee-rah-sOH-leh] Sunflower.

Giro [jEE-ro] Turn; refers to the turns of the laminated dough used in preparing puff pastry (*sfoglia*).

Gliumariedd [lyee-oo-mah-ree-EHd] See *Gnumeredd.*

Gnocchetti cacio e ouva [nyoh-kEHt-yee kAH-chee-oh eh oo-OH-vah] Egg and cheese dumplings.

Gnocchetti di fegato [+ dee fEH-gah-to] Liver dumplings.

Gnocchetti sardi [+ sAHr-dee] Short rolled bullet or "sardine" shaped pasta.

Gnocchi [nyOH-key] Small tender dumplings made from semolina flour, wheat flour, or potatoes; served like pasta.

Gnocchi alla romana [+ AHl-lah roh-mAH-no] Dumplings made with semolina, eggs, milk, and cheese.

Gnocchi di farina [+ dee fah-rEE-nah] Flour dumplings.

Gnocchi di latte [+ dee lAHt-teh] Dumplings boiled in milk.

Gnocchi di magro [+ dee mAHg-ro] Dumplings made with whole-wheat and rye flours.

Gnocchi di patata [+ dee pah-tAH-tah] Potato dumplings.

Gnocchi di riso [+ dee rEE-so] Rice dumplings.

Gnocchi verdi [+ vEHr-dee] Spinach dumplings.

Gnocco [nyOHk-ko] (*Emilia-Romagna*) Flat bread.

Gnocco fritto [+ frEEt-to] Fried dough cooked in lard.

Gnumeredd [nyoo-meh-rEHd] (*Southern Italy*) Roasted baby goat or lamb; there are several regions enjoying their own versions of this dish.

Gnummarieddi [nyoom-mah-ree-EHd-dee] See *Gnumeredd.*

Gò [goh] Goby; a small sea fish.

Gobidi [goh-bEE-dee] A local word for *gò*; see *Gò.*

Goccia [gOH-chee-ah] Drop.

Gonfietti [gohn-fee-EHt-tee] Small pastry turnovers stuffed with cheese and fried; served as an antipasto.

Gorgonzola [gohr-gohn-tsOH-lah] A famous blue-veined cheese from Gorgonzola, near Milan; made with cow's milk.

Gorgonzola bianco [+ bee-AHn-ko] White Gorgonzola.

Gragnano [grah-nyAH-no] A red wine produced in Naples.

Gramigna [grah-mEE-nyah] Thin, short, tubed pasta. Also called *gramigna bucata.*

Gramigna Rigata [+ ree-gAH-tah] Ridged *gramigna.*

Grana [grAH-nah] The collective term for hard, grainy, grating Italian cheeses.

Granatina [grah-nah-tEE-nah] A drink made with fruit syrup and crushed ice; pomegranate syrup.

Gran bollito misto [grahn bohl-lEE-to mEEs-to] See *Bollito misto.*

Gran Bui [grahn-bOO-ee] The name in Piedmont for *bollito misto.*

Granceola/granseola [grahn-chEH-oh-luh/grahn-sEH-oh-luh] Spider crab.

Granchio [grAHn-key-o] A variety of small crab.

Grande [grAHn-deh] Big.

Grande fritto misto [+ frEEt-to mEEs-to] See *Fritto misto.*

Granelli [grah-nEHl-lee] Testicles; sheep and calf testicles are most commonly eaten.

Grani di carvi [grAH-nee dee kAHr-vee] Caraway seeds.

Granita [grah-nEE-tah] A sweetened, frozen dessert ice; commonly flavored with lemon or coffee.

Grano [grAH-no] Grain; wheat.

Grano saraceno [+ sah-rah-chEH-no] Buckwheat.

Grano turco [grAH-noh tOOr-ko] Maize; corn.

Granseole [grahn-sEH-oh-leh] A local Sardinian name for a variety of crab.

Grappa [grAHp-pah] A clear Italian liqueur made from grape seeds and skins left in the wine press after the juice has been extracted.

Grasso [grAHs-so] Fat.

Grata [grAH-tah] Grating.

Gratella [grah-tEHl-lah] A cast iron stove top grill.

Gratellata [grah-tehl-lAH-tah] Grilled meat.

Graticola [grah-tEE-koh-lah] Gridiron; broiler.

Gratinata [grah-tee-nAH-tah] Refers to dishes that are topped with bread crumbs and grated cheese and browned in the oven or under the broiler.

Grattato [graht-tAH-to] Grated.

Grattugia [graht-tOO-gee-ah] Hand grater.

Grattugiatto [graht-too-jee-AHt-to] Grated.

Greco [grEH-ko] A white wine grape.

Greco di Tufo [+ dee tOO-fo] (*Campania*) A dry white wine of fine quality.

Gremolada/gremalata [greh-mah-lAH-dah/greh-mah-lAH-tah] A combination of grated lemon rind, chopped garlic, and chopped parsley. Sometimes anchovies are added to the mixture; used as a seasoning.

Grießnocken [grEHs-nOk-ahn] (*Trentino*) Dumpling soup.

Grifole [gree-fOH-leh] A variety of wild mushroom.

Grigio [grEE-jee-o] Gray.

Griglia [grEE-lyee-ah] Grill.

Griglia, alla Grilled.

Grigliata [gree-lyee-AH-tah] Grilled foods, usually an assortment.

Grigliata di carne [+ dee kAHr-neh] Assorted grilled meats.

Grignolino [gree-nyoh-lEE-no] A red table wine from Piedmont.

Grissini [grees-sEE-nee] (*Turin*) Bread sticks.

Grissini rubata [+ roo-bAH-tah] *Grissini* somewhat larger than the typical product.

Grissini stira [+ stEE-rah] Long thin grissini.

Grive [grEE-veh] A pork liver sausage flavored with juniper; from Piedmont.

Gronco [grOHn-ko] Conger eel; also spelled *grongo*.

Grongo [grOHn-go] See *Gronco*.

Grosso rigato [grOHs-so ree-gAH-to] A short fat pasta noodle; ridged.

Groviera italiano [groh-vee-EH-rah ee-tah-lee-AH-no] An Italian version of Gruyère cheese.

Guancia/guanciale [goo-AHn-chee-ah/goo-ahn-chee-AH-leh] Cured pork's jowl; similar to pancetta.

Guarnito [goo-ahr-nEE-to] Garnished.

Guarnitura [goo-ahr-nee-tOO-rah] Garnish.

Guastella [goo-ahs-tEHl-lah] (*Sicily*) Stuffed bread.

Guazzetto [goo-ahts-tsEHt-to] An aromatic stew.

Guazzetto, in Describes fish that is cooked in a white wine sauce.

Guelfus [goo-ayl-foos] (*Sardinia*) A type of pastry made with almonds.

Gustare [goos-tAH-reh] Taste.

Gustosa, salsa [sAHl-sah goos-tOH-zah] A spicy cold sauce composed of mayonnaise, gherkins, capers, onions, chili peppers, freshly ground black pepper, and salt; served with fish and meat.

Hamin [hAH-meen] Pasta noodles tossed with goose fat, pine nuts, and raisins and baked; from Ferrara (Emilia-Romagna).

Idrati di carbonio [ee-drAH-tee dee kahr-bOH-nee-o] Carbohydrates.

Imbottito [eem-boht-tEE-to] Stuffed.

Impanadas [eem-pah-nAH-dahs] (*Sardinia*) A savory meat turnover.

Impanare [eem-pah-nAH-reh] To roll in bread crumbs.

Impanato [eem-pah-nAH-to] Breaded.

Impannata, mozzarella [moh-tsah-rEHl-lah eem-pahn-nAH-tah] Mozzarella slices breaded and fried.

Impastare [eem-pahs-tAH-reh] Knead; blend.

Impasto [eem-pAHs-to] Bread dough.

Imposata [eem-poh-sAH-tah] A type of ricotta; often sweetened and used as a cannoli filling.

Incanestrato [een-kah-nay-strAH-to] "In a basket"; refers to cheeses drained in a basket.

Incasciata [een-kah-shee-AH-tah] A type of savory pie made with ground meat, tomatoes, hard-cooked eggs, and grated cheese.

Incavolata [een-kah-voh-lAH-tah] A hearty white bean soup with red cabbage, tomatoes, and bacon; from Tuscany.

Indivia [een-dEE-vee-ah] Chicory; endive.

Indivia Belga [+ bEHl-gah] Belgian endive. Also called *indivia belga*.

Inferno [een-fEHr-no] A popular wine from the Valtellina Valley (Lombardy).

Infusione [een-foo-see-OH-neh] Infusion.

Inglese, all [ahl een-glEH-seh] "In the style of England"; describes certain dishes served with melted butter.

Insaccato [een-sahk-kAH-to] A word for sausages that are enclosed in a casing.

Insalata [een-sah-lAH-tah] Salad.

Insalata di campo [+ dee kAHm-po] Dandelion.

Insalatiera [een-sah-lah-tee-EH-rah] Salad bowl.

Insaporire [een-sah-poh-rEE-reh] Flavor.

Insipido [een-sEE-pee-do] Insipid; tasteless.

Intestino [een-tehs-tEE-no] Entrails.

Intingolo [een-tEEn-goh-lo] A thick sauce or stew from southern Italy; typically served with bread.

Intinto [een-tEEn-to] Sauce.

Involtini [een-vohl-tEE-nee] Thinly sliced stuffed meat or fish.

Involtini saporiti [+ sah-poh-rEE-tee] (*Abruzzi*) Thinly sliced veal strips stuffed with mortadella sausage seasoned with herbs.

Iota friulana [ee-OH-tah free-oo-lAH-nah] (*Friuli*) A hearty soup containing beans; also spelled *jota*.

Iota triestina [+ tree-ays-tEE-nuh] (*Venezia Giulia*) Soup made from beans, cabbage, potatoes, and smoked pork.

Italia [ee-tAHl-ee-ah] Italy.

Italico [ee-tAH-lee-ko] The collective name for certain soft cheeses similar to Belpaese.

'J Jàbre [eej jAHb-reh] (*Eastern Emilia-Romagna*) Sun-dried apple slices.

Jota, la [lah jOH-tuh] See *Iota triestina* and *Iota fruilana*.

Kanostrelle [kah-noh-strEHl-leh] A small basket-shaped pastry.

Kapriol [kahp-ree-OHl] A juniper-flavored liqueur.

Kastanientorte [kahs-tAHn-ee-ayn-tOHr-teh] A chestnut tart; from Alto Adige.

Knodel/knoedel [nyoh-duhl] A type of dumpling from Alto Adige.

Knolle [nyoh-leh] (*Valle d'Aosta*) A type of gnocchi made from flour and cornmeal.

Krapfen [krAHp-fehn] (*Alto Adige*) Filled doughnuts; cream puffs.

Krapfen tirolese [+ tee-roh-lEH-seh] (*Alto Adige*) Jelly doughnuts.

Kuscus [kOOs-koos] (*Sicily*) A dessert made with couscous and nuts.

Laàn [lah-AHn] A flat, wide noodle similar to fettuccine; from Basilicata.

Lacciada [lah-chee-AH-dah] (*Lombardy*) A simple crepe typically flavored with grapes or grape seeds; see *Laciaditt*.

Laciaditt [lah-chee-ah-dEEt] A sweet crepe flavored with sugar and spices.

Lacrima Christi [lAH-kree-mah krEEs-tee] A notable red or white wine from Campania.

Ladano [lah-dAH-no] A large freshwater fish popular in parts of northern Italy.

Lagane [lAH-gah-neh] A local word for lasagne (noodle) in parts of southern Italy.

Laganelle [lah-gah-nEHl-leh] A long, wide noodle.

Laganum [lah-gah-noom] An ancient name for lasagna.

Lambrusco [lahm-brOOs-ko] Famous semi-dry sparkling red wines from Emilia-Romagna. Lambrusco is also the name of the grape used to produce the wine.

Lambrusco di sorbara [+ dee sohr-bAH-rah] One of the finest Lambrusco wines; from Modena.

Lampascioni [lahm-pah-shee-OH-nee] A bitter, edible bulb used like onions in southern Italy.

Lampone [lahm-pOH-neh] Raspberry.

Lampreda [lahm-prEH-dah] Lamprey eel.

Lardellare [lahr-dayl-lAH-reh] To lard; to stud or insert fat (lard, pancetta, ham, salt pork, and so on) into a lean piece of meat.

Lardelli [lahr-dEHl-lee] Larding fat; see *Lardellare*.

Lardo [lAHr-do] Lard. *Lardo* sometimes refers to bacon.

Lasagna da fornel [lah-sAH-nyah dah fOHr-nehl] (*Veneto*) Lasagna noodles sweetened with sugar, poppy seeds, nuts, and raisins; a traditional holiday dish.

Lasagne [lah-sAH-nyeh] A wide, flat noodle sometimes having a curly edge. Lasagnza is typically prepared by layering the noodles with sauce, cheese, meat, vegetables, etc.

Lasagnette [lah-sah-nyEHt-teh] See *Mafalde*.

Lasca [lAHs-kah] A highly regarded freshwater fish found in Lake Trasimeno (Umbria).

Lattaiolo [[laht-tah-ee-OH-lo] A dessert custard made from milk, eggs, and sugar.

Latte [lAHt-teh] Milk.

Latte alla grotta [+ AHl-lah grOHt-tah] A Ligurian dessert featuring sweet meringue poached in milk or syrup.

Latte brusco [+ brOOs-ko] (*Liguria*) Small squares of firm (chilled) savory custard dipped in bread crumbs and fried.

Lattemiele [laht-tay-mee-EH-leh] Sweetened whipped cream; a popular Milanese dessert.

Lattuga [laht-tOO-gah] Lettuce.

Lattuga romana [+ roh-mAH-nah] Romaine lettuce.

Lattume [laht-tOO-meh] Soft roe.

Lauro [lAH-oo-roh] Laurel; bay leaf.

Laziale, alla [AHl-lah lAH-tsee-ah-leh] "Latium-style"; usually indicates that onions are highlighted in a dish.

Lazio [lAH-tsee-o] See *Rome*.

Lebernocken [lEH-buhr-nOH-kuhn] (*Veneto*) Liver dumplings.

Leberreis [lEH-buhr-rahys] A type of rice dumpling from Veneto.

Legumi [lay-gOO-mee] Legumes; vegetables.

Lenticchia [layn-tEE-kee-ah] Lentil.

Lenticchie e fagioli [layn-tee-kee-eh eh fah-jee-OH-lee] A dish popular in Tuscany featuring lentils and beans.

Lenticchie stufate [+ stoo-fAH-teh] Lentil stew.

Lepre [lEH-preh] Hare.

Lepre alla maremmana [+ AHl-lah mah-rEHm-mah-nah] Stewed hare served in a sweet and sour sauce.

Lepre alla veneta [+ AHl-lah vEH-neh-tah] Hare cooked on a spit.

Lepudrida [leh-poo-dree-dah] (*Sardinia*) A hearty meat stew.

Lessare [lehs-sAH-reh] To boil.

Lesso [lEHs-so] (1) Boiled meat. (2) Boiled.

Lesso Misto [+ mEEs-to] The word for *bollito misto* in parts of Italy; see *Bollito misto*.

Libum [lEE-boom] A savory cheese cake of ancient Roman.

Lievitare [lee-eh-vee-tAH-reh] Rise; leaven.

Lievito di birra [lee-EH-vee-to dee bEEr-rah] Yeast.

Lievito in polvere [+ een pOHl-veh-reh] Baking powder.

Lievito naturale [+ nah-too-rAH-leh] Sourdough starter.

Liguria [lee-gOO-ree-ah] Fresh fruits, vegetables, and herbs play a major role in this coastal region's local cuisine. Fish stews, honey, and tripe are also much utilized, as are pine nuts and olive oil.

Limonata [lee-moh-nAH-tah] Lemonade.

Limone [lee-mOH-neh] Lemon.

Lingua [lEEn-goo-ah] Tongue.

Lingua di bue [+ dee bOO-eh] Ox tongue.

Lingue di passero [lEEn-goo-eh dee pAHs-seh-ro] "Sparrow's tongue"; a long thin pasta noodle.

Linguine [leen-goo-EE-nee] A long, thin, flat pasta noodle.

Liquido [lEE-kwee-doh] Liquid.

Liquirizia [lee-kwee-rEE-tsee-ah] Licorice.

Liquore [lee-kwOH-reh] Liquor.

Liquore di cerasoli [+ dee cheh-rah-sOH-lee] A cherry liqueur.

Liquore di mele cotogne [+ dee mEH-leh koh-tOH-nyeh] A type of spiced quince liqueur.

Liquoroso [lee-kwoh-rOH-so] Term for certain strong sweet wines.

Lisca [lEEs-kah] Fishbone.

Lisci [lEE-shee] Describes "smooth" pasta, as opposed to ridged.

Lista dei vini [lEEs-tah deh vEE-nee] Wine list.

Lista delle vivande [+ dEHl-leh vee-vAHn-deh] "List of foods"; menu.

Litro [lEE-tro] Liter.

Lodigiano [loh-dee-jee-AH-no] A *grana*-type cheese made with cow's milk from Lodi (Lombardy).

Lombardia [lohm-bahr-dEE-ah] Several well-known dishes are found throughout this large northern region; polenta, risotto, minestrone, osso buco, and ravioli to name a few. Gorgonzola, grana, Belpaese, and mascarpone are some of the renowned cheeses produced in Lombardy.

Lombata [lohm-bAH-tah] Loin.

Lombatine [lohm-bah-tEE-neh] Filet steak.

Lombo [lOHm-bo] Loin.

Lombo capriolo [+ kah-pree-OH-lo] Saddle of venison.

Lonza [lOHn-tsah] (1) A pork sausage similar to *coppa*. (2) A regional name for pork loin.

Lucanica [loo-kAH-nee-kah] (1) A pork sausage originating in Basilicata now made in many parts of Italy. (2) The Latin name for Basilicata which is sometimes still used in some areas.

Luccio [lOO-chee-o] Pike.

Luccioperca [loo-chee-oh-pEHr-kah] Perch-pike.

Lugana [loo-gAH-nah] A pleasant white sparkling wine from Lombardy.

Luganega [loo-gAH-neh-gah] A type of sausage. See *Lucanica*.

Lujanis [loo-jah-nees] A spicy pork sausage from Veneto and Friuli.

Lumaca/lumache [loo-mAH-kah/ loo-mAH-keh] Snails/snail. *Lumache* is also a type of snail-shaped pasta.

Lumache alla cappuccina [+ AHl-lah kahp-poo-chEE-nah] (*Lombardy*) Snails stewed in stock and olive oil.

Lumache medie [loo-mAH-keh mEH-dee-eh] Small pasta resembling snail shells.

Lungo-vermicelli coupe [lOOn-ghoh vehr-mee-chEHl-lee koop] Vermicelli cut into short strands.

Lupo di mare [lOO-po dee mAH-reh] Sea bass.

Luppoli [lOOp-poh-lee] Hops.

Macaron' fatt' in casa [mah-kah-rOH-nee fAH-tee een kAH-sah] Refers to homemade pasta.

Maccarello [mahk-kah-rEHl-lo] Mackerel.

Maccarones [mahk-kah-rOH-nehs] (*Sardinia*) Pasta with tomatoes, garlic, and meat.

Maccheroncelli [mahk-keh-rohn-chEHl-lee] (1) Thin twisted pasta. (2) Another name for *maccheroncini*.

Maccheroncini [mahk-keh-rohn-chEE-nee] Hollow macaroni of various lengths.

Maccheroni [mahk-keh-rOH-nee] A hollow tubed macaroni longer than *maccheroncini*.

Maccheroni alla chitarra [+ AHl-lah key-tAHr-rah] See *Chitarra*.

Macco di fave [mAHk-ko dee fAH-veh] (*Calabria*) A spicy bean soup.

Maccu [mAHk-koo] (*Sicily*) Pureed fava beans.

Macedonia di frutta [mah-kah-dOH-nee-ah dee frOOt-tah] Fruit compote.

Macedonia di verdura [+ dee veh-dOO-rah] Describes vegetables that are cut into small uniform squares.

Macellaio [mah-chehl-lAH-ee-o] Butcher.

Macelleria [mah-chehl-leh-rEE-ah] Butcher's shop.

Macerare [mah-cheh-rAH-reh] To macerate.

Macinacaffè [mah-chee-nah-kahf-fEH] Coffee mill.

Macinapepe [mah-chee-nah-pEH-peh] Pepper mill.

Macinare [mah-chee-nAH-reh] To mill or grind.

Macinino del pepe [mah-chee-nEE-no dehl pEH-peh] Pepper shaker.

Mafalde [mah-fAHl-deh] A flat, broad ripple-edged noodle; a narrow lasagna noodle. Also called *lasagnette*; see *Malfadine*.

Mafaradda [mah-fah-rAHd-dah] A type of clay plate.

Maggiorana [mah-jee-oh-rAH-nah] Marjoram.

Maggiordomo [mah-jee-ohr-dOH-mo] Maître d'hôtel; headwaiter.

Maggiordomo, burro [bOOr-ro +] Maître d'hôtel butter; butter mixed with lemon juice and parsley.

Magro [mAHg-ro] Lean.

Magro, di A meatless tomato sauce, sometimes flavored with beef or chicken stock.

Maiale [mah-ee-AH-leh] Pork; pig.

Maiale al latte [+ ahl lAHt-teh] Pork cooked in milk.

Maiale ubriaco [+ oob-ree-AH-ko] Pork cooked in red wine.

Maialino [mah-ee-ah-lEE-no] Suckling pig.

Maionese [mah-ee-oh-nEH-seh] Mayonnaise.

Maiorchino [mah-ee-ohr-kEE-no] A Sicilian cheese produced in Catania made from sheep's milk.

Mais [mAH-ees] Corn.

Malfadine [mahl-fah-dEE-neh] A long ripple-edged noodle; similar to thin *mafalde*; see *Mafalde*.

Malfatti [mahl-fAHt-tee] A type of gnocchi made with spinach; from northern Italy.

Malloreddus [mahl-loh-rEHd-doos] A popular Sardinian dumpling made from cornmeal or semolina and seasoned with saffron.

Maltagliati [mahl-tah-lyAH-tee] A flat pasta cut in narrow, elongated diamonds; used in vegetable soups.

Malto [mAHl-to] Malt.

Malvasia [mahl-vah-sEE-ah] A popular grape used throughout Italy for red and white wines.

Malvasia delle Lipari [+ dEHl-leh lEE-pah-ree] A sweet white Sicilian wine.

Mamertino [mah-mehr-tEE-no] A local white Sicilian wine.

Mamme [mAHm-meh] (*Tuscany*) Large artichokes.

Mammola [mAHm-moh-lah] A variety of artichoke popular in Rome and southern Italy. Also called *romanesco* and *romagnolo*.

Mandarino [mahn-dah-rEE-no] Mandarin orange; tangerine.

Mandilli di sea [mahn-dEEl-lee dee sEH-eh] (*Liguria*) Square-shaped pasta noodles about 6 in. x 6 in.

Mandléina [mahnd-lEH-ee-nah] An almond-flavored confection; from Bologna.

Mandorla [mAHn-dohr-lah] Almond.

Mandorla amara [+ ah-mAH-rah] Bitter almond.

Mandorlato [mAHn-dohr-lah-to] Nougat; almond milk. See *Miracolo, il.*

Mandorlini [mAHn-dohr-lee-nee] (*Emilia-Romagna*) A type of macaroon.

Manfrigul [mahn-frEE-gool] Egg barley.

Mangiabile [mahn-jee-AH-bee-leh] Edible.

Mangiafoglie [mahjeah-fOH-lyeh] Leaf-eaters; a term referring to residents of certain areas in Italy where vegetables are a large part of the daily diet.

Mangiare [mahn-jee-AH-reh] To eat.

Maniche [mAH-nee-keh] "Sleeves"; a type of large tubed macaroni.

Manicotti [mah-nee-kOHt-tee] Stuffed tubes of pasta.

Manina [mah-nEE-nah] A type of small light bread.

Manteca/manteche [mahn-tEH-kah/mahn-tEH-kah] A semi-soft cheese from Basilicata; made from buffalo's or cow's milk.

Mantovane [mAHn-toh-vAH-neh] A yeast bread from Mantua (Lombardy).

Manzo [mAHn-tso] Steer; beef.

Manzo lesso [+ lEHs-so] Boiled beef.

Manzo salato [+ sah-lAH-to] Corned beef.

Manzo secco [+ sEHk-ko] Dried beef.

Manzo, stracotto di [+ dee strah-kOHt-to] Pot roast.

Manzo stufato [+ stoo-fAH-to] Beef stew.

Marasca [mah-rAHs-kah] See *Amarena*.

Marasche [mah-rAHs-keh] See *Amarena*.

Maraschino [mah-rahs-kEE-noh] A clear cherry liqueur made from the marasca cherry.

Maraschino, salsa al A dessert sauce composed of sugar, cream, and maraschino liqueur.

Marche [mAHr-keh] A coastal, mountainous region in eastern Italy best known for the hearty fish stew *brodetto* and *vinigrassi*. Marche is also one of Italy's largest producers of truffles.

Margarina [mahr-gah-rEE-nah] Margarine.

Margherita [mahr-gheh-rEE-tah] A term sometimes used to describe certain dishes prepared with mozzarella cheese, tomatoes, and basil.

Margherite [mahr-gheh-rEE-teh] A type of pasta.

Mariconde [mah-ree-cOHn-deh] (*Lombardy*) Small gnocchi made from bread crumbs and cheese.

Marina [mah-rEE-nah] The name in Emilia-Romagna for a variety of squash.

Marinara, alla [AHl-lah mah-ree-nAH-rah] "Sailor's style"; describes dishes served with a sauce made up of tomatoes, garlic, olive oil, and olives; seafood (clams, mussels) may or may not be present.

Marinata [mah-ree-nAH-tah] Marinade; pickled.

Maritata, alla Describes certain dishes prepared with mushrooms and herbs.

Maritozzi romani [mah-ree-tOH-tsee roh-mAH-nee] (*Rome*) A soft roll made with pine nuts and raisins; traditionally eaten at Christmas.

Marmellata [mahr-mehl-lAH-tah] Jam.

Marmellata d'arance [+ dee-ah-rAHn-cheh] Orange marmalade.

Marmora [mAHr-moh-rah] See *Mormora/marmora*.

Marro [mAHr-ro] Sheep's entrails cooked with herbs; from Abruzzi.

Marronata [mahr-roh-nAH-tah] Chestnut tart.

Marroni [mahr-rOH-neh] Large chestnuts; see *Castagne*.

Marsala [mahr-sAH-lah] A famous wine from Marsala (Sicily) fortified with brandy; dry, sweet, or semi-sweet.

Marsala speciali [+ spay-chee-AH-lee] Flavored marsala wines.

Martin sec [mAHr-teen sehk] A variety of pear.

Marubini [mah-roo-bEE-nee] Small ravioli from Lombardy.

Maruzzelle [mah-roo-tsEHl-leh] A type of Italian pasta.

Marzapane [mahr-tsah-pAH-neh] Sweetened almond paste.

Màsaro [mAH-zah-ro] Wild duck.

Mascarpone [mahs-kahr-pOH-neh] A fresh, creamy cow's-milk cheese; often sweetened and used in dessert dishes.

Mascherpone [mahs-kehr-pOH-neh] Mascarpone cheese.

Massancolle [mahs-sahn-kOHl-leh] See *Mazzancolle*.

Mastrich [mahs-treesh] A custard-like dessert made with mascarpone cheese.

Matterello [maht-teh-rEHl-lo] Rolling pin.

Mattone [maht-tOH-neh] Literally "brick"; in cooking parlance this term refers to a heavy earthenware lid.

Mattone, pollo al [pOHl-lo ahl +] Whole split chicken roasted on a clay dish while being weighed down with a *mattone*; see *Mattone*.

Maturo [mah-tOO-ro] Ripe.

Mazzafegati [mah-tsah-fEH-gah-tee] Pork liver sausage; from Umbria.

Mazzamuru [mah-tsah-mOO-roo] Thin Sardinian bread (*carasau*) drizzled with olive oil and heated.

Mazzancolle [mah-tsahn-kOHl-leh] (*Lazio*) A type of prawn; also spelled *massancolle* and *mezzancolle*.

Mazzetto odoroso [mah-tsEHt-to oh-doh-rOH-so] Aromatic herbs used to season soups and stocks.

Medaglione [meh-dah-ly-OH-neh] Meat patties; round beef fillets.

Megalolo [may-gah-lOH-lo] A variety of citrus fruit grown in Calabria.

Mela [mEH-luh] Apple.

Mela cotogna [+ koh-tOH-nyah] Quince.

Melagrana [meh-lah-grAH-nah] Pomegranate.

Melanzana [meh-lahn-tsAH-nah] Eggplant; enormously popular in Italy.

Melanzane sott'olio [+ soht-OH-lee-o] Marinated eggplant.

Melanzanine [meh-lahn-tsah-nEE-nah] Baby eggplant.

Melassa [meh-lAHs-suh] Molasses.

Melone [meh-lOH-neh] Melon.

Melone bianco [+ bee-AHn-ko] Honeydew melon.

Melone e prosciutto [+ eh proh-shee-OO-to] A popular appetizer composed of melon slices wrapped with thinly sliced prosciutto.

Menta [mEHn-tah] Mint.

Mentuccia [mehn-tOO-chee-ah] Mint.

Merenda [meh-rEHn-dah] Snack.

Meringa [meh-rEEn-gah] Meringue; prepared by slowly incorporating sugar syrup to whipped egg whites.

Meringhe [meh-rEEn-gheh] See *Meringa*.

Merlano [mehr-lAH-no] Whiting.

Merlot [mEHr-loht] A red wine grape used in northern Italy.

Merluzzo [mehr-lOO-tso] Cod.

Merluzzo fresco [+ frEHs-ko] Fresh cod.

Mescolare [mehs-koh-lAH-reh] Mix.

Messicani [mehs-see-kAH-nee] Rolled veal scallops stuffed with ground sausage.

Meticcio [meh-tEE-chee-o] A cross between a domestic pig and wild boar; the meat makes excellent pork products, i.e., sausage, salami, and so forth.

Mezzaluna [meh-tsah-lOO-nah] A two-handled knife with a "half-moon" shaped blade; used for mincing foods.

Mezzancolle [meh-tsahn-kOHl-leh] (*Tuscany*) See *Mazzancolle*.

Mezzani [may-tsAH-nee] Smooth tubular pasta smaller than ziti.

Mezza zita [mEH-tsah zEE-tah] Long, large tubular pasta.

Mezzo Cotto [mEH-tso kOHt-to] Medium-done; refers to cooked meat.

Michetta [mee-kEHt-tah] A light crusty roll.

Midollo [mee-dOHl-lo] Bone marrow.

Miele [mee-EH-leh] Honey.

Miglio [mEE-lyo] Millet.

Mignestris di ris vert A rice dish from Venezia Giulia composed of onions, celery, spinach, green onions, and carrots sautéed in butter; raw rice tossed in and lightly browned; broth added gradually until rice is cooked al dente; seasoned with salt and freshly ground black pepper; sprinkled with grated Parmesan cheese and served piping hot.

Mignozzi [mee-nyOH-tsee] A sweet fritter.

Mignucchie/Mignuice [mee-nyOO-key-eh/mee-nyOO-ee-cheh] (Apulia) Semolina gnocchi.

Milanese, alla [AHl-lah mee-lah-nEH-seh] Often describes foods coated with Parmesan cheese and bread crumbs and fried in butter.

Milano [mee-lAH-no] (1) An industrial city in western Lombardy; Milanese cuisine is best characterized by the use of butter; minestrone, risotto, polenta, and ossobuco are popular dishes common to the area. (2) A version of Belpaese cheese made in Milan. (3) A salami produced in Milan.

Millecosedde [meel-lay-koh-sEHd-deh] A hearty soup featuring beans, pasta, and vegetables.

Millefiori [meel-leh-fee-OH-ree] A liqueur made from a variety of herbs and flowers.

Millefoglie [meel-leh-fOH-lyah] A dessert featuring alternating layers of pastry cream and puff pastry.

Milza [mEEl-tsah] Spleen.

Minestra [mee-nEH-strah] (1) Soup. (2) The first course of a meal.

Minestra asciutta [+ ah-shee-OOt-tah] Literally "dried soup"; this term is sometimes used to describe pasta or the pasta course.

Minestra mariconda [+ mah-ree-kOHn-dah] Consommé garnished with light dumplings.

Minestra maritata [+ mah-ree-tAH-tah] (*Naples*) A rich vegetable soup made with cabbage, cheese, and *pezzentelle*; also called *pignato grasso*.

Minestrina [mee-nehs-trEE-nah] Consommé garnished with tiny cooked pasta.

Minestrone [mee-nehs-trOH-neh] A hearty vegetable soup of which there are numerous versions.

Minestrone alla genovese [+ AHl-lah jeh-noh-vEH-seh] Vegetables flavored with pesto.

Minestrone friulano [+ free-oo-lAH-no] A hearty potato soup with tomatoes.

Minuta [mee-nOO-tah] Menu.

Miracolo, il [eel mee-rAH-koh-lo] Honey-almond nougat; also called *mandorlato*.

Miringhe [mee-rEEn-gheh] Meringue; see *Meringa*.

Mirtillo [meer-tEEl-lo] Blueberry.

Mirtillo rosso [+ rOHs-so] Cranberry.

Missoltit [mees-sohl-teet] Dried preserved fish.

Misticanza [mees-tee-kAHn-tsah] (1) A type of salad green. (2) A mixed green salad.

Mistigriglia [mees-tee-grEE-lyah] "Mixed grill"; assorted grilled meats.

Misto [mEEs-to] Mixed.

Mitili [mEE-tee-lee] Mussels.

Mitili all'agro [+ ahl-AHg-ro] Marinated mussels.

Mocetta [moh-chEHt-tah] See *Motzetta*.

Mocnik del Carso [mOHk-neek dehl kAHr-so] A thick potato soup; from Veneto.

Modena [mOH-deh-nah] A city in Emilia-Romagna producing the finest balsamic vinegar in Italy.

Mohrenköpfe [mOH-rehn-kOp-fuh] A pastry dessert from Trento featuring chestnuts and chocolate.

Moka, la [lah mOH-kah] A manual Italian coffeepot.

Moleca [moh-lEH-kah] A variety of crab caught in and around Venice; also spelled *moleche*.

Moleche [moh-lEH-keh] See *Moleca*.

Moliterno [moh-lee-tEHr-no] A cow's- or ewe's-milk cheese from Luciana; similar to *Caciocavallo*.

Molle/mollet [mOHl-leh/mOHl-leht] Soft-boiled (egg).

Mollica [mohl-lEE-kah] Bread crumbs.

Molluschi [mohl-lEEs-key] Mollusks.

Molto secca [mOHl-to sEHk-kah] Very dry.

Moncenisio [mohn-chay-nEE-see-o] A blue-veined cheese produced from cow's milk.

Mondeghili [mohn-deh-ghee-lee] Fried meat croquettes.

Monica [mOH-nee-kah] A grape used to produce sweet Sardinian wines.

Monsù/monzù [mohn-sOO/mohn-zOO] The Italian pronunciation of the French word *monsieur* (sir); a regional term from northern Italy.

Montanara, alla [AHl-lah mohn-tah-nAH-rah] "In the style of the mountains"; describes dishes prepared with a variety of root vegetables.

Montasio [mohn-tAH-see-o] A cow's-milk cheese eaten fresh or aged and used as a grating cheese.

Montepulciano d'Abruzzo [mohn-teh-pool-chee-AH-no dah-brOO-tso] An outstanding dry red wine produced in Abruzzi and Molise; also called *Montepulciano Molise*.

Montesodi [mohn-teh-sOH-dee] A red Tuscan Chianti wine.

Montone [mohn-tOH-neh] Mutton.

Monza [mOHn-tsah] A type of sausage.

Monzù See *Monsù/monzù*.

Morbido [mOHr-bee-do] Soft.

More [mOH-reh] Mulberries; black currant.

More di rove [+ dee rOH-veh] Blackberries.

Mormora/marmora [mOHr-moh-rah/mAHr-moh-rah] A sea fish related to the cod.

Morseddu [mohr-sEHd-doo] See *Murzeddu*.

Morsello [mohr-sEHl-lo] A very hot sausage from Abruzzi flavored with red pepper.

Mortadella [mohr-tah-dEHl-lah] A large sausage originating in Bologna made from pork, pork fat, and beef. There are several imitations of this famous sausage, few of which compare in quality to the original.

Mortadella di Amatrice [+ dee ah-mah trEE-cheh] A spicy, aromatic version of mortadella from Amatrice (Lazio).

Mortadella di Campotosto [+ dee kahm-poh-tOHs-to] Mortadella studded with lard and heavily flavored with garlic.

Mortadella di fegato [+ dee fEH-gah-toh] Mortadella made with pork's liver.

Mortaio [mohr-tAH-ee-o] Mortar; see *Pestello*.

Mortelle di palude [mohr-tEHl-leh dee pah-lOO-deh] Cranberries.

Mosca, con la [kohn lah mOHs-kah] "With the fly"; Sambuca garnished with a coffee bean; see *Sambuca*.

Moscardini [mohs-kahr-dEE-nee] (1) The name in northern Italy for a variety of clam. (2) A tiny octopus; much esteemed.

Moscatello [mohs-kah-tEHl-lo] See *Moscato*.

Moscato [mohs-kAH-to] A sweet wine grape.

Moscato di Pantelleria [+ dee pahn-tehl-leh-ree-ah] A sweet white sparkling wine of excellent quality; from Sicily.

Mosciame [moh-shee-AH-meh] See *Musseddu*.

Mostaccioli [moos-tah-chee-OH-lee] "Mustaches" (1) A sweet chocolate-almond pastry popular in parts of southern Italy. (2) A type of pasta noodle.

Mostaccioli rigati [+ ree-gAH-tee] "Ridged mustaches"; a type of ridged pasta.

Mosta di Frutta [mOHs-tah dee frOOt-tah] Another name for *mostarda di Cremona*.

Mostarda [mohs-tAHr-dah] Relish.

Mostarda di carpi [+ dee kAHr-pee] (*Emilia-Romagna*) A type of fruit relish made with red wine mustard.

Mostarda di cremona [+ dee kreh-mOH-nah] A fruit relish from Cremona (Lombardy); served with cold boiled meats.

Mostarda d'uva [+ dOO-vah] A relish-like condiment made with grape must and mustard; served with boiled meats.

Mostazit [mohs-tah-tsEEt] A local name for *mostaccoili*.

Mosto [mOHs-to] Must; freshly pressed grape juice before fermentation.

Motzetta [moht-tsEHt-tah] Cured meat from certain animals (goat, chamois); also spelled *mocetta*.

Mozzarella [moh-tsah-rEHl-lah] A famous soft cheese made from buffalo's milk (see *Mozzarella di Bufala*) or cow's milk.

Mozzarella affumicata [+ ahf-foo-mee-kAH-tah] Smoked mozzarella cheese.

Mozzarella di bufala [+ dee bOO-fah-lah] (*Campania*) A fresh cheese made from buffalo's milk; one of the world's great cheeses.

Mozzarella in carrozza See *Mozzarella in carrozza* Part I, *Antipasti* Section.

Mozzarella milanese [+ mee-lah-nEH-seh] Breaded slices of Belpaese cheese fried in oil.

Mucci [mOO-chee] Sugar-coated almonds often used as party favors at various religious feasts.

Muffa nobile [mOOf-fah nOH-bee-leh] Nobile rot; mold developed

Muffa nobile (cont.)
on certain grapes resulting in the concentration of sugars.

Muffuliette [moof-foo-lee-EHt-teh] (*Sicily*) A type of sweet tea pastry.

Muflone [moof-lOH-neh] (*Sardinia*) Mountain sheep.

Muggine [mOO-jee-neh] Grey mullet.

Mugnaia, alla [AHl-lah moo-nyAH-ee-ah] Describes certain fish dishes sautéed in butter and dressed with lemon juice and parsley.

Mulliatelle [mool-lee-ah-tEHl-leh] A spicy sausage made from calf's offal; from Naples.

Murena [moo-rEH-nah] An eel-like fish.

Murzeddu [moor-tsEHd-doo] A spicy peasant dish from southern Italy composed of pig's offal stewed in a spicy tomato sauce.

Mus [moos] (*Veneto*) Cornmeal mush.

Muscoli [mOOs-kOH-lee] Mussels.

Muset/musetto [mOO-seht/moo-sEHt-to] A spicy sausage from Friuli made from pork and pork fat.

Museti padovana [moo-zeh-tee pah-doh-vAH-nah] (*Veneto*) A type of pork sausage.

Musetti [moo-sEHt-tee] (*Veneto*) Pork cracklings.

Muso bi bue [mOO-so dee bOO-eh] Muzzle; ox cheek.

Musseddu [moos-sEHd-doo] Dried salted fish (tuna, dolphin, swordfish).

Mustazzoli [moos-tah-tsOH-lee] A type of sweet almond biscuit from southern Italy.

Mustica [moos-tee-kah] Anchovy eggs preserved with chili peppers; see *Bianchetti*.

Nadalin [nah-dah-leen] A sweet pastry cake from Veneto traditionally prepared for Christmas.

Napoletana, alla [AHl-lah nah-poh-leh-tAH-nah] "In the style of Naples"; often with cheese, tomato sauce, and herbs.

Napoletana, la A manual Italian coffeepot.

Napoli [nAH-poh-lee] Naples. A port city in Campania synonymous with pizza and ice cream. Tomato sauce is used heavily in Naples.

Nasello [nah-sEHl-lo] Hake; whiting.

Natale [nah-tAH-leh] Christmas.

Naturale [nah-too-rAH-leh] Dishes served plain; without sauce, dressing, etc.

Navone [nah-vOH-neh] Turnip.

'Ncapriata [een-kahp-ree-AH-tah] A puree of fava beans and seasonings.

'Ncasciata [een-kah-shee-AH-tah] (*Sicily*) A rich pasta casserole dish made with several ingredients which vary from area to area; typical components include anchovies, pancetta, tomatoes, eggplant, sausage, etc.

'Ndocca 'ndocca [een-dOHk-kah] A type of ragout made with pig's offal; from Abruzzi e Molise.

'Nduglie [een-dOO-lyeh] A spicy sausage flavored with red pepper; from central Italy.

Necci [nEH-chee] Crepes made from chestnut flour.

Nepitella [neh-pee-tEHl-lah] An

herb from the mint family.

Nepitelle [neh-pee-tEHl-leh] A sweet pie featuring currants, chocolate, and nuts; from southern Italy.

Nero [nEH-ro] Black.

Nero, al Describes pasta dishes prepared with squid and squid ink, which turns the dish black.

Nervetti [nehr-vEHt-tee] Marinated calf's feet.

Nespola [nEHs-poh-lah] Medlar; a tree bearing an edible fruit used in jams and preserves.

Neuleddi [neh-oo-lEHd-dee] (*Sardinia*) Sweet buns.

Nevi di Firenze [nEH-vee-dee fee-rEHn-tsah] A type of pasta noodle from Florence.

Nnuije [noo-ee-jeh] (*Abruzzi*) A braised pork dish.

Nocchette [noh-kEHt-teh] A smaller version of *farfalle*.

Nocciole [nOH-chee-oh-leh] Hazelnuts.

Nocciolo [nOH-chee-oh-lo] Kernel.

Noce [nOH-cheh] (1) A cut of veal from the leg. (2) Walnut; nut.

— *del Brasile* [+ dehl brah-sEE-leh] Brazil nut.

— *di cocco* [+ dee kOH-ko] Coconut.

— *moscata* [+ mohs-kAH-tah] Nutmeg.

Nociata [noh-chee-AH-tah] A type of praline from Lazio made from walnuts and honey.

Noci attorrati [nOH-chee aht-tohr-rAH-tee] See *Nociata*.

Nocino [nOH-chee-no] A walnut-flavored liqueur; from Emilia-Romagna.

Noci, salsa di [sAHl-sah dee nOH-chee] A sauce composed of crustless white bread soaked in water to soften and ground in a mortar with olive oil, walnuts, and garlic; ricotta mixed in and seasoned with salt and pepper; from Genoa (Lombardy).

Nodini di vitello [noh-dEE-nee dee vee-tEHl-lo] A cut of veal from the loin; veal medallions.

Non troppo cotto [nohn trOHp-po kOHt-to] Medium done.

Norcineria [nohr-chee-neh-rEE-ah] A shop specializing in pork products.

Nostrale [nohs-trAH-leh] Various cow's-milk cheeses produced in Piedmont.

Nostrano [nohs-trAH-no] Local.

Novello [noh-vEHl-lo] New.

Nunnate [noon-nAH-teh] See *Gianchetti*.

Oca [OH-kah] Goose.

Occhi di lupo [OH-kee dee lOO-po] A short hollow pasta noodle similar to *rigatoni*; smooth-sided.

Odore [oh-dOH-reh] Smell; aroma.

Odori [oh-dOH-ree] Aromatic herbs and vegetables used to flavor soups, sauces, stocks, and so on.

Offelle [ohf-fEHl-leh] A sandwich cookie filled with a spicy jam (*di marmellata*) or almond paste.

Olio [OH-lee-o] Oil.

Olio di lino [+ dee lEE-no] Linseed oil.

Olio di semi [+ dee sEH-mee] Vegetable oil.

Olio d'oliva [+ dee-oh-lEE-vah] Olive oil.

Olio santo [+ sAHn-to] Olive oil infused with hot red peppers; a specialty of Abruzzi.

Oliva [oh-lEE-vah] Olive.

Olive all'ascolana [oh-lEE-veh ahl-AHs-koh-lah-nah] Stuffed olives from Ascoli.

Olive nere [+ nEH-reh] Black olive.

Olive schiacciate [+ skee-ah-chee-AH-teh] An olive paste seasoned with garlic and anchovies.

Olivette [oh-lee-vEHt-teh] See *Bocconcini*.

Ombrina [OHm-bree-nah] A pleasant-tasting sea fish.

Onda, all' [ahl-OHn-dah] Creamy; smooth.

Orata [oh-rAH-tah] Sea bream; a good eating fish.

Orecchie [oh-rEH-kee-eh] "Ears"; small ear-shaped pasta.

Orecchiette [oh-ray-kee-EHt-teh] (*Apulia*) "Little ears"; a smaller version of *orecchie*; in some places of Italy it is called *recchietelle* and *'recchie*.

Orecchioni [oh-reh-kee-OH-nee] A stuffed ear-shaped pasta; from Emilia-Romagna.

Oreganato [oh-reh-gahn-AH-to] With oregano.

Origano [oh-rEE-gah-no] Oregano.

Orlandese, salsa [sAHl-sah ohr-lahn-dEH-seh] Hollandaise sauce; an emulsion sauce made by briskly whisking melted butter into beaten egg yolks.

Ortaggio [ohr-tAH-gee-o] Vegetables.

Ortica [ohr-tEE-kah] Nettle; an herbaceous plant used to season various dishes.

Ortolano [ohr-toh-lAH-no] (1) Produce vendor. (2) Ortolan; a small game bird.

Orzo [OHr-tso] (1) Barley. (2) Rice-shaped pasta.

Orzo brillato [+ breel-lAH-to] Pearl barley.

Ossa da mordere [OHs-sah dah mOHr-deh-reh] "Bone-shaped cookies flavored with almonds and lemon; also called *osso da morto*.

Oss bus [ohs boos] (*Milan*) Ossobuco.

Osso [OHs-soh] Bone.

Ossobuco [+ bOO-ko] Veal shank braised with herbs and vegetables in white wine, stock, and tomato sauce.

Ossobuco alla milanese [+ AHl-lah mee-lah-nEH-seh] Veal shanks breaded and fried; braised in white wine, stock, tomato sauce, and *gremolada*.

Ossocollo [ohs-soh-kOHl-lo] A fatty pork sausage from Veneto.

Osterie [ohs-tEH-ree-ah] The word for "inn" in Rome.

Ostrica/ostriche [OHs-tree-kah/OHs-tree-keh] Oyster/oysters.

Ostriche alla veneziana [+ AHl-lah veh-neh-tsee-AH-nah] Oysters with caviar.

Ostriche appetitose [+ ahp-peh-tee-tOH-sah] Baked stuffed oysters.

Ovini [oh-vEE-nee] Relating to lamb or sheep.

Ovoli [oh-vOH-lee] See *Ovolina/ovoli*.

Ovolina/ovoli [oh-vo-lEE-nah/OH-voh-lee] Small mozzarella cheeses.

Ovolo [OH-voh-lo] An orange-colored edible mushroom.

Pabassinas [pah-bahs-see-nahs] A rich Sardinian cake made with dried fruit and nuts.

Padella [pah-dEHl-lah] Frying pan; skillet.

Padella, in Panfried.

Paesana, alla [AHl-lah pah-eh-sAH-nah] "In the peasant style"; refers to dishes simply prepared with local ingredients; often with pork and root vegetables.

Pagello [pah-jEHl-lo] Sea bream.

Paglia e fieno [pAH-lyee-ah eh fee-EH-no] Literally "straw and hay"; a combination of egg and spinach *tagliolini*; often served in white sauce.

Pagliarino [pAH-lyee-ah-ree-no] A strong, somewhat soft cheese from Piedmont made from cow's milk.

Pagnotta [pah-nyOHt-tah] A round peasant bread loaf.

Pagro [pAHg-ro] Sea bream.

Paiuolo [pah-ee-oo-OH-lo] A large copper kettle in which polenta is cooked.

Pajata di vitello [pah-jAH-tah dee vee-tEH-lo] (*Rome*) Veal entrails.

Palato [pah-lAH-to] Palate.

Palomba [pah-lOHm-bah] Wild pigeon; also known as *palombaccio*.

Palombo [pah-lOHm-bo] A large, firm-fleshed fish related to the shark.

Pampepato [pahm-peh-pAH-to] A sweet bun flavored with pine nuts, almonds, and honey; spiced with pepper.

Panada [pah-nAH-dah] See *Pantrid maridà*.

Panbagnato [pahn-bah-nyAH-to] A peasant salad composed of moistened bread, crumpled and tossed with tomatoes, onions, garlic, and greens; also called *pan molle*.

Pan bigio [pahn bEE-gee-o] A dark, rustic bread loaf.

Pancetta [pahn-chEHt-tah] Italian cured bacon; sometimes, but not often, smoked.

Pancia [pAHn-chee-ah] Belly.

Pancòt [pahn-kOHt] See *Pancotto*.

Pancotto [pahn-kOHt-to] A peasant soup made by soaking bread in broth with herbs and vegetables; sprinkled with grated cheese.

Pandaluts [pahn-dah-loots] (*Venezia-Giulia*) A hard, sweet biscuit.

Pan di Genova [pahn dee jEH-noh-vah] A sweet almond cake.

Pan di mort [+ dee mohrt] (*Lombardy*) A nut-fruit cake flavored with chocolate.

Pan di sorgo [+ dee sOHr-go] A sweet Venetian pastry made from corn flour.

Pan di Spagna [+ dee spAH-nyah] Sponge cake.

Pandolce [pahn-dOHl-cheh] (*Liguria*) A sweet yeast cake containing candied fruit, pine nuts, raisins, and fennel seeds.

Pandoro di Verona [pahn-dOH-ro dee veh-rOH-nah] "Golden bread"; a rich, sweet yeast cake from Verona (Veneto).

Pane [pAH-neh] Bread.

Pane abbrustolito [+ ahb-broos-toh-lEE-to] Toasted bread.

Pane carasau [pAH-neh kah-rAH-sah-oo] See *Carasau*.

Pane casareccio [+ kah-sah rEH-chee-o] Homemade bread.

Pane caserellio [+ kah-seh-rEHl-lee-o] Homemade bread.

Panedda [+ pahn-EHd-dah] See *Casiglioli*.

Pane di Natale [+ dee nah-tAH-leh] "Christmas bread"; sweet yeast bread with dried fruits and nuts.

Pane di Segale [+ dee sEH-gah-leh] Rye bread.

Pan ed Nadel [pahn ehd nAH-dehl] See *Pane di Natale*.

Pane dorato [+ doh-rAH-to] French toast.

Pane fratau [pAH-neh frah-tAH-oo] Sardinian flat bread (*carasau*) layered in a casserole with meat and cheese; baked like lasagne.

Pane grattugiato [+ graht-too-jee-AH-to] Bread crumbs; also spelled *pangrattato*.

Pane integrale [+ een-tah-grAH-leh] Whole grain bread; whole wheat bread.

Panella [pah-nEHl-lah] See *Casigliolo*.

Panella Chickpea flour fritters.

Pane nero [+ nEH-ro] Rye bread.

Pane scuro [+ skOO-ro] Dark bread.

Panetteria [pah-neht-teh-rEE-ah] Bakery.

Panettiere [pahn-neht-tee-EH-reh] Baker.

Panettone [pah-neht-tOH-neh] (*Milan*) A famous sweet yeast cake sometimes flavored with raisins and nuts; traditionally served at Christmas.

Panforte di Siena [pahn-fOHr-teh dee see-EH-nah] A rich nut-fruit cake from Sienna (Tuscany).

Pan giallo [pahn jee-AHl-lo] A sweet nut-fruit cake served at Christmas; from Lazio.

Pangrattato [pahn-graht-tAH-toh] Bread crumbs; also spelled *pane grattugiato*.

Paniccia [pah-nEE-chee-ah] (*Liguria*) Baked polenta made from chickpea flour.

Panini di Pasqua [pah-nEE-nee dee pAHs-kwah] Easter bread; a sweet corn flour yeast cake studded with raisins.

Panino [pah-nEE-no] Roll.

Panino gravido [+ grAH-vee-do] Sandwich.

Panino imbottito [+ eem-boht-tEE-to] Stuffed roll; sandwich.

Paniotelle [pah-nee-oh-tEHl-leh] Toasted bread spread with anchovy paste.

Paniscia, la [lah pah-nEE-shee-ah] (1) Minestrone made with vegetables and beans. (2) Risotto cooked in red wine and minestrone.

Panissa [pah-nEEs-sah] See *Paniccia*.

Pan Molle [pahn mOHl-leh] See *Panbagnato*.

Panna [pAHn-nah] Cream.

Panna cotta [+ kOHt-tah] A rich cream custard.

Panna montata [+ mohn-tAH-tah] Whipped cream.

Pannarone [pahn-nah-rOH-neh] (*Lombardy*) Also spelled *pannerone*; a creamy blue-veined cheese made from cow's milk.

Pannato [pahn-nah-to] Breaded.

Pan pepato [pahn peh-pAH-to] A name sometimes given to gingerbread.

Pan sciocco [+ shee-OH-ko] Bread made without salt.

Pansôti/pansotti [pahn-sOH-tee/pahn-sOHt-tee] Pasta stuffed with herbs and cheese.

Panspeziale [pahn-speh-tsee-AH-leh] A sweet, spicy fruit cake traditionally prepared at Christmas.

Pan tostato [+ tohs-tAH-to] Toasted bread.

Pantrid maridà [pAHn-treed mah-ree-dAH] A bread soup from Lombardy flavored with eggs and cheese.

Panzanella, la [pahn-tsah-nEHl-lah] Bread salad; a peasant dish featuring bread pieces soaked in olive oil and accompanied with fresh vegetables.

Panzarotti [pahn-tsah-rOHt-tee] Pastry dough stuffed with meat and cheese and fried; pasta dough is used in some parts of Italy.

Papardlén [pah-pahrd-lEHn] See *Pappardellini.*

Paparot [pah-pah-rOHt] A spinach and cornmeal soup; from northern Italy.

Papassinos [pah-pahs-see-nohs] See *Pabassinas.*

Papavero [pah-pAH-veh-ro] Poppy.

Papero [pAH-peh-ro] Gosling.

Pappa al pomodoro [pAHp-pah ahl poh-moh-dOH-ro] A soup composed of bread soaked in stock with tomatoes, garlic, and basil.

Pappardelle [pahp-pahr-dEHl-leh] A long, flat pasta noodle usually ¹/₂-to 1-in. wide.

Pappardelle con la lepre [+ kohn lah leh-preh] (*Tuscany*) Hare stewed in red wine and stock with aromatic vegetables and herbs; thickened with cream. One of the best-known pasta dishes using *pappardelle.*

Pappardellini [pahp-pahr-dehl-lEE-nee] Small squares of pasta; also called *papardlén.*

Paprica [pAHp-ree-kah] Paprika.

Parma [pAHr-mah] A major culinary city in Emilia-Romagna equally famous for two products: *Parmigiano-reggiano* cheese (Parmesan cheese) and prosciutto ham.

Parmigiana, alla [AHl-lah pahr-mee-jee-AH-nah] "Parma style"; with Parmesan cheese; sometimes indicates that prosciutto is present in a dish.

Parmigiano reggiano [pahr-mee-jee-AH-no rEH-jee-ah-no] The undisputed king of Italian cheeses; this straw-colored grating cheese from Parma (Emilia-Romagna) is made from cow's milk and is typically aged for 18 to 36 months.

Parrozzo [pahr-rOH-tso] A sweet cake flavored with chocolate and sweet and bitter almonds; from Pescara (Abruzzi).

Pasqua [pAHs-kwah] Easter.

Passata di mele [pahs-sAH-tah dee mEH-leh] Apple sauce.

Passatelli [pahs-sah-tEHl-lee] A soup from Emilia-Romagna of tiny dumplings in broth. The dumplings are made with eggs, bread crumbs, spinach, and Parmesan cheese; with or without meat; sometimes called *passatini.*

Passatelli alla bolognese [+ AHl-lah boh-loh-nyEH-seh] Tiny dumplings made from bread crumbs, eggs, Parmesan cheese, and beef marrow; served in broth.

Passatini [pahs-sah-tEE-nee] See *Passatelli.*

Passato [pahs-sAH-to] Pureed; creamed. Often refers to smooth soups.

Passera [pAHs-say-rah] Flounder; sole.

Passito [pahs-sEE-to] The term for certain sweet strong wines made from sun-dried grapes. See *Vin santo*.

Passoliate [pahs-soh-lee-AH-teh] A type of almond paste confection; from Apulia.

Pasta [pAHs-tah] (1) Dough; paste. A basic pasta dough is made up of semolina or white flour, eggs, water, and salt; formed into hundreds of different shapes. (2) Noodles.

Pasta alla frutta [+ AHl-lah frOOt-tah] Fruit pie; fruit tart.

Pasta all'uova [+ ahl-oo-OH-vah] Egg pasta.

Pasta asciutta [+ ah-shee-OO-tah] See *Pastasciutta*.

Pasta asciutta alla marchigiana [+ AHl-lah mahr-key-jee-AH-nah] Noodles made from yeast dough.

Pasta briciolata [+ bree-chee-oh-lAH-tah] Pie dough.

Pasta compra [+ kOHm-prah] Factory-made pasta.

Pasta con le sarde [+ kohn leh sAHr-deh] Pasta tossed with sautéed sardines and seasoned with pine nuts and fennel; from Palermo (Sicily).

Pasta con tonno [+ kohn tOHn-no] An Italian favorite combining pasta with olive oil, spices, and tuna.

Pasta corta [+ kOHr-tah] Describes short pasta noodles.

Pasta di mandorla [+ dee mAHn-dohr-lah] Marzipan; almond paste.

Pasta fatta in casa [+ fAHt-tah een kAH-sah] Homemade pasta.

Pasta filata [+ fee-lAH-tah] Describes certain cheese such as mozzarella, provolone, *scamorze*, and so forth having a rubber-like consistency.

Pasta frolla [+ frOHl-lah] Shortdough pastry; prepared with flour, sugar, butter, and eggs.

Pasta frolla fragile [+ frAH-jee-leh] A fragile shortdough pastry made with hard-cooked egg yolks.

Pasta genovese [+ jeh-noh-vEH-seh] Génoise; a basic cake made of butter, eggs, sugar, and flour.

Pasta grattata [+ graht-tAH-tah] Grated pasta used in soups.

Pasta margherita [+ mahr-gheh-rEE-tah] Potato-flour sponge cake.

Pasta mezza frolla [+ mEH-tsah frOHl-lah] Shortdough pastry prepared with milk instead of water.

Pastarasa [pahs-tah-rAH-sah] Small gnocchi made from bread crumbs and Parmesan cheese; used in soups.

Pasta reale [+ reh-AH-leh] Small soup dumplings.

Pastasciutta [pAHs-tah-shee-OOt-tah] A term referring to pasta served with a sauce; also spelled *pasta asciutta*.

Pasta sfoglia [+sfOH-lyee-ah] Puff pastry; also called *sfogliata*.

Pasta soffiata [+ sohf-fee-AH-tah] Cream puff pastry.

Pasta tirata [+ tee-rAH-tah] A name sometimes given to fresh pasta dough.

Pasta verde [+ vEHr-deh] Green pasta; spinach pasta.

Paste [pAHs-teh] A word used to describe small pastries and confections.

Pastella [pahs-tEHl-lah] Batter; flour and water batter.

Pastella con lievito [+ kohn lee-EH-vee-to] Yeast batter.

Pastella semplice [+ sEHm-plee-cheh] Egg batter used for deep-frying.

Paste lunghe [+ lOOn-gheh] A term referring to long pasta noodles.

Pasticceria [pahs-tee-chay-rEE-ah] Pastry shop; pastries.

Pasticciata [pahs-tee-chee-AH-tah] (1) A type of meat stew (2) A baked pasta or polenta dish layered with meat, tomato sauce, *besciamella*, vegetables, cheese, and so forth; similar to lasagne.

Pasticciere [pahs-tee-chee-EH-reh] Pastry chef.

Pasticcini [pahs-tee-chEE-nee] Pastries.

Pasticcio [pahs-tEE-chee-o] (1) Pie; an old dish similar to the French pâté; meat, vegetables, or pasta baked in a pastry shell. (2) Pie crust.

Pasticcio alla ferrarese [+ AHl-lah fehr-rah-rEH-seh] A savory pie from Ferrara (Emilia-Romagna) filled with pasta, meat sauce, *besciamella*, and cheese.

Pastiera napoletana [pahs-tee-EH-rah nah-poh-leh-tAH-nah] (*Naples*) A traditional Easter tart featuring *pasta frolla* filled with ricotta, pastry cream, rose water, and softened wheat kernels.

Pastificio [pahs-tee-fEE-chee-o] Pasta factory.

Pastina [pahs-tEE-nah] Tiny pasta of various shapes; used in soups.

Pastina acini [+ AH-chee-nee] Tiny egg-shaped pasta.

Pastinaca [pahs-tee-nAH-kah] Parsnip.

Pastina all'uovo [+ ahl oo-OH-vo] Pastina made from egg pasta.

Pastina stelline [+ stayl-lEE-neh] Tiny star-shaped pasta.

Pastina tempestina [+ tehm-pehs-tEE-nah] Tiny pasta.

Pastine fantasia alla milanese [+ fahn-teh-sEE-ah AHl-lah mee-lah-nEH-seh] (*Milan*) Rich almond cookies flavored with candied fruit.

Pastizzada [pahs-teets-tsAH-dah] (*Veneto*) A dish of stewed beef of which there are several versions.

Pasto [pAHs-to] Meal; lunch, dinner.

Pastorella [pahs-tOH-rEHl-lah] A small version of Belpaese cheese.

Pastuccia [pahs-tOO-chee-ah] (*Abruzzi*) A savory roll baked with pancetta or sausage meat.

Pastu mistu [pAHs-too mEEs-too] (*Sardinia*) An interesting dish featuring roasted pig stuffed with a smaller animal.

Patata [pah-tAH-tah] Potato.

Patata al forno [+ ahl fOHr-no] Baked potato.

Patata dolce [+ dOHl-cheh] Sweet potato.

Patata foglia [+ [fOH-lyah] Potato chips.

Patata naturale [+ nah-too-rAH-leh] Boiled potato.

Patata novella [+ noh-vEHl-lah] New potato.

Patata paglia [+ pAH-lyah] Straw-cut potatoes; fried.

Patate passate [+ pahs-sAH-teh] Mashed potato.

Patate saltate [+ sahl-tAH-teh] Sliced sautéed potato.

VOCABULARY

Patate stacciate [+ stah-chee-AH-teh] Mashed potato.

Patate tenere [+ tEH-neh-reh] New potato.

Patatine [pah-tah-tEE-neh] New potatoes.

Paternostri [pah-tehr-nOHs-tree] A local pasta noodle from Calabria.

Pattona, la [lah pah-tOH-nah] A sweet cake made from chestnut-flour; from Emilia-Romagna.

Pavese [pah-vEH-seh] Soup garnished with poached eggs and croutons.

Pavone [pah-vOH-neh] Peacock.

Peará [peh-ah-rAH] Pepper sauce made with stock, bread crumbs, butter, and pepper; served with boiled meats; also called *peperata* and *peverada*. See *Peverada*.

Pecora [pEH-koh-rah] Ewe.

Pecorino [pEH-koh-ree-no] Cheeses made from ewe's milk.

— *romano* [+ roh-mAH-no] A famous hard ewe's-milk cheese from Rome; one of the oldest of Italian pecorino cheeses.

— *sardo* [+ sAHr-do] A ewe's-milk cheese from Sardinia.

— *siciliano* [+ see-chee-lee-AH-no] A hard grating cheese similar to pecorino romano; also called *Canestrato*.

Pellagrine [pehl-lah-grEE-neh] The word for scallops in parts of northern Italy.

Peluria [peh-lOO-ree-ah] Peel; skin.

Penne [pEHn-neh] A quill-shaped, tubular pasta.

Pennette [pehn-nEHt-teh] Small penne.

Pennoni [pehn-nOH-nee] Small penne.

Pentola [pEHn-toh-lah] Pot; pan.

Peoci [pay-OH-chee] Mussels.

Pepatelli [peh-pah-tEHl-lee] Sweet almond buns seasoned with pepper.

Pepato [peh-pAH-to] (1) Peppery. (2) Pecorino romano cheese seasoned with crushed peppercorns.

Pepe [pEH-peh] Pepper.

Pepe bianco [+ bee-AHn-kah] White pepper.

Pepe di caienna [+ dee kah-ee-EHn-nah] Cayenne pepper.

Pepe di giamaica [+ dee jee-ah-mAH-ee-kah] Allspice.

Pepe di Guinea [+ dee goo-ee-nEH-uh] Guinea pepper; a spice similar to cardamom possessing a mild peppery taste.

Pepe forte [+ fOHr-teh] Dried, crushed red pepper flakes.

Pepe, grano di [grAH-no dee +] Peppercorn.

Pepe nero [+ nEH-ro] Black pepper.

Peperata [peh-peh-rAH-tah] See *Peará*.

Peperonata [peh-peh-roh-nAH-tah] Peppers sautéed in olive oil with garlic and tomatoes.

Peperoncini [peh-peh-rohn-chEE-nee] Chili peppers.

Peperoni [peh-peh-rOH-nee] Sweet bell peppers.

Peperoni rossi [+ rOHs-soh] Hot red peppers.

Pepe rosso [pEH-peh rOHs-soh] Paprika.

Pepini [pay-pEE-nee] Tiny pasta bits; served in broth.

Pepolino [pay-poh-lEE-no] The name for thyme in parts of Italy.

Pera [pEH-rah] Pear.

Peradivacca/pera di vacca [pEH-rah-dee-vAHk-kah] See *Casigliolo*.

Perciatelli [pehr-chee-ah-tEHl-lee] See *Bucatini*.

Perciatelloni [pehr-chee-ah-tehl-lOH-nee] A long hollow pasta noodle.

Perfetto amore [payr-fEHt-to Ah-mOH-reh] "Perfect Love"; a liqueur from Lombardy flavored with citron.

Pernice [pehr-nEE-cheh] Partridge.

Pesca/pesche [pEHs-kah/pEHs-keh] Peach/peaches.

Pesca noce [+ nOH-cheh] Nectarine.

Pescati carbonaretti [pehs-kAH-tee kahr-boh-nah-rEHt-tee] Fish cooked on live coals.

Pescatrice [pehs-kah-trEE-cheh] Anglerfish; monkfish.

Pesce [pEH-sheh] Fish.

Pescecane [peh-sheh-kAH-neh] Shark.

Pesce persico [+ pEHr-see-ko] Perch.

Pesce San Pietro [+ sahn pee-EH-tro] John Dory.

Pesce spada [+ spAH-duh] Swordfish.

Pesche [pEHs-keh] Peaches.

Pescheria [pehs-keh-ree-ah] Fish market.

Pesciaiola [pEH-shee-ah-ee-oh-lah] Fish kettle.

Pesciolini [peh-shee-oh-lEE-nee] Tiny fish.

Pescivendolo [peh-shee-vEHn-doh-lo] Fishmonger.

Pestà [pehs-tUH] Describes sauces that have been made by crushing or grinding ingredients to a paste. See *Pesto*.

Pestazzule [pehs-tahts-tsOO-leh]

(*Apulia*) A pasta similar to *orecchiette*; see *Orecchiette*.

Pestello [pehs-tEHl-lo] Pestle.

Pesto [pEHs-to] (1) Ground; crushed. (2) A sauce made from crushed basil, pine nuts, garlic, grated pecorino cheese, and olive oil; a specialty of Genoa (*Pesto Genovese*).

Pesto genovese [+ jeh-noh-vEH-seh] See *Pesto*.

Pesto romano [+ roh-mAH-no] Pesto made with egg yolks and lemon.

Petonchio [pay-tOHn-kee-o] The word for scallop in parts of Italy.

Pettine, il [eel pEHt-teen-eh] A comb-like tool used for making *garganelli* or other ridged pasta; fresh pasta is rolled over tight strings producing a corduroyed texture. See *Garganelli*.

Pettine maggiore [+ mah-jee-OH-reh] The word for scallop in parts of Italy.

Petto [pEHt-to] Breast.

Petto di manzo [+ dee mAHn-tso] Beef brisket.

Petto di pollo [+ dee pOHl-lo] Chicken breast.

Pettole [peht-toh-leh] (*Apulia*) Sweet fritters.

Pettue [pEHt-too-eh] A local name for fritters in parts of southern Italy.

Peverada [peh-veh-rAH-dah] (1) A sauce served with fowl composed of ground sausage, chicken livers, olive oil, and seasonings. (2) Another name for *pearà*; see *Pearà*.

Pezzente [pehts-tsEHn-teh] A highly spiced pork sausage from Basilicata.

Pezzentelle [pehts-tsehn-tEHl-leh] A type of pork sausage.

Piacentinu [pee-ah-chehn-tEE-noo] A local cheese from Sicily seasoned with saffron.

Piacere, a [ah pee-ah-chEY-reh] Refers to dishes prepared to the guests choosing.

Piada [pee-AH-dah] The word in parts of Italy for yeast dough.

Piadina/piadone [pee-ah-dEE-nah/pee-ah-dOH-nah] A very thin, chewy bread of Emilia-Romagna; cooked on a hot griddle.

Piatto [pee-AHt-to] Plate; course.

Piatto del giorno [+ dehl jee-OHr-no] Specialty of the day.

Piatto di mezzo [+ dee mEHts-tso] Food tidbits eaten between meal courses.

Piatto di resistenza [+ dee ree-zees-tEHn-tsah] The climax of a meal; an elaborate main course.

Piatto fondo [+ fOHn-do] Soup and pasta plate.

Piatto forte [+ fOHr-teh] Entrée; main course.

Piatto primo [+ prEE-mo] The first course.

Piatto tipico [+ tEE-pee-ko] Typical dishes (of a region).

Piccagge [pee-kAH-jeh] Wide lasagne-like noodles from Liguria.

Piccante [pee-kAHn-teh] Highly seasoned; piquant.

Piccata [pee-kAHt-tah] Thin cutlets; usually refers to veal; also known as *piccatine*. See *Scaloppine*.

Piccatine [pee-kaht-tEE-neh] See *Piccata*.

Piccione [pee-chee-ON-neh] Pigeon.

Piccoli crostini fritti [pEE-koh-lee kroh-stEE-nee frEEt-tee] Croutons.

Piccolo [pEE-koh-lo] Small.

Pici [pEE-chee] A Tuscan specialty composed of pasta tossed with olive oil and toasted bread crumbs.

Picolit [pee-koh-lEEt] A strong, sweet white wine from Veneto.

Piconi [pee-kOH-nee] Small turnovers filled with a sweetened ricotta mixture; from central Italy.

Piede [pee-EH-deh] Foot; trotter.

Piedone [pee-eh-dOH-neh] See *Crescentina*.

Piemonte [pee-eh-mOHn-teh] A northern Italian region bordering Switzerland and France; synonymous with white truffles. Piedmont is also one of the best producers of wines in Italy.

Piemontese, alla [pee-eh-mohn-tEH-zeh] "Piedmont-style"; with white truffles and sometimes risotto.

Pieno [pee-EH-no] Refers to full-bodied wines.

Pietanza [pee-eh-tAHn-tsah] (1) Dish; course. (2) With bread.

Pietrafendola [pee-eht-rah-fEHn-doh-lah] A hard cookie.

Pignato grasso [pee-nyAHt-tah grahs-so] See *Minestra maritata*.

Pignatta [pee-nyAHt-tah] A terra-cotta (or copper) pot used to cook cannellini beans or store preserved goose.

Pignolata [pee-nyoh-lAH-tah] See *Strufoli*.

Pignoli [pee-nyOH-lee] Pine nuts.

— *salsa di* Cream sauce flavored with pine nuts.

Pillas [pEEl-lahs] (*Sardinia*) A layered pasta dish similar to lasagne featuring cheese and prosciutto.

Pimiento [pee-mEHn-to] Sweet red pepper.

Pinaroli [pee-nah-rOH-lah] A variety of small wild mushroom.

Pinci [pEEn-chee] Round, individually rolled noodles resembling thick spaghetti; from Siena (Tuscany).

Pinci di montalcino [+ dee mohn-tahl-chEE-no] *Pinci* topped with a rich sauce of ground pork, sausage meat, garlic, olive oil, tomatoes, and red wine; from Tuscany.

Pincigrassi [peen-chee-grAHs-see] The Abruzzese version of lasagna; called *vincigrassi* in Marche where it is typically flavored with prosciutto and truffles.

Pinoccate [pee-noh-kAH-teh] Almond and pine nut brittle.

Pinocchiate [pee-noh-kee-AH-teh] A pine nut flan.

Pinoli [pee-nOH-lee] Pine nuts.

Pinot grigio [pee-nOHt-grEE-jee-o] A fine white wine produced in northern Italy from grapes with the same name.

Pinta [peen-tah] Pint.

Pinza [pEEn-tsah] Describes several different sweet pastries from northern Italy.

Pinzimonio [peen-tsee-mOH-nee-o] Olive oil, salt, and pepper; used as a dipping sauce for raw vegetables; from Lazio.

Piovanello pancia nera [pee-oh-vah-nEHl-lo pAHn-chee-ah nEH-tah] An Italian name for snipe.

Pipe rigate [PEE-peh ree-gAH-tee] Ridged pasta resembling fat elbows.

Pippiare [pee-pee-AH-reh] A low simmer.

Pirciatu, u [oo peer-chee-AH-too] The name for *bucatini* in Palermo and parts of Sicily; see *Bucatini*.

Pirichittus [pee-ree-keet-toos] An orange-flavored pastry; from Sardinia.

Pisari e fasò [pEE-sah-ree eh fah-zO] Gnocchi made from bread crumbs and cheese.

Pisci d'ovu [pEE-shee dOH-voo] (*Sicily*) Small savory fritters made with eggs, bread crumbs, and Parmesan cheese.

Piselli [pee-zEHl-lee] Peas.

Pisellini [pee-zehl-lEE-nee] Very young, small peas.

Piselli novelli [+ noh-vEHl-lee] Young tender peas.

Pissaladeira [pees-sah-lah-dEH-ee-rah] An olive and anchovy pizza.

Pistacchio [pee-stAH-key-o] Pistachio nut.

Pistocheddus [pees-toh-kehd-duus] (*Sardinia*) A sweet bun.

Pitta [pEEt-tah] (*Calabria*) Pizza; topped with local ingredients.

Piviere/pivieressa [pee-vee-EH-reh/pee-vee-eh-rEHs-sah] Plover.

Pizza [pEEts-tsah] (1) Pie; cake. (2) Flat bread topped with a variety of ingredients.

Pizza al formaggio [+ ahl fohr-mAH-jee-o] See *Crescia*.

Pizza alla napoletana [+ AHl-lah nah-poh-leh-tAH-nah] (*Naples*) Pizza topped with tomatoes, anchovies, olive oil, capers, mozzarella cheese, and herbs; the classic pizza.

Pizza dolce [+ dOHl-cheh] Sweet breads or cakes usually prepared with yeast dough.

Pizzaiola [peets-tsah-ee-OH-lah] (1) A sauce composed of tomatoes, garlic, and basil. (2) Beef, chicken, or fish prepared with *pizzaiola* sauce and mozzarella cheese.

Pizza margherita [+ mahr-geh-rEE-tah] Pizza topped with basil, tomatoes, and mozzarella cheese; represents the colors of the Italian flag.

Pizza pasqualina [+ pahs-kwah-lEE-nah] A sweet bread made with ricotta.

Pizza quattro stagioni [+ kwAHt-tro stah-jee-OH-nee] "Four seasons" pizza; each quarter topped with different ingredients.

Pizza rustica [+ rOOs-tee-kah] (*Abruzzi*) A pie featuring sweet dough (*pasta frolla*) containing a rich savory filling of sausage, prosciutto, cheese, and herbs.

Pizza sardenaria [+ sahr-deh-nAH-ree-ah] Pizza topped with sardines, tomatoes, and black olives.

Pizzette [peets-tsEHt-teh] Little pizzas.

Pizzicati [peets-tsee-kAH-tee] Sweet honey fritters.

Pizzicheria [peets-tsee-keh-rEE-ah] Deli shop.

Pizzichi [pEEts-tsee-key] Small bowtie-shaped pasta.

Pizzicotti dei romani [pEEts-tsee-kohHt-tee day roh-mAH-nee] Dumplings made from chopped spinach, ricotta, eggs, and Parmesan cheese; served with an herb-butter sauce.

Pizzoccheri/pizzòcher [peets-tsOH-keh-ree/peets-tsOH-kehr] Buckwheat pasta; arranged in layers with potatoes and cabbage and topped with cheese.

Pociacche [po-chee-AH-keh] Large *orecchiette*; see *Orecchiette*.

Polenta [poh-lEHn-tah] Cornmeal mush; often chilled, sliced, and grilled; from northern Italy.

Polenta cunscia [+ kOOn-shee-ah] Polenta layered with garlic.

Polenta e osei [+ eh oh-zEH-ee] (*Lombardy*) Small roasted game birds served on a bed of sliced polenta; also called *polenta e uccelli*.

Polenta e uccelli [+ eh oo-chEHl-lee] See *Polenta e Osei*.

Polenta grassa [+ grAHs-sah] Polenta seasoned with pepper and cheese.

Polenta nera [+ nEH-rah] "Black polenta"; made with buckwheat flour, giving the dish a dark color.

Polenta pastizzada [+ pahs-teets-tsAH-dah] Polenta layered with vegetables and a rich tomato-meat sauce; from Veneto.

Polenta taragna [+ tah-rah-nyah] Buckwheat polenta; from Lombardy.

Polipo [pOH-lee-po]Octopus; squid.

Pollame [pohl-lAH-meh] Fowl.

Pollastra/pollastrello [pohl-lAHs-trah/pohl-lahs-trEHl-lo] Young chicken.

Pollastro [pohl-lAHs-trah] Chicken.

Pollo [pOHl-lo] The Italian word for chicken.

Pollo ai ferri [+ AH-ee fEHr-ree] Broiled chicken.

Pollo al babi [+ ahl bAH-bee] Chicken sautéed in olive oil and seasoned with pepper.

Pollo novello [+ nOH-vEHl-lo] Spring chicken.

Polmone [pohl-mOH-neh] Lungs; lights.

Polpa [pOHl-pah] (1) Pulp. (2) Boneless stew meat.

Polpette [pohl-pEHt-teh] Meatballs; croquettes.

Polpettini [pohl-peht-tEE-nee] Small meatballs.

Polpettone/polpettine [pohl-peht-tOH-neh/pohl-peht-tEE-neh] Seasoned ground meat; meatloaf.

Polpi in purgatorio [pOHl-pee een poor-gah-tOH-ree-o] "Octopus in purgatory"; sautéed in olive oil with tomatoes, garlic, and pepper.

Polpo [pOHl-po] Octopus.

Polsonetto/ponzonetto [pohl-sohnEHt-to/pohn-tsoh-nEHt-to] A copper saucepan; usually used to prepare dessert custards and creams.

Pomino [poh-mEE-no] A dry white Tuscan wine.

Pommarola [pohm-mah-rOH-lah] A rich tomato sauce from Naples.

Pommarola 'ncoppa [+ een-kOHp-pah] A pasta dish from Naples featuring spaghetti topped with a sauce of tomatoes, bacon, garlic, and olive oil.

Pomodori al riso [poh-moh-dOH-ree ahl rEE-zo]Fresh tomatoes, tops sliced off and reserved, cored and filled with raw rice, olive oil, chopped garlic, chopped basil, salt, pepper, and the tomato pulp mixed with tomato juice; covered with tomato tops and baked until rice is tender. Cooled slightly before serving.

Pomodori in bottiglia [+ een bohttEE-lyee-ah] "Bottled tomatoes"; refers to preserved tomatoes.

Pomodori pelati [+ peh-lAH-tee] Small plum tomato.

Pomodori penduli [+ pEHn-doo-lee] A variety of small tomato; also called *pomodoro al filo*.

Pomodoro [poh-moh-dOH-ro] Tomato.

Pomodoro, al With tomato sauce.

Pomodoro al filo [+ ahl fEE-lo] See *Pomodori penduli*.

Pomodoro fresco, sugo di [sOO-go dee poh-moh-dOH-ro frEHs-ko] Fresh tomato sauce.

Pomodoro, salsa di Tomato sauce.

Pomodoro, sugo di [sOO-go dee +] Tomato sauce.

Pompelmo [pom-pEHl-mo] Grapefruit.

Pompie [pOHm-pee-eh] Candied bitter orange.

Ponce [pOHn-cheh] Punch; mixed fruit beverage, sometimes containing alcohol.

Ponzonetto [pon-tsoh-nEHt-to] See *Polsonetto*.

Popone [poh-pOH-neh] Melon.

Porceddu [pohr-chEHd-doo] See *Porchetta*.

Porcellana [pohr-chehl-lAH-nah] China; porcelain.

Porcellino [pohr-chehl-lee-no] Piglet.

Porchetta [pohr-kEHt-tah] Roasted suckling pig.

Porchetta umbra al girarosto [pohr-kEH-tah-OOm-brah-ahl-jee-rah-rOHs-to] (*Umbria*) Baby pig roasted with rosemary and fennel.

Porcinelli [pohr-chee-nEHl-lee] A variety of wild mushroom.

Porcini [pohr-chEE-nee] Boletus; a variety of wild mushroom.

Porco [pOHr-ko] Pork.

Porrata [pohr-rAH-tuh] A savory leek pie.

Porrino [pohr-rEE-no] Chive.

Porro [pOHr-ro] Leek.

Portulaca [pohr-too-lAH-kah] Purslane; an herbaceous plant used as a salad green and seasoning.

Posillipo, alla [AHl-lah poh-sEEl-lee-po] Typically refers to shellfish served with tomato sauce.

Potacchio [poh-tAH-kee-o] Cooked in olive oil, wine, tomato sauce, and herbs.

Poveraccia [poh-veh-rAH-chee-ah] A variety of clam.

Pranzare [prahn-tsAH-reh] Dine.

Pranzo [prAHn-tso] Lunch; dinner.

Prataioli [prah-tah-ee-OH-lee] A variety of mushroom.

Preboggion [preh-boh-jee-ohn] (*Liguria*) A blend of herbs used in various local preparations.

Preboggion col pesto [+ kohl pEHs-to] A soup from Genoa (Liguria) composed of chicken broth, mixed chopped greens, and rice; flavored with pesto.

Preddas [prehd-uhs] A cheese similar to *caciocavallo*.

Pregadio [preh-gah-dEE-o] A small shellfish.

Prescinsena [preh-sheen-sEH-nah] A fresh cow's-milk cheese from Liguira.

Presnitz/presniz [prehs-neetz] An Easter pastry from Trieste (Venezia-Giulia) featuring puff pastry filled with dried fruits and nuts.

Pressato [prehs-sAH-to] A soft cow's-milk cheese.

Prestinara, alla [AHl-lah prehs-tee-nAH-rah] Describes certain dishes prepared with garlic and olive oil.

Prezzemolo [prehts-tsEH-moh-lo] Parsley.

Prezzemolo, al With parsley.

Prezzo [prEHts-tso] Price.

Prezzo fisso [+ fEEz-zo] Fixed price.

Prima colazione [prEE-mah koh-lah-tsee-OH-neh] Breakfast.

Primavera [pree-mah-vEH-rah] Spring; refers to dishes prepared with fresh spring vegetables.

Primizie [pree-mEE-tsee-eh] Spring fruit and vegetables.

Primo [prEE-moh] First; typically refers to the first course of a meal (*primo piatto*).

Primo cameriere [+ kah-meh-ree-EH-reh] Headwaiter.

Primo sale [+ sAH-leh] A type of Sicilian cheese.

Profumo [proh-fOO-mo] Aroma.

Prosciutto [proh-shee-OOt-to] Unsmoked, uncooked, salt-cured ham; the finest prosciutto come from Parma, Friuli (San Daniele), and Veneto.

Prosciutto alla toscana [+ AHl-lah tohs-kAH-nah] Ham from Tuscany; ham cured the Tuscan way.

Prosciutto di cinghiale [+ dee cheen-gee-AH-leh] Ham made from wild boar.

Prosciutto cotto [+ kOHt-to] Cooked ham.

Prosciutto crudo [+ krOO-do] Raw ham.

Prosciutto di Parma [+ dee pAHr-mah] Regarded as the finest Italian ham; from Langhirano near Parma (Emilia-Romagna).

Prosciutto di San Daniele [+ dee

sahn dahn-ee-EH-leh] A highly regarded ham from San Daniele (Friuli).

Prosciutto d'oca [+ dOH-kah] Cured goose.

Prosecco di conegliano [proh-sEH-ko dee koh-neh-lyee-AH-no] (*Veneto*) Dry or sweet white sparkling wines enjoying a fine reputation.

Provatura [proh-vah-tOO-rah] A buffalo's- or cow's-milk cheese similar to mozzarella.

Provola [prOH-voh-lah] A mozzarella-like cheese made from cow's or buffalo's milk.

Provolona di pecora [proh-voh-lOH-nah dee pEH-koh-rah] A hard, ewe's-milk cheese from Sorrento (Campania).

Provolone [proh-voh-lOH-neh] A popular cheese produced from cow's or buffalo's milk; it is sometimes smoked.

Prugna [prOO-nyah] Plum.

Prugna secca [+ sEHk-kah] Prune.

Puddica [pood-dEE-kah] A savory bread containing olives and anchovies; from Apulia.

Puddighinus a pienu [pood-dee-ghEE-noos ah pee-EH-noo] (*Sardinia*) Chicken stuffed with giblets.

Puglia [pOO-lyee-ah] Apulia, Italy's "heel"; sweet peppers, olives, tomatoes, fennel, and grapes are among the excellent produce grown in Apulia. Because of its long coastline (440 miles), seafood also plays an important culinary role.

Pulcino [pool-chEE-no] Baby chicken.

Pulilgionis [poo-leel-jee-OH-nees] Pasta stuffed with spinach and cheese; from Sardinia.

Pulmentum [pool-mehn-tOOm] An ancient staple food of Rome similar to polenta.

Puls [pools] A type of coarsely ground flour used in ancient times.

Punta [pOOn-tah] Point; tip.

Punta di asparagi [+ dee ahs-pAH-rah-jee] Asparagus tip.

Punta di petto [+ dee pEHt-to] A cut of veal from the breast.

Punta di vitello [+ dee vee-tEHl-lo] See *Punta di petto*.

Puntarelle [poon-tah-rEHl-leh] A variety of wild chicory.

Punto, al [ahl pOOn-to] Refers to meat cooked medium-done.

Pupurate [poo-poo-rAH-teh] A ring-shaped yeast cake spiced with cinnamon, cloves, and pepper.

Pura semolina [pOO-rah seh-moh-lEE-nah] Pure semolina flour; durum wheat flour.

Purea [poo-rEH-ah] Puree.

Puro [pOO-ro] Pure; clean.

Putizza [poo-tEEts-tsah] A small sweet yeast cake flavored with chocolate, raisins, and nuts.

Puttanesca/putenesca, salsa alla [poot-tah-nEHs-kuh/poo-teh-nEHs-kuh] "In the style of a prostitute"; a pasta sauce composed of olive oil, fresh chopped tomatoes, anchovies, black olives, capers, and herbs; the sauce can be cooked or uncooked.

Quadretti in brodo [kwahd-rEHt-tee een brOH-do] Tiny pasta squares in broth.

V O C A B U L A R Y

Quadrucci [kwahd-rOO-chee] "Tiny squares"; small square-shaped pasta.

Quaggiarid [kwah-jee-ah-reed] (*Apulia*) Stuffed sheep's tripe.

Quaglia [kwAH-lyee-ah] Quail.

Quagliata [kwah-lyee-AH-tah] The name used in parts of Italy for rennet; see *Quaglio.*

Quagliette di vitello [kwah-lyee-EHt-teh dee vee-tEHl-lo] Stuffed, rolled veal resembling birds.

Quaglio [kwAH-lyee-o] Rennet.

Quarantini [kwah-rahn-tEE-nee] A variety of yellow string bean.

Quartirolo [kwahr-tee-rOH-lo] A soft, creamy cow's-milk cheese from Lombardy; similar to Belpaese.

Quattro stagioni [kwAHt-tro stah-jee-OH-nee] See *Pizza quattro stagioni.*

Quinquinelle [kween-kwee-nEHl-leh] Quenelle; a light dumpling made of finely ground poultry, beef, or fish and bound with eggs, cream, panada, and so on.

Rabarbaro [rah-bAHr-bah-ro] Rhubarb.

Radicchio [rah-dEE-kee-o] (1) Red-leafed chicory. (2) The word sometimes used for radish.

Radicchio di Treviso [+ dee treh-vEE-so] A crisp variety of chicory sweet and slightly pink in color; grown in Treviso (Veneto).

Radichella [rah-dee-kEHl-lah] Dandelion.

Radici [rAH-dee-chee] Radishes.

Rafano [rAH-fah-no] Horseradish.

Raffiuoli [rahf-fee-oo-OH-lah] Small lemon-flavored pastries; from Apulia.

Raffreddare [rahf-frehd-dAH-reh] Cool; refresh.

Ragno [rAH-nyo] Sea bass.

Ragù [rah-gOO] A hearty meat and tomato sauce for pasta; a meat and tomato stew.

Ragù abruzzese [+ ahb-roots-tsEH-zeh] (*Abruzzi*) Mutton stew; cooked in wine and tomato sauce with pancetta, onions, garlic, and herbs; served with pasta.

Ragù alla bolognese [+ AHl-lah boh-loh-nyEH-seh] (*Bologna*) Ground beef, pork, ham, tomatoes, and herbs cooked in olive oil and butter; enriched with cream.

Ragù alla cacciatora [+ AHl-lah kah-chee-ah-tOH-rah] Aromatic herbs and vegetables, garlic, ground beef, and mushrooms simmered in red wine and tomato sauce.

Ragù alla napoletana [+ AHl-lah nah-poh-leh-tAH-nah] Ground pork, garlic, onions, and tomatoes, simmered in red wine and tomato paste.

Ragusano [rah-goo-zAH-no] A cow's-milk cheese from Ragusa (Sicily); eaten fresh or aged and grated.

Rana pescatrice [rAH-nah pays-kah-trEE-cheh] Monkfish; also called *rospo.*

Rane [rAH-neh] Frogs.

Rane, cosciette di [kOHs-chee-eht-teh dee +] Frog's legs.

Rapa [rAH-pah] Turnip.

Rapa Svedese [+ sveh-dEH-seh] Rutabaga.

Ratafia di cerasoli [rah-tah-fEE-ah dee cheh-rah-sOH-lee] A cherry-flavored liqueur.

Ravanello [rah-pah-nEHl-lo] Radish.

Ravenelli [rah-veh-nEHl-lee] Large radishes.

Raviggiolo [rah-vee-jee-OH-lo] A soft ewe's-milk cheese from Tuscany and Umbria.

Ravioli [rah-vee-OH-lee] Square, round, or half-moon shaped stuffed pasta. Ravioli, originally dumplings similar to gnocchi, originated in the Riviera and are one of the oldest of Italian stuffed pastas; traditional fillings include borage, sweetbreads, spinach, ground meat, cheese, eggs, and bread crumbs.

Ravioli alla fiorentina [+ AHl-lah-fee-oh-rehn-tEE-nah] See *Ravioli nudi.*

Ravioli grassi [+ grAHs-see] Ravioli filled with meat.

Ravioli magri [+ mAH-gree] Meatless ravioli.

Raviolini [rah-vee-oh-lEE-nee] Small ravioli.

Ravioli nudi [+ nOO-dee] Gnocchi made with spinch, ricotta, Parmesan, eggs, and flour; also called *Ravioli alla Fiorentina.*

Rayon [rAH-yohn] A hard grating cheese from northern Italy.

Razza [rAHtz-tzah] Skate; ray. Also spelled *arzilla.*

Reale [reh-AH-leh] (1) Royal; describes rich or hearty dishes. (2) A cut of veal from the upper shoulder.

Reblèque [rehb-lEH-kweh] A fresh cream cheese from the Valle d'Aosta; often sweetened and eaten as a snack.

'*Recchie* [ee-rEH-kee-eh] See *Orecchiette.*

Recchietelle [reh-key-eh-tEHl-leh] See *Orecchiette.*

Recioto amarone della valpolicella [reh-chee-OH-to ah-mah-rOH-neh dEHl-lah vahl-poh-lee-chEHl-lah] A dry red wine produced in Veneto; outstanding quality.

Recipiente [reh-chee-pee-EHn-teh] Container.

Recipiente per frutta [+ pehr frOOt-tah] Fruit plate.

Reclèque [reh-klEH-kweh] A soft cream cheese often sweetened and eaten for dessert.

Regaglie [reh-gAH-lyeh] See *Rigaglie.*

Reggiano [rEH-jee-ah-no] A hard grating cheese made with cow's-milk; from Reggio-Emilia.

Reginette [reh-jee-nEHt-teh] A pasta resembling thin lasagna noodles; also called *lasagnette.*

Rete [rEH-teh] Pluck; the heart, liver, lungs, and spleen of an animal; often prepared in a stew.

Rhum [room] Rum.

Ribes [rEE-behs] Currants.

Ribes bianco [+ bee-AHn-ko] Gooseberries.

Ribes nero [+ nEH-ro] Black currants.

Ribes rosso [+ rOHs-so] Red currants.

Ribollita [ree-bohl-lEE-tah] "Reboiled"; (1) A soup made with leftover beef, beans, and vegetables. (2) Minestrone prepared a day ahead; the next day the soup is "reboiled" and served.

Ricciarelli di Siena [rEE-chee-ah-rEHl-lee dee see-EH-nah] A crispy almond cookie from Tuscany.

Ricci di donna [rEE-chee dee dOHn-nah] Literally "women's curls"; a local pasta from Calabria.

Ricci di mare [+ dee mAH-reh] Sea urchins.

Riccini [ree-chEE-nee] A curled horn-shaped pasta, usually ridged.

Riccioli [ree-chee-OH-lo] A type of curly (*riccio*) pasta.

Ricciolina [ree-chee-oh-lEE-nah] Endive.

Ricciolini [ree-chee-oh-lEE-nee] Small *riccioli*.

Ricetta [ree-chEHt-tah] Recipe.

Ricotta [ree-kOHt-tah] A fresh cow's-milk cottage cheese; often sweetened and used in dessert dishes; in Italy ricotta is not considered a cheese.

— *forte* [+ fohr-teh] Fermented ricotta.

— *infornata* [+ een-fohr-nAH-tah] Baked ricotta.

— *romana* [+ roh-mAH-nah] Firm ricotta cheese.

— *salata* [+ sah-lAH-tah] Dried ricotta; used as a grating cheese.

Rigaglie [reh-gAH-lyeh] Giblets; also spelled *regaglie*.

Rigati [ree-gAH-tee] Ridged, as for pasta.

Rigatoni [ree-gah-tOH-nee] Large tubed pasta; ribbed. Also called *denti di cavallo*.

Riola [ree-OH-lah] A soft goat's- or ewe's-milk cheese.

Ripieno [ree-pee-EH-no] Filled; stuffed; also stuffing.

Ris [rees] Rice.

Riserva [ree-sEHr-vah] A wine term indicating the wine has been aged for a specific amount of time.

Risi e bisi [rEE-zee eh bEE-zee] (*Veneto*) A thick rice and pea soup.

Riso [rEE-zo] Rice.

Risotto [ree-zOHt-to] A method of cooking rice in which *arborio* rice is sautéed and liquid is slowly added in intervals until the rice is cooked al dente.

Risotto certosina [+ chehr-toh-zEE-nuh] Risotto with shrimp.

Risotto nero [+ nEH-ro] Rice cooked with squid and squid ink.

Ristorante [rees-toh-rAHn-teh] Restaurant.

Ristretto [rees-trEHt-to] (1) Reduced; refers to stocks and sauces which are gently simmered so as to reduce volume and concentrate flavors. (2) Consommé; a highly reduced and flavorful soup stock.

Ritagli [ree-tAH-lyee] Parings.

Ritortelli [ree-tohr-tEHl-lee] A word sometimes used for crepes in parts of Italy.

Robiola [roh-bee-OH-lah] A *stracchino*-type cheese from Piedmont and Lombardy made from cow's or goat's milk; also called *tuma*.

Robiola del bec [+ dehl behk] A version of *robiola* made at certain times of the year.

Rocciata [roh-chee-AH-tah] A sweet pastry from central Italy featuring fresh and dried fruit, nuts, and spices.

Roccio [rOH-chee-o] A rich orange-raisin yeast bread; from central Italy.

Rognonata [roh-nyoh-nAH-tah] See *Rognone, salsa di*.

Rognone, salsa di [roh-nyOH-neh]

A thick sauce composed of diced veal kidneys, red wine, beef stock, juniper berries, rosemary, and seasonings; for beef and veal.

Rognoni [roh-nyOH-nee] Kidneys.

Rollatini [rohl-lah-tEE-nee] Thinly sliced meat or poultry stuffed and rolled.

Roma [rOH-mah] Italy's capital city located in Lazio. Although Romans love to eat out and boast perhaps of more restaurants than any other Italian city, simple local fare still dominates; lamb and kid are popular as is beef and beef offal. Pasta, beans, vegetables (particularly artichokes), and pecorino cheeses are also essential to Rome's cuisine.

Romagna [roh-mAH-nyah] See *Emilia-Romagna*.

Romagnola [roh-mah-nyOH-lah] An esteemed variety of artichoke; also called *mammolo*.

Romagnola, alla Denotes certain dishes served with tomato sauce.

Romana, alla [roh-mAH-nah] Describes various dishes prepared in the Roman fashion; often denotes the use of onions or meat sauce.

Romanello [roh-mah-nEHl-lo] "Little romano"; a hard sharp grating cheese made from cow's milk.

Romanesco [roh-mah-nEHs-ko] A high-quality variety of artichoke; also called *mammolo*.

Romano [roh-mAH-no] A hard grating cheese of which there are several versions; see *Pecorino*. Pecorino is Italy's oldest cheese.

Romano, caprino [kah-prEE-no +] Pecorino cheese made from goat's milk.

Romano, vacchino [vah-kEY-no +] Pecorino cheese made from cow's milk.

Rombo [rOHm-mo] Turbot; brill.

Rombo chiodato [+ key-oh-dAH-to] Turbot.

Rombo liscio [+ lee-shee-o] Brill.

Rosa canina [rOH-sah kah-nEE-nah] Rose hip.

Rosatello [roh-zah-tEHl-lo] Rosé wine.

Rose [rOH-zah] The name sometimes used for a variety of radicchio.

Rosmarino [rohs-mah-rEE-no] Rosemary.

Rosolare [roh-zoh-lAH-reh] To brown in butter or oil; sauté.

Rosolate [roh-zoh-lAH-teh] Roasted.

Rosolio di anice [roh-zOH-lee-oh dee AN-nee-cheh] An anise-flavored liqueur.

Rospo [rOHs-po] Monkfish; also called *rana pescatrice*.

Rossa, salsa [sAHl-sah rOHs-sah] "Red sauce"; a simple tomato sauce.

Rossetti [roh-sEHt-tee] Fried whitebait.

Rosso [rOHs-so] Red.

Rosticceria [rohs-tee-cheh-rEE-ah] (1) Rôtisserie. (2) Sandwich shop; snack shop.

Rosticiada [rohs-tee-chee-AH-dah] (*Lombardy*) Slices of pork and sausage served in a spicy onion-white wine sauce.

Rosticini [rohs-tee-chII-nee] Roasted lamb.

Rosumado [roh-zoo-mAH-do] A beverage composed of red wine to which egg yolks and sugar have been incorporated.

Rotoli [rOH-toh-lee] "Rolls"; thinly sliced meat, pasta, bread, and so on stuffed with various fillings and rolled.

Rotolo di Natale [rOH-toh-lo dee nah-tAH-leh] Sweet yeast dough rolled thin and layered with pine nuts, candied fruit, and raisins; rolled up and baked.

Rotolo di Pasta [+ dee pah-stah] A pasta sheet spread with various fillings; rolled up and cooked.

Ruchetta [roo-kEHt-tah] A plant common to southern Italy used as a vegetable.

Rucola [rOO-koh-lah] Arugula; also spelled *rughetta*, *rugula*, and *rugola*.

Rughetta [roo-ghEHt-tah] See *Rucola*.

Ruote di carro [ruu-OH-teh dee kAHr-ro] Cart wheel-shaped pasta.

Ruotini [roo-oh-tEE-nee] Small *ruoti*.

Russole [rOOs-soh-leh] A variety of wild mushroom.

Rustutu cu'sammurigghiu [roos-tOO-too koo-sahm-moo-rEE-ghee-oo] (*Sicily*) Fried breaded swordfish.

Saba [sAH-bah] Concentrated wine must.

Sagne chine [sAH-nyeh kEE-neh] (*Calabria*) Lasagne.

Sagnettine [sah-nyeht-tEE-neh] (*Abruzzi*) Linguine.

Sala da pranzo [sAH-lah dah prAHn-tso] Dining room.

Salama da sugo [sah-lAH-mah dah sOO-go] A pork sausage from Ferrara and Felino flavored with wine and brandy (Emilia-Romagna).

Salame [sah-lAH-meh] Salami; large salt-cured sausages made from pork, pork fat, and flavorings.

Salame da sugo [+ dah sOO-go] A spicy pork and liver sausage; a specialty of Ferrara (Emilia-Romagna) and other parts of northern Italy.

Salame di Fabriano [+ dee fah-bree-AH-no] (*Marche*) A pork and veal sausage of excellent quality.

Salame di Napoli [+ dee nAH-poh-lee] See *Salame napoletano*.

Salame Felino [+ feh-lEE-no] See *Salama da sugo*.

Salame finocchiona [+ fee-noh-key-OH-nuh] See *Finocchiona*.

Salamella [sah-lah-mEHl-lah] A spicy sausage.

Salame Milano [+ mee-lAH-no] A salami from Milan made from lean pork and beef speckled with pork fat.

Salame napoletano [+ nah-poh-leh-tAH-no] A pork and beef salami seasoned with pepper; also called *salame di Napoli*.

Salamin d'la duja [sah-lah-mEEn dee lah dOO-juh] A local salami of Piedmont.

Salamoia [sah-lah-mOH-ee-ah] Brine.

Salatini [sah-lah-tEE-nee] A salty cracker.

Salato [sah-lAH-to] Salted; cured.

Sale [sAH-leh] Salt.

Salignon [sah-lee-nyOHn] A fresh goat's- or ewe's-milk cheese from the Italian Alps; flavored with sweet red peppers and herbs.

Salmì [sahl-mEE] A game stew.

Salmistra [sahl-mEEs-trah] Another name for *Aostin*; see *Aostin*.

Salmone [sahl-mOH-neh] Salmon.

— *affumicato* [+ ahf-foo-mee-kAH-to] Smoked salmon.

Salmoriglio [sahl-moh-rEE-lyee-o] A sauce for grilled meats and fish composed of olive oil, lemon, garlic, oregano, and salt and pepper.

Salsa [sAHl-sah] The Italian word for sauce.

— *di cren* [+ dee kren] Horseradish sauce.

— *di noci* [+ dee nOH-chee] A Genoese sauce made by grinding bread (which has been immersed in milk or water), walnuts, olive oil, and fresh garlic in a mortar until smooth; enriched with ricotta and Parmesan cheese and seasoned to taste.

— *secca* [+ sEHk-kah] A highly reduced, concentrated tomato sauce.

— *verde* [+ vEHr-deh] Piquant green sauce; describes sauces of which there are several versions composed mainly of green herbs, olive oil, and seasonings.

Salsicce cotte nella cenere [sahl-sEE-cheh kOHt-teh nEHl-lah chEH-neh-reh] (*Sicily*) Sausage cooked in live cinders.

Salsiccia [sahl-sEEk-kee-ah] Sausage.

— *a metro* [+ uh mEHt-ro] A long, thin pork sausage.

Saltare/saltate [sahl-tAH-reh/sahl-tah-teh] Sauté; sautéed.

Saltata in padella [+ een pah-dEHl-lah] Literally "sautéed in a frying pan"; this term refers to foods, particularly pasta, tossed in the pan with the sauce prior to serving.

Saltimbocca [sahl-teem-bOHk-kah] (*Rome*) A famous dish featuring thin slices of veal topped with prosciutto and fresh sage; cooked in butter and white wine.

Salumeria [sah-loom-eh-rEE-ah] A gourmet shop; deli.

Salumi [sah-lOO-mee] Cured processed pork products; cold cuts.

Salvia [sAHl-vee-ah] Sage.

Salviata [sahl-vee-ah-tah] A type of crustless quiche flavored with sage and cheese.

Sambuca [sahm-bOOk-kah] A clear anise-flavored liqueur. See *Sambuco*.

Sambuco [sahm-bOOk-ko] Elder; a flowering shrub whose berries are used in the production of *Sambuca*. See *Sambuca*.

Sana cucina [sAH-nah koo-chEE-nah] Healthy cooking.

Sanato [sah-nAH-to] Veal raised in Piedmont; of excellent quality.

Sangiovese [sahn-jee-oh-vEH-seh] The major red Chianti grape.

Sangue [sahn-ghOO-eh] Blood.

Sangue, al Very rare.

Sangue di raboso [+ rah-bOH-so] A liqueur produced in Veneto.

Sanguinacci [sahn-ghoo-ee-nAH-chee] A wild mushroom grown in central Italy.

Sanguinaccio [sahn-ghoo-ee-nAH-chee-o] (1) Blood pudding. (2) A sweet dessert pudding from Naples made with pig's blood and flavored with chocolate.

Sanguinante [sahn-goo-ee-nAHn-teh] Rare; undercooked.

San Marzano [sahn mahr-tsAH-no] A variety of plum tomato excellent for sauces.

VOCABULARY

Saor [sAH-ohr] (*Veneto*) Fish marinated in vinegar and seasonings.

Sapa [sAH-pah] A sweet syrup made from concentrated wine must.

Saparoso [sah-pah-rOH-so] Relish.

Sappada [sahp-pAH-dah] Smoked ham.

Saraghine [sah-rah-ghEE-neh] The word for sardine in parts of Emilia-Romagna.

Sarago [sah-rAH-gho] Sea bream.

S'aranzata [sah-rahn-tsAH-tuh] Candied orange peel; from Sardinia.

Sarde [sAHr-deh] Sardines; pilchards.

Sardegna [sahr-dEH-nyah] Sardinia; a large Mediterranean island off the west coast of Italy. Livestock, especially pigs and sheep, seafood, and pecorino cheeses are major food staples. Game animals and fresh fruit and vegetables are abundant and of excellent quality.

Sardenaira [sahr-deh-nAH-ee-rah] A Ligurian word for pizza.

Sardine [sahr-dEE-neh] Sardines; plichards.

Sardo [sAHr-do] See *Fiore sardo*.

Sardoni [sahr-dOH-nee] Sardine; anchovy.

Sardoni a scotadeò [+ ah skoh-tah-deh-O] (*Veneto*) Fire-roasted sardines.

Sargnon [sahr-nyon] A creamy cheese made from a mixture of various cheese and alcohol; from Piedmont.

Sartizzu [sahr-tEEts-tsoo] (*Sardinia*) A spicy pork sausage.

Sartù [sahr-tOO] (*Naples*) A hearty dish featuring cooked rice, chicken giblets, sausage, meatballs, and mozzarella cheese baked in tomato sauce.

Sassella [sahs-sEHl-lah] Dry red wine from Lombardy.

Sassicaia [sahs-see-kAH-ee-ah] Dry red wine from Tuscany; one of Italy's finest.

Sassolini [sahs-soh-lEE-nee] A type of sausage similar to *zampone* from Modena (Emilia-Romagna).

Sassolino [sahs-soh-lEE-no] (*Emilia-Romagna*) An anise-flavored liqueur from Sassuola.

Saueresuppe [sah-weh-ray-zOOp-pah] Tripe soup; from Trentino.

Sauro [sAH-oo-ro] Sorrel.

Saussa d'avie [sah-OOs-suh dAH-vee-eh] A spicy sauce form Piedmont composed of mustard, ground nuts, and honey; served with boiled meats.

Savoiardi [sah-voh-ee-AHr-dee] Ladyfingers; small oval of sponge cake used in several sweet preparations.

Savor [sah-vohr] (*Emilia-Romagna*) A relish-like condiment composed of diced apples and quince stewed in grape must.

Sbira [sbEE-rah] (*Genoa*) Tripe soup.

Scabeccio [skah-bEH-chee-o] (*Liguria*) Marinated fried mullet.

Scaccia [skAH-chee-ah] A savory vegetable and cheese pie.

Scalogno [skah-lOH-nyo] Shallot.

Scaloppe/scaloppine [shah-lOHp-peh/skah-lohp-pEE-neh] Thin veal cutlets; other local names include *piccata* and *piccatine*.

Scamorza [skah-mOHr-tsah] A

pear-shaped cheese eaten fresh or aged; made from buffalo's or cow's milk.

Scampi [skAHm-pee] A variety of shrimp from the Adriatic Sea.

— ***fra diavole*** [+ frah dee-AH-voh-leh] A famous dish featuring sautéed shrimp served in a hot tomato sauce.

Scamponi [skahm-pOH-nee] Large shrimp.

Scapace/scapece [skah-pAH-cheh/ skah-pEH-cheh] Pickled fish; boneless fish fried in oil and marinated in vinegar and spices (including saffron).

Scarola [skah-rOH-lah] Escarole.

Scarpazza [shahr-pAHts-tsah] See *Scarpazzone*.

Scarpazzit [skahr-pahts-tsEEt] Spinach fritter.

Scarpazzone [skahr-pahts-tsOH-neh] (*Emilia-Romagna*) A vegetable and cheese pie; also called *erbazzone* and *scarpazza*.

Scatagghiett [skah-tah-ghee-EHt] A dessert pastry from Apulia flavored with honey.

Scatola [skAH-toh-lah] Box; can.

Scheggino [skay-jEE-no] A town in Umbria noted for black truffles.

— ***pasta di*** [pAH-stah dee +] Fresh pasta served with a sauce composed of pureed trout, black truffles, tomato paste, chicken stock, and seasonings. See *Scheggino*.

Schiacciata [skee-ah-chee-AH-tah] A flat yeast bread.

Schiacciata unta alla fiorentina [+ OOn-tah AHl-luh fee-oh-rayn-tEE-nah] (*Florence*) Flat bread made with beef stock in place of some of the water.

Schiaffettoni [skee-ahf-feht-toh-nee] Baked pasta stuffed with meat and cheese.

Schiava [skee-AH-vah] A red wine grape.

Schiena [skee-EH-nah] Saddle (*venison; hare*).

Schienali [skee-eh-nAH-lee] Spinal marrow; used in stuffings or prepared like sweetbreads; also called *filone*.

Schiumoni [skee-oo-mOH-nee] (*Sicily*) Almond meringue pastries.

Schneckensuppe [shehk-ehn-sOO-peh] Snail soup; from Trentino.

Schüttelbrot [shOO-tehl-broht] A local bread of Trentino.

Schwammerlsuppe [shvAHm-mehrl-sOO-peh] Mushroom soup; from Trentino.

Schwartzplentene [shvAHrts-plEHn-teh-neh] (*Alto Adige*) A dumpling made from rye and buckwheat flours.

Sciabbaccheddu [shee-ah-bah-kEHd-doo] Fried whitebait; from Sicily.

Sciatt [shee-AHt] (*Lombardy*) Sweet fritters.

Sciroppo [shee-rOHp-po] Syrup.

Sciroppo, alla Cooked in syrup.

Sciuetta [shee-oo-EHt-tah] Marzipan confections.

Sciumette alla grotta [shee-oo-mEHt-teh AHl-lah grOHt-tah] A famous dessert featuring sweet meringue mounds poached in milk and served in a pistacchio-custard sauce.

Scorfano/scorpena [skOHr-fah-no/ skohr-pEH-nah] Rascasse; scorpion fish. An expensive sea fish

Scorfano/scorpena (cont.) prepared similarly to bream; often used in fish soups and stews.

Scorza [skOHr-tsah] Peel; skin.

Scorza candita [+ kahn-dEE-tah] Candied citrus peel.

Scorzetta [skohr-tsEHt-tah] Zest.

Scorzonera [skohr-tsoh-nEH-rah] Salsify.

Scottadito [skoht-tah-dEE-to] Grilled lamb chops served piping hot.

Scottare [skoht-tAH-reh] (1) Burn; scald. (2) To cook in very hot fat.

Scottiglia [skoht-tEE-lyee-ah] Meat stew.

Scotto [skOHt-to] Overcooked.

Scripelle [skree-pEHl-leh] See *Crispelle 'mbusse*.

Scungili [skoon-jEE-lee] Whelk; conch.

Scuro [skOO-ro] Dark; refers to certain preparations possessing a dark color.

Sebadas [seh-bah-dahs] A sweet Sardinian dessert fritter.

Secco [sEHk-koh] Dry.

Secondo piatto [seh-kOHn-do pee-AHt-to] Second course.

Sedanini [seh-dah-nEE-nee] Small narrow rigatoni.

Sedano [sEH-dah-no] Celery.

Sedano di Verona [+ dee veh-rOH-nah] Celeriac.

Sedano rapa [+ rAH-pah] Celeriac.

Seicentenario [say-ee-chehn-teh-nAH-ree-o] (*Tuscany*) A red wine of superb quality.

Sèller [sEHl-lehr] (*Lombardy*) Celery.

Selvaggina [sehl-vah-jEE-nuh] Game.

Selvatica [sehl-vAH-tee-kah] Wild.

Sementare [seh-mehn-tAH-reh] Baby eels.

Semini di melo [seh-mEE-nee dee mEH-lo] Tiny teardrop-shaped pasta.

Semola [sEH-moh-lah] See *Semolino*.

Semolina [seh-moh-lEE-nah] Semolina porridge; see *Semolino*.

Semolino [seh-moh-lEE-no] Semolina flour.

Semplice [sEHm-plee-cheh] Plain.

Senape [sEH-nah-peh] Mustard.

Senatori [seh-nah-tOH-ree] The name in Veneto for large mature peas.

Seppie [sEHp-pee-eh] Cuttlefish; a squidlike fish popular in several parts of Italy.

Seràs/serò [seh-rUHs/seh-rO] A fresh cow's-milk cheese from Aosta.

Serpentaria [sehr-pehn-tAH-ree-ah] Tarragon.

Serpillo [sehr-pEEl-lo] Wild thyme.

Servizio [sehr-vEE-tsee-o] (*Restaurant*) Service.

Setaccio [seh-tAH-chee-o] Sifter.

Seuppa [seh-OOp-pah] A local word for soup in parts of Italy.

Sfilatini [sfee-lah-tEE-nee] A long loaf of bread.

Sfinciuni [sfeen-chee-OO-nee] Sicilian pizzas; savory buns with toppings.

Sfingi [sfEEn-jee] Cream puffs; small pastries.

Sfogi in saor [sfOH-jee een sAH-ohr] (*Venice*) Fish braised in wine and vinegar; prepared during the *Festa del Redentore* (Feast of the Redeemer).

Sfoglia [sfOH-lyee-ah] A sheet of pastry; puff pastry. See *Pasta sfoglia*.

Sfoglia, la A sausage and cheese pie.

Sfogliata [sfoh-lyee-AH-tah] See *Pasta sfoglia*.

Sfogliatelle [sfoh-lyee-ah-tEHl-leh] A Neapolitan dessert featuring puff pastry filled with (usually) pastry cream.

Sfogliatine [sfoh-lyee-ah-tEE-neh] A puff pastry turnover stuffed with mozzarella cheese, tomato sauce, and oregano; served as an entrée or appetizer.

Sformato [sfohr-mAH-to] Flan.

Sformato di maionese [+ dee mah-ee-oh-nEH-seh] Mayonnaise mold; fresh mayonnaise mixed with liquid gelatin and chilled in a mold; served with boiled fish or meat.

Sfotzato [sfoht-tsAH-to] (*Lombardy*) A dry red wine.

Sfrappole/sfrapel [sfrAHp-poh-leh/ sfrah-pEHl] A sweet braided pastry; from Emilia-Romagna.

Sgombero [sgOHm-beh-ro] Mackerel.

Sgombro [sgOHm-bro] Mackerel.

Sguazeto [sguu-ah-tseh-to] Lamb stew.

Sicilia [see-chEE-lee-ah] Sicily; The largest Mediterranean island located at the "toe" of Italy. Seafood and fresh produce dominate the Sicilian diet which often results in robust pasta dishes; famous for elegant pastries and rich ice creams.

Siciliana, alla [AHl-lah see-chee-lee-AH-nah] Describes several different dishes prepared "Sicilian style"; often denotes the presence of eggplant or seafood.

Siero [see-EH-ro] Buttermilk.

Siero di latte [+ dee lAHt-teh] Whey.

Silvestro [seel-vEHs-tro] An herb liqueur.

Sivet [see-veht] A game stew thickened with the animal's blood.

Smacafam [smah-kah-fahm] (*Veneto*) A type of polenta made from buckwheat flour.

Smejassa [smeh-jAHs-sah] (*Veneto*) Sweet polenta mixed with dried fruits and nuts; served as a dessert.

Soave [soh-AH-veh] A dry white wine from Veneto.

Sobbollire [sohb-bohl-lEE-reh] A low simmer.

Sode, uova [oo-OH-vah sOH-deh] Hard-boiled eggs.

Sodo [sOH-do] Hard.

Sodro [sOH-dro] Cider.

Soffocato [sohf-foh-kAH-to] Sweat; to cook vegetables over low flame in a heavy covered pot.

Soffriggere [sohf-frEE-gheh-reh] To fry lightly.

Soffritto [sohf-frEEt-to] (1) Chopped aromatic herbs and vegetables lightly fried in butter or oil; the flavoring for numerous soups, stews, sauces, and so on. (2) To lightly fry.

Sogliola [soh-lyee-OH-lah] Sole.

Solaia [soh-lah-ee-ah] A red wine from Tuscany; fine quality.

Soncino [sohn-chEE-no] Lamb's lettuce; mâche; also called *valerianella* in parts of Italy.

Sopa [sOH-pah] The word for soup in parts of Italy.

Sopa coada [+ koh-AH-dah] (*Veneto*) Pigeon meat and giblets covered with stale bread; moistened with broth and baked.

Sopa friulana [+ free-oo-lAH-nah] Celery soup.

Soppressa [sohp-prEHs-sah] A large pork sausage from Veneto; *soppressa veneta* (Valpolicella) and *soppressa bellunese* (Belluno) are the most popular.

Soppressata [sohp-prays-sAH-tah] A spicy smoked pork sausage; a specialty of Basilicata.

Sora [sOH-ruh] A fresh goat's-milk cheese from Piedmont.

Sorbetto [sohr-bEHt-to] Sorbet; flavored iced dessert sometimes containing cream or egg whites.

Sospiri [sohs-pEE-ree] (*Sardinia*) A sweet almond confection; also spelled *suspirus*.

Sottaceti [soht-tah-chEH-tee] Pickled vegetables.

Sott'aceto [soht-tah-chEH-to] Pickled.

Sottofesa [soht-toh-fEH-zah] A cut of veal from the upper leg.

Sott'olio [soht OH-lee-o] Preserved in oil.

Spaccatina [spahk-kah-tEE-nah] A type of bread.

Spaghetti [spah-ghEHt-tee] A long, round, thin noodle; the most popular of all pastas.

Spaghettini [spah-ghayt-tEE-nee] Thin spaghetti.

Spago [spAH-go] Cord; the word from which spaghetti derives its name.

Spalla [spAHl-lah] Shoulder.

Spannocchi [spahn-nOH-kee] Prawn.

Sparagio [spAH-rah-jee-o] Asparagus.

Specialità [spay-chee-ah-lee-tAH] Specialty.

Speck [spehk] Smoked ham or bacon from Alto Adige.

Spezie [spEH-tsee-eh] Spices.

Spezzatino [spehts-tsah-tEE-no] Cubed meat usually stewed; stew.

Spianatoia [spee-ah-nah-tOH-ee-ah] Pasta board; a special wooden board on which pasta dough is kneaded and rolled out.

Spicchio di aglio [spEE-kee-o dee AH-lyee-o] Garlic clove.

Spiedini [spee-eh-dEE-nee] (1) Skewers. (2) Kebab; skewered food. (3) Small hollow pasta noodles; ridged.

Spiedo [spee-EH-do] Spit.

Spigola [spee-gOH-lah] See *Branzino*.

Spinaci [spee-nAH-chee] Spinach.

Spirale [spee-rAH-leh] A short pasta formed into spirals.

Spongarda/spongata [spohn-ghAHr-dah/spohn-ghAH-tah] A sweet pie filled with candied and dried fruits, nuts, and jam.

Spugnola, la [lah spoo-nyOH-lah] A local lasagne from Modena featuring *spugnole* mushrooms.

Spugnole [spoo-nyOH-lah] A variety of large wild mushroom.

Spuma [spOO-mah] Foam; describes light foamy (sometimes frozen) desserts.

Spumante [spoo-mAHn-teh] Sparkling.

Spumone [spoo-mOH-neh] A custard-based ice cream lightened with whipped cream or egg whites.

Spuntino [spoon-tEE-no] Snack.

Stacchiotte [stah-kee-OHt-teh] Shell-shaped noodles.

Staghiotte [stah-ghee-OHt-teh] Square or rectangle-shaped pasta.

Stagionare [stah-jee-oh-nAH-reh] To season.

Stagione, di [dee stah-jee-OH-neh] In season.

Stampo [stAHm-po] Mold.

Starna [stAHr-nah] Partridge.

Stecchi [stEH-kee] Small skewered tidbits breaded and fried.

Stellette [stehl-lEHt-teh] Star-shaped pasta.

Stelline [stehl-lEE-neh] See *Pastina stelline*.

Stenderello [stehn-day-rEHl-lo] Rolling pin.

Stiacciata [stee-ah-chee-AH-tah] A sweet pastry; cookie.

Stinco [stEEn-ko] (Calf's) shin.

Stivaletti [steeivah-lEHt-tee] "Little boots"; a type of pasta noodle.

Stoccafisso [stoh-kah-fEEs-so] Stockfish; dried salted cod.

Stomaco [stOH-mah-koh] Stomach.

Storione [stoh-ree-OH-neh] Sturgeon.

Storni [stOHr-nee] Starling.

Straca dent' [strAH-kah dehnt] A crunchy almond cookie from Emilia-Romagna.

Stracchino [strah-kEY-no] Describes certain creamy cheeses from northern Italy made from cow's milk; Gorgonzola is a type of *stracchino* cheese.

Stracci [strAH-chee] Short flat soup noodles; also called *carte da giuoco*.

Stracciatella [strah-chee-ah-tEHl-lah] Egg drop soup; boiling broth to which a mixture of beaten eggs and Parmesan cheese are added.

Stracciato [strah-chee-AH-to] Scrambled.

Stracotto [strah-kOHt-to] (1) Pot roast. (2) Over cooked.

Stramaldetta [strah-mahl-dEHt-tah] A name once used for polenta.

Strangolapreti [strahn-ghol-ah-prEH-tee] Small pasta dumplings made from hard-wheat flour.

Strapazzato [strah-pahts-tsAH-to] Scrambled.

Strascenate [strah-sheh-nAH-teh] (1) A tubed pasta noodle. (2) Square or rectangle-shaped pasta.

Strascinari [strah-shee-nAH-ree] (*Basilicata*) A local, hard-wheat pasta; called *strascinati* outside of Basilicata.

Strascinati [strah-shee-nAH-tee] See *Strascinari*.

Strattu [strAHt-too] Tomato paste; concentrated tomatoes.

Stravecchio [strah-vEH-key-o] Very old; Parmesan cheese which has been aged for three years. This term also refers to wine.

Stravecchione [strah-veh-key-OH-neh] Parmesan cheese that has been aged over four years.

Strega [strEH-gah] A sweet herb liqueur.

Stria [strEE-ah] (*Emilia-Romagna*) A local flat bread of Modena; flavored with herbs and sometimes studded with pancetta.

Strinù [stree-nOO] (*Lombardy*) A spicy pork and beef sausage.

Strucolo [strOO-koh-lo] (*Veneto*) A sweet rolled pastry filled with ricotta, dried fruits, and nuts.

Struffoli [strOOf-foh-lee] Small sweet honey fritters; also called *pignolata*.

Strutto [strUUt-to] Lard; pork fat.

Stufato [stoo-fAH-to] Braised meat; meat stew. Also called *stufatino*.

Stuzzicadenti [stoouts-tsee-kah-dEHn-tee] Toothpick.

Succo [sOOk-ko] Juice.

V O C A B U L A R Y

Succulento [sook-koo-lEHn-to] Succulent

Succu tundu [sOOk-koo tOOn-doo] See *Frègula*.

Suffle [sOOf-fleh] Soufflé.

Sugna [sOO-nyuh] Lard; suet.

Sugo [sOO-go] Juice; sauce; gravy.

— *al* With sauce.

— *di pomodoro* [+ dee pohm-oh-dOH-ro] Tomato sauce.

Suina, carne [kAHr-neh soo-EE-nah] Pork.

Sulla vena [sOOl-lah vEH-nah] A semisweet Frascati wine.

Sultanina [sool-tah-nEE-nah] Sultana; golden raisin.

Suppa [sOOp-pah] The word for soup in parts of Italy.

Supplì [soop-plEE] Croquettes; typically made with rice.

Supplì al telefono [+ ahl teh-leh-fOH-no] Rice croquettes made with mozzarella cheese. When bitten into, the melted cheese becomes stringy, resembling telephone wires.

Supplì di riso [+ dee rEE-zo] Rice croquettes.

Suprema di pollo [soop-rEH-mah dee pOHl-lo] Boneless, skinless chicken breast.

Susina [soo-sEE-nah] Plum; prune.

Suspirus [soos-pEE-roos] See *Sospiri*.

Taberna vinaria [tah-bEHr-nah vEE-nAH-ree-ah] A winery in ancient Rome.

Tacchinella [tah-key-nEHl-lah] Young turkey.

Tacchino [tah-key-no] Turkey.

Taeddas [tah-ehd-dahs] A cheese similar to *Caciocavallo*.

Tagliare, per [pehr tah-lyee-AH-reh] Cutting utensils; knives.

Tagliarini [tah-lyee-ah-rEE-nee] See *Fedelini*.

Tagliatelle [tah-lyee-ah-tEHl-leh] The traditional Bolognese pasta noodle; similar to fettuccine, but slightly wider.

Tagliato [tah-lyee-AH-to] Sliced.

Tagliente [tah-lyee-EHn-teh] Sharp.

Taglierini [tah-lyee-eh-rEE-nee] See *Fedelini*.

Tagliere [tah-lyee-EH-reh] Cutting board.

Taglio [tAH-lyee-o] A pasta noodle.

Tagliolini [tah-lyee-oh-lEE-nee] See *Fedelini*.

Tagliuzzare [tah-lyee-ootz-tzAH-reh] Dice; cut into small pieces.

Tajarin [tah-jah-reen] (*Piedmont*) A long flat pasta noodle; *tagliolini*.

Taleggio [tah-lEH-jee-o] A soft *stracchino*-type cheese made with cow's milk from Bergamo (Lombardy).

Talfino [tahl-fEE-no] Another name for *Taleggio* cheese.

Taralli [tah-rAHl-lee] (1) Sweet ring-shaped pastries. (2) Savory pretzel-like pastries; from Apulia.

Tarantello [tah-rahn-tEHl-lo] A tuna sausage; from Taranto (Apulia).

Targoncello [tahr-ghohn-chEHl-lo] Tarragon.

Tarocco [tah-rOHk-ko] A variety of orange.

Tarollo [tah-rOHl-lo] (*Apulia*) A simple bun; sometimes flavored with various spices.

Tartarà [tahr-tah-rAH] (1) A sweet almond pudding. (2) A savory custard made from eggs, milk, cheese, and spices.

Tartaruga [tahr-tah-rOO-ghah] Turtle.

Tartelletta [tahr-rehl-lEHt-tah] Tartlet.

Tartina [tahr-tEE-nah] Canapé.

Tartufata [tahr-too-fAH-tah] Truffle; also *tartufo*.

Tartufo [tahr-tOO-fo] Truffle; Italy's finest truffles come from Piedmont.

— *bianco* [+ bee-AHn-ko] White truffle.

— *d'alba* [+ dAHl-bah] Piedmontese white truffle.

— *di mare* [tahr-tOO-fo dee mAH-reh] A variety of clam.

— *nero* [+ nEHr-o] Black truffle.

Tartufoli [tahr-tOO-foh-lee] A former Italian word for potato.

Tatliu [taht-lee-oo] (*Sardinia*) Grilled sheep's offal; also spelled *trattaliu*.

Taurasi [tah-oo-rAH-zee] (*Campania*) One of the region's best red wines.

Taverna [tah-vEHr-nah] Tavern.

Tavola [tAH-voh-lah] Table.

Tavola fredda [+ frEHd-dah] Cold buffet.

Tavoletta [tah-voh-lEHt-tah] Bar.

Tè [teh] Tea.

Tegamaccio [tay-ghah-mAH-chee-o] Compote.

— *di verdure* [+ dee vehr-dOO-reh] Vegetable compote.

Tegame [teh-gAH-meh] A copper saucepan.

— *al* Describes certain dishes prepared in a *tegame*; sautéed.

Tegamino [tah-gah-mEE-no] A small *tegame*.

Teglia [tEH-lyee-ah] A sheetpan.

— *alla* Describes foods cooked on a *teglia*.

Teiera [teh-ee-EH-rah] Teapot.

Tellina [tehl-lEE-nah] The name in Emilia-Romagna for a type of small clam.

Temolo [tEH-moh-lo] Grayling; a freshwater fish related to the trout.

Tempestina [tehm-pehs-tEE-nah] See *Pastina tempestina*.

Tenero [tEH-neh-ro] Tender.

Testa/testina/testarella [tEHs-tah/tehs-tEE-nah/tehs-tah-rEHl-lah] Head; referring to the head.

— *di vitello* [+ dee vee-tEHl-lo] Calf's head.

Testo [tEHs-to] A terracotta griddle.

Testun [tehs-toon] A hard grating cheese from parts of Piedmont.

Tiella [tee-EHl-lah] A casserole dish featuring layers of different ingredients. Sliced potatoes, tomatoes, rice, olive oil, fish, and meat are commonly used to prepare this dish.

Tielle [tee-EHl-leh] A clay pot.

Tiepido [tee-EH-pee-do] Tepid.

Tigelle [tee-jEHl-leh] A peasant flat bread cooked between clay disks; from parts of northern Italy.

Tiglio [tEE-lyee-o] Lime.

Timballo [teem-bAHl-lo] Timbale; a preparation baked in a timbale or mold; the mold is often lined with pastry and filled with various forcemeats, rice, pasta, vegetables, and so on.

Timo [tEE-mo] Thyme.

Tinca [tEEn-kah] Tench; a European freshwater fish.

Tinche [tEEn-keh] See *Tinca*.

Tiramisú [tee-rah-mee-sOO] A popular dessert cake made with sweetened mascarpone cheese, espresso, and chocolate.

Tirolerkrapfen [tee-rOHl-uhr-krAHp-fehn] (*Alto Adige*) Cream puffs filled with fruit jam.

Tocco [tOHk-ko] (1) (*Genoa*) Tomato sauce. (2) Tomato sauce made with wild mushrooms or meat.

Toma [tOH-mah] A rich cow's-milk cheese from Piedmont.

— **veja** [+ vEH-juh] A version of *Toma* cheese.

Tomaxelle [toh-mahks-EHl-leh] Baked stuffed veal.

Tometta [toh-mEHt-tah] Fresh *Toma* cheese.

Tomini [toh-mEE-nee] Small very fresh *Toma* cheeses.

Tomini del Talucco [+ dehl tah-lOOk-ko] A goat's-milk cheese from Piedmont.

Tonnarelli [tohn-nah-rEHl-lee] Thin square-shaped pasta noodles similar to linguine.

Tonnato [tohn-nAH-tah] Describes foods served with tuna sauce; see *Tonno, salsa di.*

Tonnellini [tohn-nehl-lEE-nee] Small *tonnarelli*.

Tonno [tOHn-no] Tuna.

— **al** With tuna sauce; see *Tonno, salsa di.*

— **ragù, al** [rah-goo ahl +] See *Tonno, salsa di.*

— **salsa di** [sAHl-sah dee +] Tuna sauce; tomatoes, onions, garlic, and tuna fish (canned) sautéed in olive oil; served with pasta.

Topinamburo [toh-peen-ahm-bOO-roh] Jerusalem artichoke.

Topini di patate [toh-pEE-nee dee pah-tAH-tah] (*Florence*) Potato dumplings.

Torciolata [tohr-chee-oh-lAH-tah] (*Umbria*) A sweet pastry flavored with apples and chocolate.

Torcolo [tOHr-koh-lo] A local bread roll from Umbria.

Tordimatti [tohr-dee-mAHt-tee] Stuffed veal shaped into thrushes (*tordi*).

Tordo [tOHr-do] Thrush.

Torgiano [tohr-jee-AH-no] (*Umbria*) Dry red wines; fine quality.

Torricella [tohr-ree-chEHl-lah] (*Tuscany*) An excellent dry white wine.

Torrone [tohr-rOH-neh] Nougat; often containing candied fruits and nuts.

— **al cioccolato** [+ ahl chee-oh-koh-lAH-to] Chocolate-flavored nougat.

— **gelato** [+ jeh-lAH-to] Frozen nougat.

Torta [tOHr-tah] Pie; cake; tart.

— **di pane** [+ dee pAH-neh] Bread pudding.

— **di riso** [+ dee rEE-zo] Sweet rice pie.

— **di tagliatella** [+ dee tah-lyee-ah-tEHl-luh] Sweet tagliatelle dough filled with nuts, chocolate, dried fruit, butter, and sugar.

— **gianduia** [+ jee-ahn-dOO-ee-ah] A rich chocolate and hazelnut cake from Turin (Piedmont).

— **nera** [+ nEH-ruh] "Black tart"; a sweet tart made from chocolate, coffee and almonds.

— **pasqualina** [+ pahs-kwah-lEE-nuh] (*Liguria*) A rich vegetable pie made with puff pastry filled with various vegetables, eggs, and cheese.

Tortano [tohr-tAH-no] (*Naples*) A flat ring-shaped bread.

Tortei con la cua [tohr-tEH-ee kohn lah kOO-ah] (*Emilia-Romagna*) Pasta stuffed with herbed cheese.

Tortelletti [tohr-tehl-lEHt-tee] Large tortellini; smaller than *tortelloni*.

Tortelli [tohr-tEHl-lee] A stuffed pasta typically filled with chopped greens and cheese; a specialty of Parma.

— **d'erbette** [+ dehr-bEHt-teh] *Tortelli* stuffed with chopped herbs and greens.

Tortellini [tohr-tehl-lEE-nee] Small stuffed ring-shaped pasta; a specialty of Bologna.

— **di Novi** [tohr-tEHl-lee dee nOH-vee] *Tortelli* stuffed with squash.

— **di San Leo** [+ dee sahn lEH-o] (*Umbria*) Ravioli filled with chopped herbs and greens.

Tortelloni [tohr-tehl-lOH-nee] Large tortellini.

Tortiera [tohr-tee-EH-rah] Baking pan.

Tortiglione [tohr-tee-lyee-OH-neh] An almond-flavored cake.

Tortiglioni [tohr-tee-lyee-OH-nee] See *Vita*.

Tortina [tohr-tEE-nah] A small tart.

Tortino [tohr-tEE-noh] A savory pie or tart.

Toscana [tohs-kAH-nah] Tuscany; the cuisine of this northern region emphasizes the refined yet simple preparation of the main ingredients used; beef, pork, poultry, and game birds are grilled with olive oil; fresh vegetables are prepared with little or no sauce, as are beans and pasta. A wide variety of breads are baked here and are eaten at every meal. Italy's most famous wine, Chianti, is produced in Tuscany.

—, **alla** "Tuscan style"; often denotes the use of fresh herbs and tomatoes; see *Toscana*.

Toscanelli [tohs-kah-nEHl-lee] (*Tuscany*) A type of local bean.

Toscanello [tohs-kah-nEHl-lo] A local sheep's-milk cheese from Sardinia.

Tosella alla panna [toh-sEHl-lah AHl-lah pAHn-nah] (*Veneto*) Fresh cheese enriched with cream.

Tostapane [tohs-tah-pAH-neh] Toaster.

Tostare [tahs-tAH-reh] To toast.

Tostato [tohs-tAH-to] Toasted.

Totano [tOH-tah-no] A cephalopod similar to the squid; prepared like squid or pickled.

Tovaglia [tah-vAH-lyee-uh] Table cloth.

Tovagliolo [toh-vah-lyee-OH-lo] Napkin.

Tozzetti [tohts-tsEHt-tee] A sweet almond and hazelnut cookie; a specialty of Rome.

Tralendalbrot [trah-lEHn-dahl-broht] A local bread of Trentino/Alto Adige.

Tramezzino [trah-mehts-tsEE-no] Small cocktail sandwiches.

Trancia [trAHn-chee-ah] Slice; usually refers to fish (*trancia di pesce*).

Trattaliu [traht-tah-lee-oo] See *Tataliu*.

Trattoria [traht-toh-rEE-ah] A small restaurant or inn featuring local homemade food.

Trebbiano [trehb-bee-AH-no] A major white wine grape; used mainly in Tuscany.

Trecce [trEH-cheh] See *Treccia*.

Treccia [trEH-chee-ah] (1) Braid; plait. (2) Braided bread loaf. (3) A braided cheese; also called *trecce*.

Trenette [treh-nEHt-teh] (*Genoa*) A fine flat pasta noodle typically served with pesto.

Trentino [trehn-tEE-no] Wild mushrooms, polenta, *stoccafisso*, and fresh vegetables are staples of this northern Italian region. Like Alto Adige, Austria and Germany have influenced the cuisine of Trentino, as seen in the use of dumplings, pork, and sauerkraut. See *Alto Adige*.

Tria [trEE-ah] A local Ligurian word for linguine.

Tricolore [tree-koh-lOH-reh] Describes certain dishes featuring three colors usually red or orange, white, and green, representing the colors of the Italian flag.

Triestina, alla [tree-ays-tEE-nah] "Trieste (Friuli) style"; describes simple, hearty dishes.

Trifola [trEE-foh-lah] The word for truffle in parts of Lombardy and Piedmont.

Trifolati [tree-fohl-AH-tee] Describes vegetables, particularly sliced mushrooms, sautéed in olive oil with chopped garlic and parsley.

Triglia [trEE-lyee-ah] Red mullet.

Triglie di scoglio [+ dee skOH-lyee-o] A variety of mullet.

Trincas [treen-kahs] (*Sardinia*) A local sweet biscuit.

Tripolini [tree-poh-lEE-nee] A form of pasta.

Trippa [trEEp-pah] Tripe.

Trippate, pasta alle [pAHs-tah AHl-leh treep-pAH-teh] A dish featuring pasta tossed with a sauce composed of tripe, tomatoes, broth, olive oil, and fresh herbs; a specialty of Tuscany.

Tritato [tree-tAH-to] Minced.

Trito [trEE-to] (1) Minced or diced vegetables. (2) Hash.

Triya [trEE-yah] A word used in parts of southern Italy for pasta.

Troccoli [trOH-koh-lee] Long square pasta noodles; from Foggia (*Apulia*).

Trofie [troh-fEE-eh] A short spiral-shaped pasta noodle.

Trota [trOH-tah] Trout.

— *salmonata* [+ sahl-moh-nAH-tah] Salmon trout.

Trotelle [troh-tEHl-leh] Young trout.

Tubetti [too-bEHt-tee] Small tubular pasta.

Tubetti lunghi [+ lOOn-gee] Short, thin tubed pasta, slightly arched.

Tubettini [too-beht-tEE-nee] Tiny tubular pasta.

Tufoli [tOO-foh-lee] A type of pasta.

Tuma [tOO-mah] See *Rabolia*.

Tumet [too-meht] An aromatic cheese from Vercelli (Piedmont).

Tundus [tOOn-doos] (*Sardinia*) Homemade bread.

Tuorlo d'uovo [too-OHr-lo doo-OH-vuh] Egg yolk.

Turacciolo [too-rAH-chee-oh-lo] Cork.

Turbante [toor-bAHn-teh] A puff pastry shell used to contain various preparations.

Turcinelli [toor-chee-nEHl-lee] Short, corkscrew pasta noodles.

Turiddu [too-rEEd-doo] (*Calabria*) Sweet almond cookies.

Turta de faiscedda [tOOr-tah dee fah-ee-shEHd-dah] An egg and bean dish; from Sardinia.

Türteln [toor-tEHln] (*Trentino*) Local stuffed dumplings filled with cooked greens.

Uccelli [oo-chEHl-lee] See *Uccellini*.

Uccellini/ucelletti [oo-chehl-lEE-nee/oo-chehl-lEHt-tee] Small game birds, typically roasted.

Uccellini scappati [+ skahp-pAH-tee] (*Lombardy*) A dish composed of rolled stuffed veal or veal chunks resembling small birds and prepared grilled or roasted.

'U grane cuotte [OO ghrAH-neh koo-OHt-teh] (*Apulia*) A confection made from nuts, dried fruit, and chocolate.

Umbria [OOm-bree-ah] A small region settled in the heart of Italy. Roasted baby pig (and other pork products), freshwater fish, truffles, wild pigeons, white figs, and fennel are important components of Umbrian cookery.

Umidino [oo-mee-dEE-no] Stewed.

Umido, in [een OO-mee-do] Stew; cooked slowly in liquid.

Uova [oo-OH-vah] Eggs.

Uova al tegame [+ ahl tay-gAH-meh] Fried eggs.

Uova di Pasqua [+ dee pAHs-kwah] Easter eggs.

Uova sode [+ sOH-deh] Hard-boiled eggs.

U pirciatu [oo peer-chee-AH-too] See *Pirciatu, u.*

Uva [OO-vah] Grapes.

Uva di Corinto [+ dee koh-rEEn-to] A word sometimes used for currants.

— *passa* [+ pAHs-sah] Raisin.

— *secca* [+ sEHk-kah] Raisins.

— *spina* [+ spEE-nah] Gooseberry.

— *sultanina* [sool-tah-nEE-nah] Currants.

Uvetta [oo-vEHt-tah] Raisins.

Valerianella [vah-lay-ree-ah-nEHl-lah] See *Soncino*.

Valle a'Aosta [vAHl-leh dah-OHs-tuh] Hearty soups and stews, whole grains, cheese, and game are favorites of the Valle d'Aosta; the smallest of Italian regions, located north of Piedmont.

Vaniglia [vah-nEE-lyee-ah] Vanilla.

Vanello [vah-nEHl-lo] Plover.

Varzi [vAHr-tsee] A spicy pork sausage from Lombardy.

Vassoio [vahs-sOH-ee-o] Tray.

Vasteddi [vahs-tEHd-dee] A local bread roll from Sicily.

Vasteddi maritati [+ mah-ree-tAH-tee] (*Sicily*) A savory yeast bun filled with ricotta and herbs.

Vecchio [vEH-key-o] Old; also refers to Parmesan cheese aged for two years.

Vecchio samperi [+ sahm-pEH-ree] A dry aperitif wine from Marsala (Sicily).

Venegazzu [veh-neh-ghAHts-tsoo] Dry red and white sparkling wines from Veneto.

Veneti [vEH-neh-tee] (*Venice*) Cookies sweetened with jam.

Veneto [vEH-neh-to] (1) A region in northern Italy. Rice and polenta are the staple starches that typically accompany the diverse seafood and vegetable dishes, prepared with a tactful use of herbs and spices. (2) A sharp cow's-milk cheese from Venice

Veneto (cont.)
often compared to *Asiago*.

Venézia [vay-nEh-tsee-ah] Venice. See *Veneto*.

Venezia Giulia [+ jee-OO-lee-ah] A small northern coastal region; Prosciutto di San Daniele, from Friuli, is perhaps the most famous product from this area. Pork, seafood, polenta, beans, corn, turnips, and other vegetables and fruits are local favorites.

Veneziana, alla [veh-neh-tsee-AH-nah] "Venetian style"; usually indicates onions and white wine are present in a dish.

Ventaglio [vehn-tAH-lyee-o] The word for scallop in parts of Italy.

Ventresca [vaynt-tEHs-kah] The underbelly of tuna.

Ventricina [vayn-tree-chEE-nah] A salami from central Italy flavored with pepper, fennel, and orange.

Vera cucina italiana [vEH-rah coo-chEE-nah ee-tah-lee-AH-nah] "True Italian cooking."

Verde [vEHr-deh] Green.

— *salsa* See *Salsa verde*.

— *sardo* [vEHr-do sAHr-do] A Sardinian blue-veined cheese made from ewe's milk.

Verdello [vayr-dEHl-lo] A variety of orange.

Verdure [vayr-dOO-reh] Vegetables.

Vermicelli [vayr-mee-chEHl-lee] Thin spaghetti.

Vermicellini [vayr-mee-chehl-lEE-nee] Thin vermicelli.

Vermut [vEHr-moot] Vermouth.

Vernaccia di Oristano [vehr-nAH-chee-ah dee oh-rees-tAH-no] A white fortified wine from Sardinia.

Verza [vEHr-tsah] Green cabbage.

Verze e patate [+ eh pah-tAH-teh] (*Veneto*) Cabbage cooked with potatoes.

Vescie [vEH-shee-eh] A variety of wild mushroom.

Vestedda [vays-tEHd-dah] (*Sicily*) A flat bread; often topped with various ingredients.

Vezzena [vehts-tsEH-nah] A cheese from Trentino usually aged and grated.

Vialone nano [vee-ah-lOH-neh nAH-no] A variety of Italian rice; used in risotto and other rice dishes.

Vincisgrassi [veen-chees-ghrAHs-see] See *Pincigrassi*.

Vin cotto [veen kOHt-to] Literally "cooked wine"; describes certain strong sweet wines.

Vini neri [vEE-nee nEH-ree] Dark red wines.

Vino [vEE-no] Wine.

— *amabile* [+ ah-mAH-bee-leh] Sweet wine.

— *asciutto* [+ ah-shee-OOt-to] Dry wine.

— *bianco* [+ bee-AHn-ko] White wine.

— *da pasto* [+ dah pAHs-to] Ordinary wine served at meals.

— *da Tavola* [+ dah tAH-voh-lah] Table wine.

— *del paese* [+ dehl pah-EH-seh] Local wine.

— *di Oporto* [+ dee oh-pOHr-to] Port wine.

— *di Xeres* [+ dee jzEH-rehs] Sherry wine.

— *frizzante* [+ freets-tsAHn-teh] Sparkling wine.

— *nobile di Montepulciano* [+ nOH-bee-leh dee mohn-teh-pool-chee-AH-no] A dry red wine